Contents

CONTENTS

iv

Preface

Our aim is to provide a course which explains and gives practice in the various skills of summarising. Each of three skills is exercised separately and thoroughly, as the list of Contents makes plain, before they are combined and the fourth added. This new approach contrasts with the usual method of throwing the pupil into the deep end after a page or two of advice. Throughout the book we give prominence to worked examples – specimens of pupils' attempts – which illustrate the points made about method and provide material for discussion, thus helping pupils to become self-critical.

'Summary', in our opinion, is a much wider term than 'precis', which came to be associated with a formal, stereotyped examination exercise. Skill in it is necessary to all academic work, not only in English; it is also a vital part of the use of language, spoken and written, in our daily lives, as we explain in Chapter 1 and incidentally throughout. Training in summarising is therefore valuable, for its own sake, as an essential part of the study of English in schools, and also for its practical application in the world outside school.

As a part of the total process we would stress the importance of paraphrase. Ability to express in one's own words is a true test of comprehension. In summary work, the avoidance of the phrases, clauses and sentences of the original leads to a properly condensed version, rather than to a patchwork of ill-digested pieces lifted from the passage. This does not mean that the pupil must on no account use any single word from the original, as is sometimes suggested. We would also emphasise the need for thorough and sound training in note-making, an aspect of summarising which has wide and obvious application.

The book provides two years' work for the fourth and fifth years in secondary schools, with sufficiently varied material to allow the teacher to choose that most appropriate for the particular class. Able pupils should work quickly through the early chapters, doing many of the exercises orally, though with due emphasis on method and accuracy. Less able pupils will find it possible to work more slowly and to make progress steadily; up to the end of Chapter 9 there is much for the non-academic. Chapter 10 contains questions from recent C.S.E. and G.C.E. Ordinary Level examination papers, for those preparing for such examinations. Although there is a planned progression of work throughout the book, it would be possible to change the order in the later stages to suit individual preferences and circumstances. Some teachers might prefer, for example, to move from Exercise B of Chapter 6 (p. 67) straight to Chapter 8, returning to Chapter 6 when they finished Exercise F (p. 94) and then resuming the sequence of the book.

A large proportion of the material for study is drawn from modern authors, and good documentary writing figures prominently. We have tried to choose passages which, while suitable for the immediate purpose, are interesting and worth reading in themselves. We believe the book will assist the teaching and appreciation of summarising as a living activity, not as a series of tricks which may be performed without genuine understanding.

We should like to thank, for their help in various ways, T. D. Denner, John Dodge, J. C. Mallison, Mervyn Payne, J. I. M. Stewart, R. M. T. Evans and W. I. Browne.

G. W. DENNIS

D. W. H. SHARP

Chapter 1

The Art of Summary

Can this cockpit hold
The vasty fields of France? or may we cram
Within this wooden O the very casques
That did affright the air at Agincourt?

King Henry V: Prologue

That Shakespeare succeeded in the seemingly impossible task of portraying the battle of Agincourt and many other vast actions within the limits of the conventional stage, provides us with an extreme and very complicated example of the art of summary. Not many of us will feel able to attempt such a difficult task, though most of us will wish to discover and admire exactly how Shakespeare and other great writers perform it. One important part of the method is the selection of significant detail, and consequently the rejection of the less important material which surrounds it.

This leads us to the realisation that summarising is not something only for the Shakespeares of this world, but that it is a basic, essential human activity and one which each of us uses many times each day throughout life. Whenever we give an account of an event we have seen, we select and condense, for life is too short for every little detail to be included, and in some cases time is precious. The police and the magistrate will not be very pleased with the witness who starts a description of a road accident by giving a detailed account of what she herself was wearing at the time. How many explanations of failure to produce homework give the full story? This ability to select and condense is important in all human affairs, and its importance is increasing all the time, for modern society is becoming more and more complex, is using more and more words, spoken and written, and consequently we need more and more to select and condense in order to deal with the flow of language at home and at work.

We have all known people who fail to select and condense, who try to give a word by word account of a conversation they have heard, or a page by page description of a book they have read. They can be very boring, and we usually learn to switch off our full attention when they are pouring forth the words. Such a weakness amongst our friends can be very irritating, but it is a more serious matter if inability to summarise affects our studies or our work, and it can do so easily. This need not happen, however, for the art of summary can be learnt, and can be improved by training and practice, as this book will demonstrate, so that all the various uses of language which each of us employs can be made more effective.

So far we have used the words 'summary' and 'to summarise', but you may have come across another word with essentially the same meaning, 'précis'. In this book we have decided to use 'summary' and its verb, even though there is no basic dictionary difference in meaning between it and 'précis', because précis has come by tradition to mean a particular type of exercise found in certain examinations, demanding the reduction of a prose passage of about 500 words to one-third of its length. We wish to emphasise that summarising is a much more widely applicable activity than this stereotyped exercise would suggest, but we must also point out that we have included some work of this kind for those who need it for examinations. In any case, if you cover all the work in this book you will be able to deal with all kinds of summary (or précis) work that you are likely to come across.

Let us now consider some typical uses of summary in everyday life:

At Home

1 Your TV set breaks down in the middle of your favourite serial programme. You ask your friend for a summary of the rest of the instalment.

2 You have been out for the evening with your friends, and arrive home late. When you are asked what you have been doing, you give a condensed (and perhaps carefully selected) account of your activities.

3 Mother has had a long conversation with the next-door neighbour. When she returns you ask what they were talking about, and receive a condensed version.

4 Father has announced his intention of asking the boss for an increase in salary. When he arrives home, he gives the family a condensed version of what the boss said, unless the boss's reply was very brief ('Yes' or 'No'!).

At School

1 You are told to read two chapters in your History textbook and make brief notes of the important points.

2 The Editor of the school magazine asks you to write a brief report of Speech Day.

3 You watch a scientific experiment in the laboratory, and then write a condensed account of it in your note-book. Notice the kind of happenings you omit (e.g. breakages and interruptions).

4 The Head asks you to explain briefly what happened during the twenty minutes when your form was left alone, and a window was broken.

Outside Home and School

1 Newspaper reports of speeches, events and matches.

2 Minutes of committee and council meetings.

3 Advertisements. An advertiser is usually brief and to the point, partly because space is expensive and partly because very few people will read a 2,000-word explanation of why his product is superior.

4 A busy managing director has insufficient time to read all the reports and journal articles that he needs to read. Summaries will be carefully prepared for him.

Exercise A (Oral)

Give as many other examples as you can of the use of summary in each of the three groups:

1 At home.

2 At school.

3 Outside home and school.

It will be obvious to you by now that general language ability, the ability to understand and to use words in speech or writing, will enable you to summarise more efficiently, so that skills which are trained in other English lessons, particularly in comprehension and composition work, will be valuable here. In addition, however, there are certain skills which are especially relevant to summarising, and in the following chapters we explain and exercise each of them in turn, before combining them and asking you to summarise a passage.

These skills are:

1 Paraphrase

This means expressing other people's ideas in our own words. It is important in summary work because we cannot condense a passage simply by cutting out certain sentences or paragraphs and stringing the remaining bits together. This would be like trying to make a machine smaller by taking out some of the parts; if the resulting

3

'machine' worked at all, it certainly would not function in the same way as the original machine. A summary must be a condensed version of the original without any alteration of the ideas and attitude of the author. It would be wrong to suggest that you must avoid all words and phrases used in the original, of course, but the ability to understand, digest and reproduce ideas in a more concise form in your own words is a vital part of summarising.

2 *Abstraction*

This is the power to select important points and to relegate or reject the less important and the unimportant. When we condense a passage to, say, a quarter of its length, it is obvious that we must decide which statements, ideas or arguments we must keep and which we may omit. This kind of discrimination is essential in summarising, and indeed in all areas of academic work.

3 *Giving a Title*

A title may be regarded as a summary of a summary. Its purpose is to express in a very few words the central theme of a speech or a piece of writing. Again, you will realise that this skill is not restricted in its value to formal exercises in English.

When we summarise a complicated report, or the plot of a long novel, we use these three skills, and several others. How many others can you think of?

Making a summary, therefore, is demanded of us many times in our work and in our social life. It is also a complicated process, if done well, and one which improves our handling of language for whatever purpose.

You may well have realised while reading this chapter that not all summaries are what we call later in the book *neutral*. It often happens that the purpose of a summary is not simply to give a condensed version of what the author wrote, of what the speaker said, or of what happened. The person making the summary may quite deliberately distort the original, without in any way altering any parts of it; he does it by omitting certain aspects, or by making the important unimportant, and vice-versa. If you consider the instances listed earlier in this chapter (pages 2–3) you should be able to say on which occasions you would expect this prejudiced kind of summary to be given. You can also see how it works by comparing the reports of the same political speech in different newspapers. It is important, of course, that you should be aware that this can happen, so that you are on your guard against being persuaded on insufficient or distorted evidence. Try to think of other kinds of distorted summary with which you are familiar in your daily lives.

One other abuse of summary must be mentioned. You may have seen advertisements for the world's great literature in handy form, or words to that effect. A condensed version of a great play, novel or poem can never be an adequate substitute for the original. Why not? (A good point for discussion.) At the same time, you should remember that the ability to summarise well is an invaluable aid to literary appreciation, as you should be discovering in your own studies. This point brings us back to where we started the chapter.

Exercise B (Oral)

1   Give concise travelling directions
     (a)   from school to your home;
     (b)   from your home to the nearest theatre;
     (c)   from school to the public library;
     (d)   from your home to the dentist's;
     (e)   from your home to where you spent your last summer holiday.

2   Give a summary of the plot of
     (a)   a film or play you enjoyed;
     (b)   one episode of a television or radio serial;
     (c)   a novel you have read recently.

3   Give a brief account of a typical day in the life of
     (a)   yourself;
     (b)   a close relative;
     (c)   a well-known personality you admire (as you imagine it to be).

4   Give a brief account of your favourite leisure-time activities.

5   Make a short speech in favour of *or* against The Art of Summary.

Chapter 2

Paraphrase I

Introductory

A hopeful Irishman, walking one day along the High Street, was attracted by this notice in a jeweller's window: 'Look at this watch for ten shillings.' He looked at the watch for a few minutes, and then went into the shop to claim his money. Do you think he got it?

The notice is of course ambiguous. To the jeweller, it meant one thing; to the Irishman, another. What are those two meanings?

Exercise A

These five advertisements are clumsily expressed. Re-word them so that each says clearly what it was intended to say.

1   Try the Upminster Theatre, 8.30 p.m. Just the thing for a dull evening.

2   Why go out of Torquay to be swindled? Come to the Pull Inn.

3   Teeth extracted with the greatest pains.

4   We do not tear your clothes with machinery. We do it carefully by hand. (Laundry sign.)

5   Try our patent mosquito-destroyer coil, 15p. It is perfectly safe for mosquitoes.

Exercise B

The following also fail to convey what their authors meant. Put them right. (Is the first one, for example, intended as a promise or as a threat?)

1   We never allow a dissatisfied customer to leave the premises if we can help it. It doesn't pay.

2   After using your ointment my face started to clear up at once, and after using two jars it was gone altogether.

3   In reply to your valued enquiry, we enclose illustrations of Dining Tables of Oak, seating fourteen people with round legs and twelve people with square legs, with prices attached.

6

4 We charge low prices of admission, but they are recognised by our regular visitors as being consistent with the quality of the films being screened.

5 A jumble sale will be held in the Parish Room on Saturday next. This is a good chance to get rid of anything that is not worth keeping but is too good to throw away. Don't forget to bring your husbands.

These exercises are not difficult, but in working through them you have needed to find words of your own to convey the full and exact meaning the author intended. *To find words of your own to convey the full and exact meaning* – that is the essence of Paraphrase. In writing your re-worded version you will make the sense of the passage clear to yourself; and, as is sometimes equally important, if your paraphrase is good it will prove to others (such as examiners) that the sense is clear to you. Difficult writing becomes easier to understand if you try to put it into your own words, and the more you practise this the more readily will you be able to understand difficult matter the first time you read it. Paraphrase is also an important preliminary of summary work, because before you can condense a passage you must understand it thoroughly.

The sentences in the exercises above needed re-wording because they had been carelessly written. Usually, however, the material you will have to paraphrase is well written, and it is shortcomings in the reader that make it difficult. Many writers use a larger vocabulary and a greater range of figurative expressions than you have yet become accustomed to. For examples to illustrate their arguments, they can refer to things which for them are general knowledge, but which may not be known to you at all.

A good dictionary will simplify many of these difficulties. People often think of a dictionary merely as a book for checking spelling, but it is vastly more useful than that. It is in fact an alphabetical history of the English language, both spoken and written, and will record at least five important facts about every word in it: 'Its form, or to put it more simply, its modern spelling; its meaning, or meanings; its grammatical function or functions; its etymology, that is, the story of its origins and subsequent development; and its pronunciation'.

You will see that a dictionary which gives all this information is the most valuable reference book you can have. You should have one of your own, because you will need to use it constantly. There are other books, however, which you will sometimes want to look at. For instance, where would you turn for help in understanding allusions to literature? or to the Bible? or to a source which you did not recognise?

Exercise C

These ten sentences illustrate difficulties of the kinds discussed above. Four are proverbial expressions, three are idiomatic, and three contain allusions which you may not immediately grasp. Which sentences belong together: i.e. which present the same difficulties?

1 Prevention is better than cure.

2 Latin? – that's my Achilles heel, I'm afraid.

3 The trouble about inviting the vicar to supper is that he *will* talk shop.

4 The strike was called off at the eleventh hour.

5 Although the gates were supposed to be closed, we pulled some strings and managed to get in.

6 You can't have the penny and the bun.

7 It was a dull afternoon when the match started, but by the end the gloom was stygian.

8 In entering for both track and field events, Jill had bitten off more than she could chew.

9 More haste, less speed.

10 The last straw breaks the camel's back.

Proverbs

Proverbs are concise observations based on experience of daily life, widely known and of accepted general truth. They are usually very short; they are always 'much matter decorated into few words'; and it is not easy, however familiar they are to us, to express their full meaning in words of our own. (That is why the proverbs survive.) The proverbs in Exercise C were numbers 1, 6, 9, 10. Here are two Fourth Formers' attempts at paraphrasing the first: *Prevention is better than cure*. Which do you prefer?

a If a person is prevented from having a disease, he or she suffers no ill effects, but when that person has been cured after contracting the disease he or she is liable to suffer after-effects, such as scars or deformity.

b Taking steps to see that something unpleasant doesn't happen is better than being able to put it right when it does.

The weakness of *a* is that it does not express *some general truth*; it merely gives an example of a happening about which the proverb might be used. Consider the wisdom of a man who went to the trouble of lagging the pipes in his house during the summer, instead of waiting until winter frosts burst them before he did anything. We could equally well apply the *proverb* to his action – but not the *paraphrase*; and so it is not satisfactory. On the other hand, *b* does seize on the essence of the proverb, and does express it in suitably general terms. Could it be improved?

You will have noticed that the paraphrases are longer than the originals. This will often be so, for the better the writing the more difficult it is to express it briefly in our own words. When summarising, we select those important points which we want to keep, and express them as concisely as possible in our own words. This will become clearer in later chapters.

Exercise D

Comment on these paraphrases, and then improve them:

1 *More haste, less speed.*

a When one does something quickly, it is liable to be imperfect, and so it has to be done all over again, whereas if it was done a little slower it would probably be perfect.

b If you are in a hurry and you try to hurry more, you will make mistakes and lose time.

(The proverb comments on an ill-judged and unsuccessful attempt to do something quickly and so save time. Does either paraphrase suggest this? The writer of *a* adds two ideas of his own: which are they?)

2 *You can't have the penny and the bun.*

a You shouldn't try to make two advantages out of one, if it's impossible.

b When you have the choice of two alternatives, you cannot have the best of both.

(Is the suggestion of *advantages* in the proverb? Which two words omitted from the second part of *b* would improve it greatly? Why would you reject 'You cannot have the best of both worlds' as a *paraphrase* of this proverb?)

3 Now paraphrase: *The last straw breaks the camel's back.*

When you have written your version, compare it with others from your class, and decide whether, where they differ from yours, they are improvements or not. Take special care that, whilst the whole of the proverb's meaning has been expressed, nothing has been added, and that the paraphrase can be as widely applied as the proverb.

Keeping these aims in mind, try the following exercises. The proverbs in the first one are probably familiar to you; and even if those in the second are not, with a little care you will be able to understand, and then to paraphrase, them all.

Exercise E

1   Practice makes perfect.
2   Cut your coat according to your cloth.
3   Where there's smoke there's fire.
4   The proof of the pudding is in the eating.
5   Necessity is the mother of invention.

Exercise F

1   Great talkers are little doers.
2   When the wine is in, the wit is out.
3   Be not made a beggar by banqueting upon borrowing.
4   Flies are easier caught with honey than with vinegar.
5   Hope is a good breakfast, but is a bad supper.

Proverbs have been described above as 'general truths', and indeed two of those quoted in this section have almost identical meanings. Sometimes, however, two proverbs appear to contradict one another: *Many hands make light work* but *Too many cooks spoil the broth; Penny wise, pound foolish* but *Look after the pence and the pounds will look after themselves.* Can *both* be general truths?

Idioms

Every language has its own idioms, and native speakers use them all the time, usually unconsciously. Probably they first become aware of them when they have to translate from their own language into another. You will see the point if you have tried to find an English equivalent for 'Tiens!', or a French idiom for 'to pull someone's leg' or 'a wet blanket'. (We suggest *monter un bateau à quelqu'un* and *un vrai parapluie*; but what do these phrases mean literally?) The fact that idioms like these are in use all the time suggests that 'we know what they mean'; trying to explain their meaning to others, particularly to foreigners, suggests that perhaps we do not.

Exercise G

1   Consider these Fourth Formers' paraphrases of one of the idiomatic sentences in Exercise C above:
Although the gates were supposed to be closed, we pulled some strings and managed to get in.
a   Although the gates had been shut, we managed to pull ourselves up over them.
b   The ground was full but we wangled our way in.

(Is either version satisfactory? *a* takes the idiom literally: did they really climb the gates? *b* expresses the meaning better, but the use of *wangled* is a mistake. Before you write your own paraphrase, consider: How are puppets worked? What is a puppet government?)
2   *Paraphrase:* The trouble about inviting the vicar to supper is that he *will* talk shop.
3   *Paraphrase:* In entering for both track and field events, Jill had bitten off more than she could chew.

Compare your paraphrases with others from your class. Check that the *full and exact* meaning of the idiom has been expressed, with nothing added.

Exercise H

Paraphrase the following idioms:
1   To break the ice.
2   A breakthrough in science.
3   Burning the candle at both ends.
4   A bottleneck in production.
5   To have something up one's sleeve.

Exercise I

Paraphrase these sentences:
1   Strike while the iron is hot!
2   An iron curtain divides East from West, and helps to maintain the cold war.
3   I shall think twice before eating there again – we had to pay through the nose for a very run-of-the-mill lunch.
4   Set a beggar on a horse, and see him ride.
5   In a large family there are always a few skeletons in the cupboard; and in my father's clan there were many uncles and aunts and cousins, consequently many cupboards, consequently some skeletons.

This practice may make you aware of idioms, but no number of exercises can prepare you for all you may meet. Only alert reading can do that – reading with your eyes open. You should, however, be careful how you use them in your own writing, for reasons contained in this comment by F. L. Lucas: '*Trump-cards* are dog-eared, *burning-questions* leave us cold, and *the eleventh hour* no longer strikes.' What warning is given here, and why did Lucas express it in this way?

Allusions

Not many years ago, the author of any serious book could assume that all his readers would, like himself, have studied some Latin and Greek authors, know a good deal of classical mythology, and include the Bible among their bedside reading. As a result, the author would share with his readers a great store of common knowledge, any aspect of which he need only refer to briefly for the full purpose of his reference to be understood. Those days have gone, and it is probably only the compilers of crossword puzzles who write for similarly knowledge-able readers today. The change is not wholly a loss: people are less well read in classical literature because they are better read in other directions; and a much greater proportion of the population reads now than in the days when Latin poets used to attract greater praise in this country than English ones.

You will, however, still meet allusions in your reading, and their comparative rarity increases the difficulty of dealing with them when they do occur.

'*Latin—that's my Achilles heel, I'm afraid.*' If you look up this allusion (where?), you will probably find something like this:

Achilles. . . . When a baby, Achilles was immersed by his mother in the Styx, and was thereby rendered invulnerable, except in the heel by which she held him. It was from a wound in the heel, inflicted by Paris, that he died many years later, after a heroic career. Hence: *Achilles heel*, proverbial for a vulnerable spot.

1   Make use of the relevant part of this to write a paraphrase of the sentence above.

2   *Paraphrase:* It was a dull afternoon when the match started, but by the end the gloom was stygian. (Where will you look up that allusion?)

3   *Paraphrase:* The strike was called off at the eleventh hour. (A Biblical reference: see the parable of the labourers in the vineyard.)

As before, compare your version of each of these sentences with others in the class.

Exercise K

Trace the origins of these allusions, and then paraphrase them:

1   A labour of Hercules;
2   a good Samaritan;
3   the Midas touch;
4   to meet one's Waterloo;
5   a Napoleon of finance.

Exercise L

Paraphrase these sentences:

1   If you try to learn a foreign language without memorising its grammar, you are building on sand.
2   Some people never get far even with their native tongue; they writhe like Laocoön in the toils of the simplest sentences.
3   John had been thinking of leaving the club for some time, and when he forgot to renew his subscription he realised that he had crossed the Rubicon.
4   In writing paraphrases, you have to steer between the Scylla of omission and the Charybdis of invention.
5   Macaulay may be a Philistine; but he remains a Goliath.

The more you read, the greater will be the range of allusions you can appreciate without turning to reference books; and so the greater will be your pleasure in reading. You will be mastering some of the resources of language – learning to read it and so to have a chance of writing it with greater exactness. If you continue to practise, your skill will increase. Which proverb quoted earlier in this chapter says almost exactly that?

So far in this chapter, you have been given for paraphrase sentences whose difficulties can be largely overcome by using the right reference books. This has been useful practice in reading and writing with exactness, but its main purpose has been to prepare you to face the biggest single difficulty which adult writing presents – simply, that it is grown-up. This is not merely a question of 'hard words'. It is to do with the way adults think, with their habit of abstract thought. And the only way to be thoroughly at home with this kind of writing is to grow up yourself in your use of language.

There are examples of this kind of expression in the proverbs you have already studied. Seeing a dress or a painting you had spoilt through trying to finish in a hurry, an adult might say, 'More haste, less speed!' The comment, because it was brief and placed the blame

exactly, might annoy you more than a detailed investigation of the
causes of the accident. Karl Marx held the view that religious beliefs
so drugged working people that they ceased to be ambitious to better
themselves; and he expressed this compactly by writing, 'Religion is
the opium of the people'. It is general knowledge that people tend
to make light of the disasters which happen to them, whilst they
exaggerate the trivial discomforts they suffer; but it took Swift to
convert this knowledge into the aphorism, 'Elephants are always
drawn smaller than life, but a flea always larger'. What kind of a
person do you imagine Aunt Agatha to be, judging from P. G.
Wodehouse's remark that she 'eats broken bottles and wears barbed
wire next to the skin'? And would you like to come before his
magistrate who 'looked like an owl with a dash of weasel blood in
him'?

Exercise M

Consider carefully the meaning of each of the following, and when
you are clear about it write your paraphrase.

1   The pen is mightier than the sword.
2   To travel hopefully is better than to arrive.
3   A man that is young in years may be old in hours, if he has lost no
time.
4   I prefer old age to the alternative.
5   Genius is one per cent inspiration and ninety-nine per cent
perspiration.
6   Beauty is altogether in the eye of the beholder.
7   It is good to be without vices, but it is not good to be without
temptations.
8   When a piece of paper blows into a law-court, it may take a yoke
of oxen to drag it out again.
9   It is hard to split atoms because it is like shooting birds in the
dark, in a country where there are few birds.
10   It is better to wear out than rust out.

Jargon and Jargantuan

Here are two definitions, followed by two passages illustrating them.
Which passage goes with which definition?

a   Jargon is shop talk. Every profession and trade, every art and
science has its own technical vocabulary, consisting of exact and sometimes difficult words not intelligible to the general public, but necessary to the profession or trade, etc.

b   Jargantuan is a ponderous and fearsome dialect: long-winded, stilted, circumlocutory. It prefers the inflated cliché to the plain phrase, and is in general the enemy of exactness and precision.

c   A good camera lens focused correctly will project the object on to film at its maximum resolution, and will project other objects in acceptable focus nearer and farther from the object until those other objects are defined by circles larger than 1/100th-inch in diameter.

d   It would be very much appreciated if you would endeavour to accumulate material descriptive of conditions at present governing the activities during leisure hours of young persons under twenty-one.

A little thought will soon show that *c* is using vocabulary which, if baffling to you, would be precise and clear to a photographer. In a manual for beginners, it would need re-writing – but what would happen to its preciseness and its length? On the other hand, *d* is long winded; you should be able to paraphrase it in ten words or fewer.

You will meet writing of both these kinds every day. Textbooks, knitting patterns, model-kit manuals, car handbooks, hire-purchase agreements, sports and games – they all employ jargon in this sense: technical language, concise and exact to the expert, but unintelligible to everyone else. Because its meaning is so compressed, it can never be paraphrased briefly. In the right place, of course, it is quite acceptable; but the deliberate use of too-technical language for a non-specialist audience is indefensible, and has aptly been christened *bafflegab*. In business letters, some newspapers and much advertising you may meet jargantuan (sometimes called *gobbledygook* or *the barnacular*). When you are tired, you may even write it.

You will not often be asked to paraphrase jargantuan: such inflated, clumsy language is too easy to re-word! In the main, however, to take the long-term view, we feel bound to point out that the number of those who continually 'envisage possibilities' or 'anticipate that in the event of...' is by no means on the decrease – and a few examples are therefore included in this book. On the other hand, it is good practice to try to express jargon – i.e. acceptable technical phraseology – in layman's language: many words of technical origin find their way into everyday speech, and in using them often we become careless about their precise meaning. The first sentence below provides one example, and a short search in any good dictionary will soon reveal others.

Exercise N

Re-write as simply as possible:

1   Trespassers will be prosecuted.

2   Since CO_2 is a non-supporter of combustion, it is used to extinguish fires.

3   Learned behaviour is a series of conditioned reflexes.

4   Selective weed-killers are a great help in increasing agricultural productivity; unchecked, weeds may easily reduce yields by 25 per cent.

5   The executors of the late Mr Edwards invested the balance of his estate in gilt-edged securities.

Exercise O

Find three examples of jargon which you think your class should be able to paraphrase, and two which you hope will be too hard for them. (Have your own versions ready.)

Exercise P

Paraphrase the following, using several sentences for each if necessary.

1   Most dinosaurs were timid, and few were carnivores; they seldom ventured far from the security of their swampy habitats.

2   A change of address should be notified promptly to the Head Postmaster. Alternatively the licence should be presented at any Post Office for amendment.

3   The power requirements of industry in Britain account for only a fraction of the industrial consumption of energy.

4   A sample cross-section of consumer opinion convinced the company that there was a market for Scrubbit.

5   Crystalline rocks are excellent insulators of heat; between one crystal and another there can be a marked difference in the coefficient of expansion, and consequently in the amount of expansion which occurs within a given increase in temperature. The process produces sand and hot deserts.

General Exercise

In this last exercise, you will find examples of all the kinds of difficulty so far discussed. See if you can identify them (there are seven altogether). And remember, whether you are evolving your paraphrases orally or in writing, to aim to·re-express each sentence fully and exactly.

Exercise Q

1   All men are created equal.

2   Repetition is reputation.

3   You can skate more than one mile on one slice of bread.

4   Absence is to love what wind is to fire: it extinguishes the small, and inflames the great.

5   All animals are equal, but some animals are more equal than others.

6   He expired in indigent circumstances.

7   The man who would stoop so low as to write an anonymous letter, the least he could do would be to sign his name to it.

8   Genius does what it must, and Talent does what it can.

9   The style of an author should be the image of his mind; but the choice and command of language is the fruit of exercise.

10   All flesh is as grass. (See Isaiah, ch. 40.)

11   Work expands to fill the time available for its completion.

12   This criticism is not open, as Britishers would be, and consequently it is difficult to nail down, but, like a snake in the grass, is whispered behind a hand which covers a sneering face.

13   Gladstone is a sophisticated rhetorician inebriated with the exuberance of his own verbosity.

14   Not one of the passengers could have said, from anything he saw, what either of the other two was like; and each was hidden under almost as many wrappers from the eyes of the mind, as from the eyes of the body, of his two companions.

15   The progress of science always involves a delicate balance between critical observation and speculative theorising – between careful piecemeal investigation of particular problems and imaginative general interpretation of the results obtained.

16   Whatever is worth doing at all is worth doing well.

17   We think of a witch-doctor as a man who pretends to work miracles in the name of hidden ghosts; but he is much nearer to the craftsman than to the mystic.

18   A soft answer turneth away wrath; but grievous words stir up anger. (Proverbs ch. 15.)

19   If a thing is worth doing, it is worth doing badly.

20   First, mind it well, then pen it, then examine it, then amend it, and you may be in the better hope of doing reasonably well.

* * *

Latin, that ancient sword of Cicero, lyre of Catullus, and thunder of Virgil, has become the pallid valet of the lawyer and the doctor, laying out their double-breasted polysyllabics, workaday clichés, and full-dress circumlocutions. 'I had to let my secretary go,' a doctor told me. 'She never could remember the Latin for cod liver oil.'

JAMES THURBER: *Lanterns and Lances* ('The New Vocabularianism').

Note. The quotation about the value of dictionaries (p. 7 above) is from G. H. Vallins: *The Making and Meaning of Words*. 'Jargantuan' and 'barnacular' were coined by Ivor Brown, who has published in *Chosen Words* a selection of the material in his eight 'word books' (*A Word in Your Ear*, etc.). Sir Ernest Gowers deals fascinatingly with 'gobbledygook' in *The Complete Plain Words*. Some of the examples in this chapter, and also in Chapter 5, were first printed in Denys Parsons' collections of howlers and misprints (*It Must Be True*, etc.).

Chapter 3

Abstraction I

'It is of the highest importance in the art of detection to be able to recognize out of a number of facts which are incidental and which vital.'
The Memoirs of Sherlock Holmes

Being able to express other people's ideas in your own words is one of the basic skills which are essential in daily life as well as in summarising, and the first stages of practice in this have been covered in Chapter 2. In the present chapter we are concerned with another of these basic skills, the ability to select an important point, or important points, from a passage which contains a number of points of varying importance, including, perhaps, some which are unimportant. This power of selection, or abstraction, is an important aspect of all kinds of reporting. The radio commentator at a football or cricket match cannot hope to mention everything that he sees, so he selects those features which he considers to be important or interesting; the fashion editor who reports her visit to a dress show concentrates on the new and striking features of the clothes displayed, because they are what is important to her and her readers; the managing director will receive detailed reports from the various heads of departments responsible to him, but from these he will abstract those aspects of most vital concern, in his opinion, for his own report to the board of directors, who in turn will select certain points for discussion and decision. Examples such as this can be found in every job, at every level, and we should realise that we are all dependent in some way or other on other people's powers of abstraction, just as others are dependent on our own.

A simple example will illustrate the scale of importance:

They found John lying face down on the bed. The hilt of a dagger could be seen protruding from between his shoulder blades, and there was no doubt that he was dead. Cheerful dance music came from a transistor radio on the bedside table, the curtains were drawn and the electric light was on.

In this short passage there are several facts, but the most important, without question, is that John is dead. Next in importance, perhaps of equal importance, is the fact that he was murdered. (Why is suicide unlikely?) The other facts are not nearly so important, though they would matter to a doctor trying to determine the time of death or to a detective trying to reconstruct the crime. If we were asked to make notes of the most important points in the passage, we could write 'John dead – murdered', or even more briefly, 'John murdered'.

Note-making

When making notes in this way, the aim is to be as brief as possible. You need not use proper sentences, as can be seen from the example above, but you should make sure that the note contains enough information to remind you of the whole passage when you look at it later on. At first you may find it helpful to write down the point in your own words without concentrating on brevity, condensing this into a proper note as a second stage. You should soon be able to omit this intermediate step, however, and find yourself able to make notes straight from the passage.

Exercise A

Select in each case the most important point and make a note of it, i.e. write it down as briefly as you can.

1   The new jet plane was painted scarlet, with a silver device on each wing and its name in gold on the fuselage. On its first flight it broke the world airspeed record.

2   The housewife reported that the new soap powder cleaned her clothes well, that it had a pleasant smell and that it was sold in a charming, pink packet.

3   When Richard was learning to ride a bicycle, he fell heavily at a corner, grazing both his knees, making his nose bleed, breaking his right arm, and scratching the chromium on his handlebars.

4   The general store on the corner sold everything on Joan's shopping list, but when she got there it was closed for the lunch-hour.

5   The cat burglar broke into the Evans's flat at midnight, leaving an hour later with two pork pies, a pair of nylon stockings, a pound of tomatoes and Mrs Evans's pearl necklace and matching ear-rings.

6   When the surveyor examined the house, he found that there was a magnificent view from the front windows, that the doors fitted well and that the roof did not leak; but he also found that the roof timbers were riddled with woodworm.

7   Tony took great care with his Geography homework, looking up

the facts in his textbook and colouring his maps well, but the master returned it unmarked because the handwriting was illegible.

8   Before he set off to catch the 9.30 train, Jeremy made sure that he had his sandwiches, his train-spotter's guide and his ticket, but then he discovered that his watch was slow and that it was already 9.35.

9   Two lorries and eight cars collided in thick fog on the M.1. One lorry and three of the cars were completely wrecked, and thirty yards of crashproof fencing was badly damaged. All the drivers and passengers, however, escaped with cuts and bruises, being allowed to go home after treatment in hospital.

10   Five minutes from the end of the hockey match, Rosemary scored a simple goal to make the score 2–1 in favour of her team, and this was still the score when the final whistle went.

In Exercise A you will have noticed that most of the examples were very simple ones, but that some of them needed a little thought. You should also have noticed that in some cases it was necessary to express the main point in your own words, because it was not stated in so many words in the original sentences. This was true of the fact that John had been murdered, in the example given on page 19. Here is another simple example:

Ronald Jones was sent to prison for three months after the police had found the firm's cash-box hidden in his wardrobe, covered by a pile of old shirts and pullovers.

The main point of this sentence might be expressed as 'Ronald Jones gaoled for theft'.

We must remember, therefore, that when we abstract important points from a passage we often abstract ideas which are not actually stated in the author's own words. In this way we are combining the skills of abstraction and paraphrase.

Examples of pupils' work

1   On the present occasion the solemnity of night's approach was rendered far more striking than it is to dwellers in ordinary towns, by that time-honoured custom observed by the people of Whitby, of leaving their streets wholly unlighted: in thus making a stand against the deplorably swift advance of the ride of progress and civilisation, they displayed no small share of moral courage and independent judgment. Was it for a people of sense to adopt every new-fangled invention of the age, merely because their neighbours did?
LEWIS CARROLL: *Wilhelm von Schmitz*

Some answers showed that the pupils had grasped the main point, but had failed to express it in their notes precisely enough:

(*a*) Why keep up with the Joneses?
(*b*) Perverse to conform to contemporary municipal standards.
(*c*) Satirisation of Whitby citizens' diehard attitude over progress.
(*d*) Was it for people of sense to adopt every new-fangled invention of the age?

Good answers:

(*a*) Absence of lighting in Whitby was due to the reactionary populace.
(*b*) Whitby had unlighted streets because of conservative people
(*c*) Unlighted streets, a revolt against progress.
(*d*) Streets unlit in Whitby because of narrow-minded citizens.
Which of these do you consider to be the best?

2   But in spite of the vagaries of fashion in art and much variety in the powers of its leading practitioners, the tone of the eighteenth century was favourable to high quality in the arts and crafts. England was filled full of beautiful things of all kinds, old and new, native and foreign. Houses in town and country were as rich as museums and art galleries, but the books, the engravings, the china, the furniture, the pictures were not flaunted or crowded for exhibition, but were set in their natural places for domestic use in hospitable homes.

G. M. TREVELYAN: *English Social History*
Why are the following notes unsatisfactory?

(*a*) More high quality taste.
(*b*) Eighteenth-century England's extravagance for perfection.
(*c*) Only the best would do in the 18th century.
(*d*) In 18th-century good taste in aesthetics.

The best answers received were:

(*a*) High aesthetic standard in 18th century.
(*b*) Eighteenth-century taste appreciated good quality design.
But even these fail to include the whole of the main point, that the products of the arts and crafts were part of everyday life; so we should add 'part of everyday life' to complete the note.

3   Annual income twenty pounds, annual expenditure nineteen pounds nineteen shillings and sixpence, result happiness. Annual income twenty pounds, annual expenditure twenty pounds ought and sixpence, result misery.

CHARLES DICKENS: *David Copperfield*

This example produced the note which illustrates clearly what we are aiming at:

Living within means – happiness. Living beyond means – misery.

Exercise B

The following examples are more difficult than those in *Exercise A*, but in each case you are asked as before to express as briefly as possible, in note-form, the important point or points; where there is more than one main point, the number you should look for is given in brackets at the end of the passage.

1   Fog everywhere. Fog up the river, where it flows among green aits and meadows; fog down the river, where it rolls defiled among the tiers of shipping, and the waterside pollutions of a great (and dirty) city. Fog on the Essex marshes, fog on the Kentish heights. Fog creeping into the cabooses of collier-brigs; fog lying out on the yards, and hovering in the rigging of great ships; fog drooping on the gunwales of barges and small boats. Fog in the eyes and throats of ancient Greenwich pensioners, wheezing by the firesides of their wards; fog in the stem and bowl of the afternoon pipe of the wrathful skipper, down in his close cabin; fog cruelly pinching the toes and fingers of his shivering little 'prentice boy on deck.
CHARLES DICKENS: *Bleak House*

2   On the big new estates, and in the new towns, one can see that between the pubs, the television and the grown-up societies father and mother will get along, that the little ones, going to school, will find junior organisations to cater for them. But the situation of the teenagers seems desperate. What are they to do? There is, perhaps, nowhere to dance, and only one poor coffee bar which keeps open until about nine-thirty. Beyond that, and particularly in winter, they seem to have nowhere to go. Above all they need to find some stamping ground where they feel they belong of right. They are too young to be anything but self-conscious and out of place in adult organisations.
LESLIE PAUL: *Hot House*

3   Mr Squeers's appearance was not prepossessing. He had but one eye, and the popular prejudice runs in favour of two. The eye he had was unquestionably useful, but decidedly not ornamental: being of a greenish-grey, and in shape resembling the fan-light of a street door. The blank side of his face was much wrinkled and puckered up, which

gave him a very sinister appearance, especially when he smiled, at which times his expression bordered closely on the villainous. His hair was very flat and shiny, save at the ends, where it was brushed stiffly up from a low protruding forehead, which assorted well with his harsh voice and coarse manner.

CHARLES DICKENS: *Nicholas Nickleby*

4   Parliamentary speeches today are as thick with figures as pips in raspberry jam. This was not always so. Here is how a speech from the Chancellor of the Exchequer might have read early in January 1890: 'The country enters the new year in a fairly prosperous state: from London and a number of other towns there are widespread reports of crowded markets at Christmas, though it is true that there have been some complaints of the high prices. I am given to understand, however, that one or two places in the north may not be sharing the general prosperity; a Doncaster steel mill, I am told, has given notice to a number of labourers.'

And this is how speeches by Chancellors of the Exchequer tend to read today: 'Industrial production in December was 3 per cent higher, on a seasonally adjusted basis, than in June; and unemployment in December, also seasonally adjusted, was only 1·5 per cent of the employed population – the same figure as November. But in the northern region there was a rise in the unemployment percentage between the two months, from 2·2 to 2·5 per cent; this is partly because steel output in that region is running as much as 20 per cent below last year's level.'

FRANK T. BLACKABY: *Figures are Facts*

5   In many societies children's walking means more trouble for the adults. Once able to walk, the children are a constant menace to property – breaking dishes, spilling the soup, tearing books, tangling the thread. But in Manus, where property is sacred and one wails for lost property as for the dead, respect for property is taught children from their earliest years. Before they can walk they are rebuked and chastised for touching anything which does not belong to them.

MARGARET MEAD: *Growing up in New Guinea*   (2 points)

6   The House of Commons is in some ways the most typically English of our institutions. And certainly it has never been mirrored in all its completeness anywhere else. It has had its imitators: no comparable institution has been so freely imitated. But nowhere else, neither in foreign countries nor in the countries of the Commonwealth where the historical forms have been most closely preserved, has the

authentic atmosphere of the House of Commons been reproduced.
Oxford and Cambridge: G.C.E. O Level

7   The need for manned aircraft should be evident to anyone who
has thought at all about the problems of fighting any future war. This
is not to suggest that missiles are not of prime importance: for certain
clearly defined tasks it is an enormous advantage to be able to
dispense with a human crew, and thereby to endow a vehicle with far
greater power of manoeuvre, greater performance, and the ability
to conduct types of mission for which conventional aeroplanes are
wholly unsuited. Nevertheless, as is now fully appreciated by all
except the general public, the missile has come to supplement, and
not to supplant, the military aeroplane.
Oxford and Cambridge: G.C.E. O Level

8   Statesmen regarded the fate of agriculture with all the more
indifference because it involved no acute problem of unemployment.
The farm labourer did not remain on the land when his occupation
there was gone, as unemployed miners hang round a closed mine.
When 'Hodge' lost his job, or when his wages fell, he slipped away
to the towns and found work there. Or else he migrated overseas, for
the colonies and the United States were still receiving the over-plus of
our still rapidly rising population. As a class, the English agricultural
labourer was well accustomed to the idea of leaving the land.
G. M. TREVELYAN: *English Social History*   (2 points)

9   The trouble with most museums is that they are too big and have
too many things in them. They present too big a temptation to
wander in at the front door, and wander round looking at everything,
before wandering out without being any the wiser. Most museums,
after all, cover nearly as wide a variety of subjects as most libraries –
though often with a particular local slant.
     To use a museum properly you have to have an objective, but it is
well worth paying one quick 'sightseeing' visit just to get an idea of
what the museum has to offer. After that, a museum should be *used*
rather than just visited. You will find that a museum can be used in
somewhat the same way as you use a library.
BENEDICK RICHARDS: *It's All Free*   (2 points)

10   Even the finest natural haven has no value (except as a place of
refuge for storm-bound ships) if it is distant from centres of population
or industry. Falmouth harbour in Cornwall is one of many examples
of this, for here one of the largest and most sheltered havens in Britain

25

has never become a really great port because of its location in a non-industrial part of the country. There are dozens of equally good natural harbours on the west coast of Scotland and in Ireland which are never used, though the Navy made use of some of them in wartime.

Yet it was the existence of sheltered waterways which first created centres of population. Harbours created many towns and cities. At a time when there were no roads, or only tracks, the sea and navigable rivers were Britain's main highways, and people gathered close to their banks and shores. Ships sailed up rivers and inlets as far inland as they could without hazard. Settlements, then towns that became cities, grew at these places. London is where it is because of the Thames, Liverpool because of the Mersey, Dublin because of the Liffey, and Bristol because of the Avon.

J. LENNOX KERR: *Harbour Spotter*   (2 points)

11   From extreme evils a country is for the most part saved by entrusting the management of its affairs chiefly to the upper classes of the community. A government of gentlemen may be and often is extremely deficient in intelligence, in energy and in sympathy with the poorer classes. It may be shamefully biased by class interests, and guilty of great corruption in the disposal of political appointments, but the standard of honour common to the class at least secures it from the grosser forms of corruption and the interests of its members are indissolubly connected with the permanent well-being of the country.

Oxford and Cambridge: G.C.E. O Level

12   Railroads shall soon traverse all this country, and with a rattle and a glare the engines and trains shall shoot like a meteor over the wide night-landscape, turning the moon paler; but, as yet, such things are non-existent in these parts, though not wholly unexpected. Preparations are afoot, measurements are made, ground is staked out. Bridges are begun, and their not yet united piers desolately look at one another over roads and streams, like brick and mortar couples with an obstacle to their union; fragments of embankments are thrown up, and left as precipices with torrents of rusty carts and barrows tumbling over them; tripods of tall poles appear on hilltops, where there are rumours of tunnels; everything looks chaotic, and abandoned in fell hopelessness.

CHARLES DICKENS: *Bleak House*   (2 points)

13   Some of the ways in which the young irritate their elders are only superficialities – surface tricks (of speech or dress or behaviour)

which have no very deep significance and can be treated as tiresome trifles rather than as important fundamentals. And, the other way round, many of the habits of the elders which drive the youngsters up the wall are no more than habits – ways of talking and behaving which have become ingrained in forty or fifty years, and have no very deep significance either. The danger is that these comparatively unimportant superficial differences may drive the gap between the generations wider and deeper.

SIR JOHN WOLFENDEN: *Family Affair* (2 points)

14   But to some readers, vaguely accustomed to think of the Middle Ages as a period of chivalry and love, with knights ever on their knees to ladies, it may come as a shock to realise that, in the knightly and gentle class, the choice of partners for marriage had normally nothing whatever to do with love; often the bride and bridegroom were small children when they were pledged for life, and even if adults, they were sold by their parents to the highest bidder. The Pastons and other county families regarded the marriages of their children as counters in the game of family aggrandisement, useful to buy money and estates, or to secure the support of powerful patrons. If the victim destined for the altar resisted, rebellion was crushed – at least in the case of a daughter or female ward – with physical brutality almost incredible. Elizabeth Paston, when she hesitated to marry a battered and ugly widower of fifty, was for nearly three months on end 'beaten once in the week or twice, sometimes twice in one day, and her head broken in two or three places'. Such were the methods of her mother Agnes, a highly religious, respectable and successful controller of the large Paston household.

G. M. TREVELYAN: *English Social History* (2 points)

15   We have made peculiar difficulties for ourselves by our fantastic rate of progress in science, technology and the social sciences. The great deeds of our time are now accomplished on *unintelligible frontiers*. When heroism appeared, as it once did, mostly on the battle-field or in personal combat, everybody could understand the heroic act. The claim of the martyr or the bluebeard to our admiration or horror was easy to grasp. When the dramatic accomplishment was an incandescent lamp, a steam engine, a telegraph, or an automobile, everybody could understand what the great man had accomplished. This is no longer true. The heroic thrusts now occur in the laboratory, among cyclotrons and betatrons, whose very names are popular symbols of scientific mystery. Even the most dramatic, best-publicised

adventures into space are on the edges of our comprehension. There are still, of course, rare exceptions – a Dr Albert Schweitzer or a Dr Tom Dooley – whose heroism is intelligible. But these only illustrate that intelligible heroism now occurs almost exclusively in the field of sainthood or martyrdom. There no progress has been made for millenia. In the great areas of human progress, in science, technology, and the social sciences, our brave twentieth century innovators work in the twilight just beyond our understanding. This has obviously always been true to some extent; the work of profound thinkers has seldom been more than half-intelligible to the lay public. But never so much as today.

DANIEL J. BOORSTIN: *The Image* (3 points)

Chapter 4

Giving a Title I

We are all familiar with several common types of title. What does the title of this book tell you, before you even look at the contents? Think about other titles you know, of books, plays, films, magazines and television shows, for example. They may be divided into two groups: those which indicate very clearly the main topic of the work (e.g. *The Loneliness of the Long-Distance Runner*); and those which are not at all helpful (e.g. *Kangaroo*). We shall be concerned in our own work only with titles which must be as helpful as we can make them.

It is worth considering for a while another very common use of titles, that found in newspapers, where they are known as headlines. It has been said that some newspapers try to make their headlines as informative as possible, in order to save lazy readers the bother of reading the reports and articles, though this is not the true motive. Look at the headlines in the daily paper that you usually read, and see what conclusions you can draw about titles; in particular, decide which headlines give the best indication of what is to be found in the report or article under them.

The following headlines were taken from six national daily newspapers, and they all refer to the same event, the 1961 May-Day Parade in Moscow:

1 RUSSIA DISPLAYS HER AIR POWER.
2 RUSSIA SHOWS OFF HER AIR POWER.
3 RUSSIA DISPLAYS HER MISSILES.
4 MR K'S SKY OPENER.
5 KHRUSHCHEV SHOWS OFF.
6 THE MIGHTIEST OF ALL AIR SHOWS – BY MR K.

Many points are raised by this set, but you should consider these questions, as well as others of your own:

1 What is the difference in effect between DISPLAYS and SHOWS OFF?

2 How would you define the difference between AIR POWER and MISSILES?

3 Which of the headlines are neutral, and which clearly reveal an attitude towards the Russians?

4 Why do three use RUSSIANS, one KHRUSHCHEV and two MR K?

You will have to make decisions based on such considerations as these when you are giving titles to passages.

Newspaper headlines can also afford illustrations of the dangers to be avoided. Some may be ambiguous:

MACARTHUR FLIES BACK TO FRONT.

POLICE FOUND SAFE UNDER BLANKET.

BARKING GOALKEEPER SENT OFF.

INDIAN BRAVES FIRE.

Some may be obscure, or take time to understand, either because words are strung together in an unusual, 'shorthand' way:

COLLEGE BAR REFUSAL TO BE DISCUSSED.

RIVER NUDE MURDER HUNT.

Or because the writer uses jargon or technical terms:

PARKS SLAMS TON (a cricketer's century).

62 P.C. IN MODS GROUP ON DRUGS 'FOR KICKS' (with reference to the Purple Hearts scandal).

GALE HITS SWALLOWS (illuminated by the next sentence: 'The Swallow Class championship at Bembridge, Isle of Wight, had to be postponed yesterday owing to gale-force south-westerly winds, rain and heavy seas').

These errors, and others you may discover, should serve as warnings. The whole field of titles, and especially newspaper headlines, is a fascinating one, but we must concentrate now on our proper concern, giving a title to passages which are to be summarised. The title may be regarded as a 'miniature summary'.

Four simple **rules** will suffice:

1   The title should give an accurate indication, as fully as possible, of the main topic of the passage.

2   The student's attitude and opinions must not influence his choice of title. He is concerned with what the author of the original passage wrote, and not with his own reactions to it, except on rare and special occasions (see Chapter 6, 'Point of View', pages 67–73).

3   The title should be a serious one, and not misleading, sensational, ambiguous, obscure, deliberately mystifying or whimsical.

4   The title should generally be restricted to a maximum of eight words. A one-word title will rarely be adequate.

The application of these rules can best be studied by looking at an example.

Examples of pupils' work

A restaurant beside the road offered 'buffaloburgers' for lunch, and I stopped to ask how it was that these animals, so scrupulously preserved from extinction, should be available for this sad metamorphosis. I was told that they are restricted to a few small reservations, and since they breed fairly prolifically and cannot roam elsewhere they are outgrowing their limits; so for an unfortunate minority, whack! and there is a crate of buffaloburgers. This is an astonishing fact, for in 1889 the original mighty herds of buffalo, which positively blackened the Great Plains during the migratory season, had been reduced to 541 head, and most of those were in zoos or private preserves. Thanks to the American strain of historical romanticism, the beast has made a remarkable recovery, and there are now about 9,000 bison in the United States, most of them as free, and all of them as stupid, as the ones we saw in Wyoming.

JAMES MORRIS: *Coast to Coast*

Some tried to respond to the tone of the passage, and in so doing broke Rule 3 in various ways:

> A Fate worse than Extinction?
> A New Purpose in Life for the Buffalo.
> A Safety Valve for American Romanticism.
> Buffalo, we love you but . . .
> Out of the Range, into the Frying Pan.
> Birth-control for Buffaloes.

You can appreciate the dangers of trying to be clever, for these fail lamentably to 'give an accurate indication, as fully as possible, of the main topic of the passage'.

Better answers included:

> The Buffalo's Descent from Reservation to Restaurant.
> From Game Reservation to Food Preservation.
> The Reduced Status of the Buffalo.

But the most suitable titles given were:
> Control of the Buffalo.
> Controlling the Buffalo Population.

We think the second of these is the best of all.

Exercise A

Give a suitable title for each of the following passsages:

1   There is, I fear, at the present time, an increasing tendency to

irreverent treatment of the name of God and of subjects connected with religion. Some of our theatres are helping this downward movement by the gross caricatures of clergymen which they put upon the stage: some of our clergy are themselves helping it, by showing that they can lay aside the spirit of reverence, along with their surplices, and can treat as jests, when *outside* their churches, names and things to which they pay an almost superstitious reverence when *inside*.

LEWIS CARROLL: *Sylvie and Bruno Concluded*

2   With gadgets in general I can only suggest that we keep our heads and select. If you are the kind of person who sees in a shop window an ingenious device for removing the stones from cherries, another which is supposed to peel shrimps, a dough-nut cutter and a juice extractor, and goes in to buy the lot in the hope that one day they will come in useful, you had better move into a larger house for your credulity is going to be exploited more and more as the years pass. Some gadgets are useful, some are not, while a great many take so long to adjust and use that the work could have been done with a sharp knife in half the time.

RUPERT CROFT-COOKE: *Cooking for Pleasure*

3   It is all very well in this age of status symbols to call rat catchers 'rodent operatives', but to expect them to remove wasps' nests in addition to their other duties is to defile their noble office. Recently they have been expressing their dissatisfaction over a mere 50p bonus for every nest destroyed. This is not enough. They should persuade their union, the National Union of General and Municipal Workers, to remove this task from their hands and to press for another post – that of 'insect exterminator'. After all, a rat is not a wasp and never has been, and it is dangerous to offend a man's dignity by offering a payment for a job which is out of his province. It could cause a general strike.

Welsh Joint Education Committee: Use of English

4   The archaeologist, contrary to popular opinion, does not spend his whole working life digging up treasures in the wilder parts of the world. Some of his work is carried out in the field, it is true, but much of it is done in museum, library and study, trying to understand what he and his colleagues have found, and how it fits into the pattern of previous knowledge. He has to spend a surprisingly large part of his time reading the results of other people's work; I reckon, as an archaeologist studying the pre-history of Europe and the British Isles, that I have in the course of a year to go through at least fifteen to

twenty journals dealing with our own islands, and sixty or seventy covering the European continent. If you add marginal studies in history, philology and Oriental archaeology, the total would naturally be bigger, and, of course, does not include books and monographs.
s. PIGGOTT: *Approach to Archaeology*

5   The eighteenth century was not, although it is often supposed to have been, a golden age for the employer. Just as in Rome the social status of a man was estimated by the number of slaves that he owned, so also was the relative grandeur of our ancestors assessed by the number of footmen clinging to the backs of their chariots and the sparkle of the liveries that they wore. The tradesman's wife at Canonbury, wishing to compete with her friends in Islington, would compel her husband to engage more servants than he either wanted or could afford. As a result, London, with a total population of 650,000 in 1767, owned as many as 50,000 domestics.
Welsh Joint Education Committee: G.C.E. O Level

6   By reciting their favourite poems aloud to each other, an Australian poet and his wife often while away many of those long straight miles of road that make driving in Australia at once pleasurable and boring. They like poetry. They like it enough to make it part of themselves, and because they make it part of their memories they can share it with others. They enjoy it because they are able to speak it aloud without embarrassment, giving the printed word its fullest liberation in the sound of the human voice. They also learn new poetry as they drive along, short poems they have appreciated for their wit or longer ones they can dwell over for their fuller, more expansive treatment of some situation, experience or idea.
A Review of English Literature, Vol. 5, January 1964

7   The question 'What gives fudge its special flavour?' can now be answered in a more precise way than the usual injunction to make it by heating cream with sugar at the temperature of boiling water.

The answer is that the flavour is due to a substance 4-Cis-heptenal, which has been identified and made synthetically.

This discovery is reported in an issue of the journal *Nature* by scientists working at the Unilever Research Laboratory at Vlaardingen, Holland. The original identification was made by Miss P. Haverkamp Begemann and Miss J. C. Koster, starting with more than 200 lb. of butterfat, and ending with roughly one fifty-thousandth of an ounce of fudge flavour.

'Olfactory assessment' was used to make an initial decision between a number of closely related chemical substances synthesized by Dr K. de Jong and Dr H. van der Wel. Final tests of the identity of the natural and synthetic flavours were made chemically.
The Times, 9 May 1964

8   The motor vehicle is here to stay; numbers may increase three or four times by the end of the century, and half the total increase is likely to come within ten years. The studies indicate the kind and scale of measures required to meet the increases of traffic. But when traffic growth and the measures are compared, it is difficult to avoid the conclusion that for a long period ahead traffic will increase faster than we can hope to cope with it, even on the most optimistic assumptions of capital investment. It may even be thought that a desperate situation will arise. The further conclusion is unavoidable: that conditions as they are going to develop in this island in the next ten years or so will demand an almost heroic act of self-discipline from the public. It is not only road safety that is involved, but everything to do with the sane and civilised use of motor vehicles. Motor manufacturers, parents, and teachers will have major parts to play, but the main burden of responsibility will rest with drivers. If ever there was a need for a sixth sense, this appears to be the best example – a sense of 'motorised responsibility' appropriate to a society which is in process of acquiring mobility on a scale unknown to previous generations.
Traffic in Towns (Buchanan Report)

Exercise B

Give a suitable title for each of the passages in *Exercise B* of Chapter 3 (pages 23–28).

Chapter 5

Paraphrase II

'Father Brown laid down his cigar and said carefully: "It isn't that they can't see the solution. It is that they can't see the problem."'

The Scandal of Father Brown

If we cannot understand a piece of writing, it is always helpful to be able to discover the difficulties in it. The first exercise, which will remind you of work done in Chapter 2, should give you practice both in detecting difficulties and in comprehension.

Exercise A

Paraphrase each of the following:

1   An army marches on its stomach.

2   Adolescence is the period of apprenticeship to one's adult role.

3   The pressure and volume of a fixed mass of a gas are inversely proportional, provided that the temperature is kept constant.

4   Although a large number of children partake of free meals at the school canteens, the proportion found to be suffering from marked malnutrition is a modest one. (A genuine error.)

5   The more people use the wireless the less they listen to it.

6   Soap and education are not as sudden as a massacre, but they are more deadly in the long run.

7   Machines are not only the instruments of our livelihood; they also provide the alleviation of our leisure.

8   Liberty is precious – so precious that it must be rationed.

9   Half a million people liquidated is a statistic, but one man killed in a traffic accident is a national tragedy.

10   Climate has one advantage over weather as a subject for calculation: it is within reasonable limits deterministic.

11   Science is not a Frankenstein but a liberating force.

12   Whatever hope is yours, was my life also. (Written by a soldier killed in the First World War.)

13   Intellectuals are natural Luddites.

14   The stresses of 20th-century life, and the brainwashing of the Admen, have made us all the more ready to clutch at the straw of the pink pill, and our weaknesses are big business.

15   In the early days of industrialisation there was an increasing demand for labour. The working-class family could not help seeming to itself to be better off the bigger it was – children were economic assets.

16   It lies with man himself whether nuclear energy with all its possibilities is to become a threat or a promise to mankind, and whether the successful unlocking of the mighty forces of Nature means existence or annihilation.

17   It is necessary for technical reasons that these warheads should be stored with the top at the bottom, and the bottom at the top. In order that there may be no doubt as to which is the bottom for storage purposes, it will be seen that the bottom of each head has been plainly labelled with the word TOP.

18   The hell of politics is that it reduces everything to the average truth that can be squeezed into a slogan. It's then the ready-made, pre-packaged truth that can be marketed at elections.

19   Malaria is a difficult disease to eradicate from a country. It is a chronic infection, and even when a patient has recovered completely he is liable to reinfection, for one attack does not result in natural immunity thereafter. Nor is it possible to prevent the disease by 'artificial' immunisation.

20   Our civilisation behaves as if the Age of Leisure were staring it in the face, and as if it did not like the look of it. This is not yet true of the countries where pie is still mostly in the sky; they are still striving for it single-mindedly, but with a dynamism which might easily carry them past the goal, into the traditional tracks of successful nations.

Tone

'You have done well!' These words look like strong praise, and they may be; but they can be spoken in a tone which makes them into bitter criticism, or which suggests that your success was as accidental as a **rainbow. How would the words be said if the speaker thought that** you had done really well? That you had done well but could have done better? That you had, at some time in the past, done well, but not now? That *you* had done well, but the others had not? How would the words be said if the speaker was astonished at your achievement? or if he felt that you had done very badly indeed?

Most of the passages in this book are neutral in tone, but in many there are moments where the author intends his remarks humorously or ironically, and to fail to notice his change of tone would lead you to misunderstand his meaning, perhaps quite badly. Occasionally writers will become very angry, or very passionate, or very contemptuous; and, again, you will need to appreciate this. Whether the summary you make of their writing reflects its tone depends on the purpose of your summary – as you will be reminded in a later chapter.

Exercise B

In what tone should the following sentences be read? (Try to find *verbs* which suggest the tone: e.g., would 'boasted' be better than 'said' for (1), or does it imply that Wilde intended his remark too seriously?)

1 To Customs officers on landing at New York: 'I have nothing to declare except my genius.'
2 Beware of the dog.
3 Halt at major road ahead.
4 Drinka pinta milka day.
5 I thank thee that I am not as other men are. (S. Luke, ch. 18, v. 11.)
6 Angling – I can only compare to a stick and a string, with a worm at one end and a fool at the other.
7 Let them eat cake.
8 Sir, you have but two topics, yourself and me. I am sick of both.
9 Suffer the little children to come unto me, and forbid them not: for of such is the kingdom of God. (S. Mark, ch. 10, v. 14.)
10 We here highly resolve that this nation, under God, shall have a new birth of freedom; and that government of the people, by the people, for the people, shall not perish from the earth.
11 A cucumber should be well sliced, and dressed with pepper and vinegar, and then thrown out, as good for nothing.
12 We are waiting for the long-promised invasion. So are the fishes.
13 The Duke of Wellington, commenting on a draft sent out to him in Spain, 1809: 'I don't know what effect these men will have upon the enemy, but by God they terrify me.'
14 Oscar Wilde: 'I wish I had said that.'
    Whistler: 'You will, Oscar, you will.'
15 I received your foolish and impudent letter. Any violence offered me I shall do my best to repel; and what I cannot do for myself, the law shall do for me. I hope I shall never be deterred from detecting what I think a cheat, by the menaces of a ruffian.

Reported Speech

Some people re-tell, word for word, every fragment of every conversation they take part in or overhear; they are usually exhausting company. Most of us pass on only those parts of real interest to our listeners. We do this quite unconsciously, and very easily, and yet as we do so we are in fact practising two skills necessary in summary work: we are *abstracting* the main points, and at the same time turning the words we heard into *reported speech*. Occasionally (as in slander cases), it is important to have a verbatim record of what was originally said; but more often a shortened, reported version will do.

The following brief exchange took place at the first Motor Show, held in November 1896. Charles Jarrott was a famous racing-motorist of the day.

Questioner: 'Where is the electricity stored?'
Jarrott: 'That is not an electric machine but one driven by petrol.'
Questioner: 'What do you mean – petrol?'
Jarrott: 'Petrol is a spirit – like methylated spirit.'
Questioner: 'Good gracious! Doesn't it always blow up?'

Here are two attempts to turn these sentences into reported speech. If you think one is better than the other, try to say why.

a   The questioner asked Jarrott where the electricity was stored. Jarrott said that that car was not an electrical machine but one driven by petrol. Then the questioner asked Jarrott what petrol was, and he said that petrol was a spirit, like methylated spirit. Then the questioner said good gracious, didn't it always blow up?

b   Jarrott was asked by a questioner where the electricity was stored. He replied that the car was not an electric machine, but was driven by petrol. Then he was asked what he meant by petrol, and he explained that it was a spirit, like methylated spirit. The questioner was surprised that it didn't always blow up.

Compare the original with *b*, asking yourself: why 'is' (in line 1) becomes 'was'; why 'you' (line 3) becomes 'he'; why the questioner's final question has lost its question-mark; what has happened to the inverted commas throughout; and whether the choice of verbs bears out what was said about neutral verbs in the section on Tone above. Finally, basing them on these hints and putting them in their order of importance, write down *five rules* to help you when you have to turn direct into reported speech.

Unless you are particularly asked to, or unless the material seems to require it, you need not write summaries in reported speech. It is, however, sometimes necessary; and here is an exercise for practice.

Exercise C

Make readable versions in reported speech of the following:

1   I walked deliberately to him, took off my hat, and said:
'Dr Livingstone, I presume?'
'Yes,' said he, with a kind smile, lifting his cap slightly.
'I thank God, Doctor, I have been permitted to see you.'
He answered, 'Stanley, I feel thankful that I am here to welcome
you.'

2   Dr Neville Mercury told a local N.F.U. gathering last night: 'For
the sake of peace, I believe that people in Eastern lands must not be
encouraged to eat beef. My experience is that to give men plenty of
red meat makes them so fit and well that they become almost violent.
I think we have enough trouble with the violent people we already
have, and I suggest that we leave those people to their rice. Let us not
aggravate the situation by wanting them to start eating beef.'

3   'I shall see you again, shall I not?'
'Alas!' Miss Vandeleur answered. 'You have heard my father.
What can I do but obey?'
'Tell me at least that it is not with your consent,' returned Francis.
'Give me a keepsake.'
'If I agree,' she said, 'will you promise to do as I tell you?'
'Willingly,' replied Francis.
'Whatever you hear, whatever happens, do not return to this
house. Hurry fast until you reach the populous quarters of the city;
even there be upon your guard. You are in a greater danger than you
fancy.'

4   A British Rail punctuality drive has had unforeseen results for
the staff on some main line stations. 'People have come to rely on
trains being late,' said a Derby ticket-collector today. 'Now many are
leaving on time, and we get people dashing through the barrier at the
last minute and returning to complain that they've missed the train.
When we explain politely that the train left on time, they become
abusive.'

5   'There are cases, of course,' said Dr Borden, 'in which we can
save people's lives without their helping us. But those cases are rare.
The strongest of all medicines is faith. And your job is to justify the
faith in yourself and your colleagues. I'm afraid this sounds like a
sermon, Mr Bradley, but when I see a young man like yoursel

beginning his medical career, I like him to feel that it's a serious moment. It's full of tremendous responsibilities not only to your patients but also to yourself. Very well, Mr Bradley, that's all. I wish you good luck.'

6   Councillor Trafford took exception to the proposed notice at the entrance of South Park: 'No dogs must be brought to this Park except on a lead.' He pointed out that this order would not prevent an owner from releasing his pets, or pet, from a lead when once safely inside the Park.

The Chairman (Colonel Vine) : 'What alternative wording would you propose, Councillor?'

Councillor Trafford: ' "Dogs are not allowed in this Park without leads." '

Councillor Hogg: 'Mr Chairman, I object. The order should be addressed to the owners, not to the dogs.'

Councillor Trafford: 'That is a nice point. Very well then: "Owners of dogs are not allowed in this Park unless they keep them on leads".'

Councillor Hogg: 'Mr Chairman, I object. Strictly speaking, this would prevent me as a dog-owner from leaving my dog in the back-garden at home and walking with Mrs Hogg across the Park.'

Councillor Trafford: 'Mr Chairman, I suggest that our legalistic friend be asked to redraft the notice himself.'

Councillor Hogg: 'Mr Chairman, since Councillor Trafford finds it so difficult to improve on my original wording, I accept. "Nobody without his dog on a lead is allowed in this Park".'

Councillor Trafford: 'Mr Chairman, I object. Strictly speaking, this notice would prevent me, as a citizen who owns no dog, from walking in the Park without first acquiring one.'

Councillor Hogg (with some warmth): 'Very simply, then: "Dogs must be led in this Park".'

Councillor Trafford: 'Mr Chairman, I object. This reads as if it were a general injunction to the Borough to lead their dogs into the Park.'

Councillor Hogg interposed a remark for which he was called to order; upon his withdrawing it, it was directed to be expunged from the Minutes.

The Chairman: 'Councillor Trafford, Councillor Hogg has had three tries; you have had only two. . . .'

Councillor Trafford: ' "All dogs must be kept on leads in this Park".'

The Chairman: 'I see Councillor Hogg rising quite rightly to raise another objection. May I anticipate him with another amendment: "All dogs in this Park must be kept on the lead".'

This draft was put to the vote and carried unanimously, with two abstentions.

Minutes of a Borough Council, in ROBERT GRAVES and ALAN HODGE: *The Reader Over Your Shoulder*

The five rules which you made for your own guidance need slight modification when you turn into reported speech a conversation *in which you were concerned.*

7 Grandma made this phone call the day after Henry heard he had passed an important examination. Write the account of it which Grandfather might give. (You will be using reported speech in its most usual form.)

'Hello . . . oh, good . . . that *is* Henry, isn't it? I'm so glad. I have just heard of your wonderful success from your mother and father. It's a great result – didn't I tell you that you could do it? Grandfather and I are very proud of you.

'Well, I won't keep you long now – I expect you will be wanting to go out and celebrate or something. Grandfather and I would like to join you, but it's too far, and besides we'd be in the way. So we're sending a little present to help you enjoy your success; it should reach you tomorrow, dear. . . . No, no, you mustn't thank us . . . you've earned it! Just relax now, and then you'll be ready to work very hard when you begin again in the Autumn.

'I must ring off now – grandfather's favourite programme is just starting on television, and he'll never forgive me if I talk all through it. Bye-bye, Henry – congratulations again – bye-bye.'

8 Now write Grandma's version. Begin: 'I rang Henry because I was so pleased to have heard from . . .'

9 Finally, report this telephone call as though you were Henry.

Letters and Documents

The writer of your history book – or the writers of the history books on which it is based – consulted many documents in order to discover the facts he has now made easily available to you: war maps, old manuscripts, diaries, wills, letters. In the same way, every geography text book is based partly on scrutiny of documents such as weather maps, rainfall graphs and export figures, although it may seldom quote them directly. (If it were a different kind of book it might contain nothing else.)

You will see that it is not possible to give a hard-and-fast rule about summarising letters and documents – the kind of summary you make will depend on the purpose for which you are condensing them. You should, however, be careful not to omit any important information contained in the letter-head (e.g. who wrote the letter, and to whom). An example will make this clear.

Imagine that the proprietor of your local cinema wanted to advertise in a special way a long, colourful and expensive war film he was going to show soon. He had decided that a good way of doing this would be to put up a bright streamer, bearing the film's title, from his cinema to the building opposite – which happened to be the Town Hall. He would write to the Town Clerk for permission.

At the next Council meeting, his request would be discussed. Some doubts might be felt for the safety of the fabric of the Town Hall; but, on the other hand, most councillors would want to encourage the proprietor's initiative. One might mention that, although the film was for the public's entertainment, it was also for the cinema's profit. And so the discussion would go.

At last, one councillor would suggest something acceptable to all. His proposal would be seconded. And soon the Town Clerk would write to the cinema proprietor, giving the Council's decision.

The whole affair would be recorded in the Council's Minutes:

A request from Mr George Bear, the proprietor of the Plaza Cinema, to fix a banner approximately two feet deep by fourteen feet long to the Town Hall advertising the film 'Revenge from Space' was received. Councillor Dudley Payne moved, and Councillor Richard Evans seconded and it was RESOLVED that the application be granted for the period of the film and subject to a donation of £5 to Oxfam, and subject also to the Council being indemnified against any damage done, which should be made good by the applicant.

The initial letter from Mr Bear is summarised (and its letter-head incorporated) in the first sentence of the Minutes. The first half of the second sentence records the most important fact of the Council's discussion, and the rest of the sentence sets out conditions which the Town Clerk will have to pass on to Mr Bear when he writes to him. It would be interesting to work out in class the two letters, and also perhaps (particularly with the extract of p. 40 above in mind) to imagine the Council Meeting which came between them.

Exercise D

In reported speech, convey the important information contained in the following:

I

> THE SUBMERGED LOG COMPANY
> EAST ROAD
> GRINSTEAD
> Date as postmark

Dear Sirs,

CHRISTMAS CARDS

The Submerged Log Company has recently given consideration to the sending of Christmas Cards and, although it is certainly not without its pleasant side, we have decided regretfully to discontinue the sending of Christmas Cards from this year.

I am sure that you will appreciate that the warmth of the feelings of all in this firm who have had, and are having, dealings with you is undiminished, and that as in the past, but henceforth silently, our good wishes will be with you at this time of year.

> Yours faithfully,
>
> THE SUBMERGED LOG COMPANY

2   THE FÜHRER AND SUPREME COMMANDER OF
     THE ARMED FORCES

> FÜHRER HEADQUARTERS
> 16 July 1940
>
> 7 copies

Directive No. 16

On preparations for a landing operation against England

Since England, in spite of her hopeless military situation, shows no sign of being ready to come to an understanding, I have decided to prepare a landing operation against England and, if necessary, to carry it out.

The aim of this operation will be to eliminate the English homeland as a base for the prosecution of the war against Germany and, if necessary, to occupy it completely.

Preparations for the entire operation must be completed by the middle of August.

> *Signed:* ADOLF HITLER

3

LONDON TRANSPORT
GRIFFITH HOUSE
280 MARYLEBONE ROAD
LONDON N.W.1

Extension 102
Our reference J64/ABB
14 September 1964
Dear Sir,

   Thank you for your letter. Please use the extracts you mention in your textbook. The re-worded notice we like to quote is 'Smokers are asked to sit at the back' instead of 'Smokers are requested to occupy rear seats' – but it is, of course, your book.

Yours faithfully,

H. F. HUTCHISON

Publicity Officer

G. W. Dennis, Esq.
The College
Llandovery

4   TO THE HON. JOHN JAY, U.S.A.

KENSINGTON GORE
NEAR LONDON
10 July 1810

. . . . I am grieved to tell you that both your countrymen and my own are still carrying on the abominable traffic in human flesh, in spite of the abolition laws of their respective countries. I trust that a continuance of the vigorous methods we are using to carry our law into effect, will by degrees force our commercial men to employ their substance in some more innocent commerce. I am not without hopes of a practical, though not a formal, adoption of the only effectual expedient for suppressing the slave trade: that of the armed vessels of both our countries taking the slave ships of the other as well as those of its own.

Your faithful servant,

WILLIAM WILBERFORCE

5   Advice columns are a common feature of the English Press. In 1960 an African paper adopted the idea, and the following letters and replies were first printed in the *Central African Mail*'s 'Tell me, Josephine.'

a   'I am naturally irresistible. Many beautiful girls flock to me when I ask them. Social life is a cup of tea. Tell me why girls come flocking to a boy like me?'

   Because they are half-witted, I imagine. No sensible girl would rush to a man so full of self-conceit.

b 'When we take a walk together my silly wife complains that I wink at other women and she is angry about this, going at me like a bullet. I have patiently explained that it is the strong sunlight making me blink, but the woman will not have this. What would you do with such a silly wife?'

Wear dark glasses when walking out in the sunshine. Then only you will know what your eyes are doing.

c 'I belong to a family of men who have no hair on their heads when they are grown up. I promised to marry and she was a real happy girl till she suddenly told me she was no longer my future wife because I am of this bare family.

'She fears I may be bald when grown up, and so too may she, as my wife. The girl admits she has never seen a bald woman since she was born.

'How can I persuade her to be my wife? Is it a worm, and is it a men's disease only? If you tell her this may help me.'

Baldness in men often runs in families and is not a disease or a worm. It is something to do with 'genes' or tiny cells that make up your body from the moment you are born. Only men are affected and you cannot catch it from another person. You are not certain to go bald. Tell your girl that many distinguished people all over the world are bald. Tell her that if you do go bald in years to come, you will use the money you save on hair-cuts to buy her presents.

Simplifying

London Transport buses used to display this notice:

Dogs. Small dogs may, at the discretion of the conductor and at owner's risk, be carried without charge upon the upper deck of double-deck buses, or in single-deck buses. The decision of the conductor is final.

The notice now reads:

You can take your dog with you if it is a small one and the conductor agrees. It travels free, but at your risk. If the vehicle is a double-decker, you must both go on the upper deck.

Compare the two versions, using the following hints.

a What is the effect on the tone of the notice of the change from *Small dogs may . . . at owner's risk be carried* to *You can take your dog . . . it travels free*?

b In what way is *at your risk* an improvement on *at owner's risk*?

c Why is *dogs may be carried* less good than *you can take your dog*?

d There are many more verbs in the second version than in the first: which words do they replace?

45

e Compare the length and structure of sentences in the two notices.
f The vocabulary of the second is simpler (*discretion* and *decision* become *agrees*), although here the changes are more important for lightening the tone than simplifying the language.

From making this comparison you can work out four principles to guide you when simplifying a difficult or confused extract, particularly if its sentences are long.

Simplify the vocabulary.

Recast the piece into shorter sentences.

Use as many active verbs as you can.

Make the tone more direct – where appropriate, more personal.

In the light of these suggestions, comment on the two versions of the following notice, and then go on to *Exercise E*.

WARNING: The London Transport Board cannot be responsible for failure to adhere to the scheduled times of the buses, nor can they guarantee the running of the services to be as stated, though every effort will be made to maintain them.

You cannot hold London Transport responsible if your bus is late or does not run. London Transport does not guarantee that its services will keep to the timetable or will run at all, although, of course, it will do its best to see that they do.

Exercise E

Simplify the following. It will often be necessary to use several sentences to make clear at greater leisure a point made very concisely in the original. (See also Chapter 2, page 9.)

1 The prison is an integral part of the amenity of the Dartmoor area. It is part of the moor's character, fascination and history.

2 With the increase in power of steam locomotives both permanent way and coaching stock improved, so that the attainment of higher speeds synchronised with a growth of railway-mindedness in the country in general, and a mile-a-minute travel was accepted as a natural rather than a sensational development.

3 The increasing mobility of the public due to wider ownership of cars and the change in leisure habits have produced a threat to the existence of National Parks.

4 Evolution is a corollary to organic growth; the inorganic does not grow and does not exhibit evolution.

5   If you should die in the Civil Service, after at least **ten years** reckonable service, your wife would get a pension of one-third of the pension you would have got if you had retired because of ill-health on the day you died, or £25 a year, whichever was the greater.

6   The stern compassion of circumstances, the twinges of adversity, the spur of slights and taunts in early years, are needed to evoke that ruthless fixity of purpose and tenacious mother-wit without which great actions are seldom accomplished.

7   This is the gradation of thinking, preaching, and acting: if a man thinks erroneously, he may keep his thoughts to himself, and nobody will trouble him; if he preaches erroneous doctrine, society may expel him; if he acts in consequence of it, the law takes place.

8   The season generally associated with Forsythia is the spring; the blossoms tend to appear at the beginning or in the middle of March, but in an early season they may already be open by the end of February or the beginning of March, while in a late season one may have to wait until the end of March or the beginning of April for the first blossoms to appear.

9   We need not sentimentally under-estimate the insincerity all around us and within us, or the extent to which we reduce other people to the status of tools for our purposes; but as a thread running through it and occasionally appearing, there is in most human beings a spontaneous liking for the friendly companionship of other people.

10   The more advanced the civilisation, the larger the communities in which it lived. Lack of hygiene and medical knowledge were therefore combined with overcrowding, a state of affairs that both bred and spread disease. Improved means of communication and discovery of international trade routes had made more food available but they also spread infections which had until then been regional and to which native populations had acquired partial immunity. Introduced to fresh areas these infections often took a violently epidemic form.

11   We hold these truths to be sacred and undeniable; that all men are created equal and independent, that from that equal creation they derive rights inherent and inalienable, among which are the preservation of life, and liberty, and the pursuit of happiness.

12   When numbered pieces of toast and marmalade were dropped on various samples of carpet arranged in quality, from coir matting to

the finest Kirman rugs, the marmalade-downwards incidence varied indirectly with the quality of the carpet – the Principle of the Graduated Hostility of Things.

13 Science is directed towards understanding, and technology is directed towards use. The criteria of achievement in science can only be applied by scientists, who must be the judges of the significance of any claim to the extension of pure knowledge. The criteria of success in technology is that of the market, whether the new idea is a commercial asset or not: the final judgment here is exercised by the consumer.

14 Is television drug or stimulus? The answer must surely be that, just as its use for good or bad ends, doctrinally, will depend on the fundamental philosophy, democratic or totalitarian, religious or atheistic, of the State controlling the system, so its tactical direction will help to determine its effect as a soporific or an awakener.

15 The increasing affluence of society is reflected in the proliferation of sports and the larger number of people participating in them. Nevertheless, the increased cost of facilities in a concentrated and urbanized country and the impossibility of the immediate participants in any one sport finding and organizing sufficient resources to meet the cost of facilities means that even an affluent society must make general provision for sport if all its members are to have the opportunity of enjoying it, and if the best performers are to meet the challenge of world standards.

*   *   *

Robert Gunning, in his book *The Technique of Clear Writing*, describes writing of the sort you have been paraphrasing in this exercise as 'foggy', and has evolved a Fog Index by which you can compare the density of different examples. To arrive at this, you count the number of three-syllable words (ignoring proper nouns, compounds and verb-endings) in one hundred words from the passage. You then add the number of words in the average sentence, and multiply the sum by 0·4. If the answer is more than 12, the writing is very foggy indeed.

This chapter contains one more exercise – of ten longer passages – and then you will have had as much practice as you need in paraphrasing on its own. But the skill you have been developing will often be used in the rest of this book, as you get to grips with an extract before trying to summarise it.

Exercise F. Paraphrase:

1   The banana are a great remarkable fruit. They are constructed in the same architectural style as sausage, difference being skin of sausage are habitually consumed, while it is not advisable to eat wrapper of banana. The bananas are held aloft while consuming; sausage are usually left in reclining position. Sausage depend for creation on human being or stuffing machine, while banana are pristine product of honourable mother nature. In case of sausage, both conclusions are attached to other sausage; banana on other hand are attached on one end to stem and opposite termination entirely loose. Finally, banana are strictly of vegetable kingdom, while affiliation of sausage often undecided.
A Japanese Schoolboy, in R. SWANN and F. SIDGWICK: *The Making of Prose*

2   The history of science, more than of any other activity, shows men and women of every nation contributing to the common pool of organised knowledge and providing the means for enhancing human welfare. No respect for tradition or for our scientific heritage, however, can ever be allowed to impede the advance of science itself. Great discoverers of the past were breaking new ground, and those who would emulate them must learn the science of today in order to make tomorrow's advances.
J. JEWKES and others: *The Sources of Invention*

3   The Pickwickian Christmas did very little to stimulate consumption; it was mainly a gratuitous festivity. A few vintners and distillers and poulterers were the only people whom it greatly profited financially. This was a state of things which an ever-increasingly efficient industrialism could not possibly afford to tolerate. Christmas, accordingly, was canalised. The deep festal impulse of man was harnessed and made to turn a very respectable little wheel in the mills of industry. Today Christmas is an important economic event.
ALDOUS HUXLEY: *The Olive Tree*

4   Undoubtedly it is among the foremost duties of a historian to point out the faults of eminent men of former generations. There are no errors which are so likely to be drawn into precedent, and therefore none which it is so necessary to expose, as the errors of persons who have a just title to the gratitude and admiration of posterity. In politics, as in religion, there are devotees who show their reverence for a departed saint by converting his tomb into a sanctuary for crime.

5 A Judge cannot compel a Jury to agree, but he can remind the Jurors. It is most important that the Jury should agree if it is possible to do so; that, with a view to agreeing, there must inevitably be some give and take; and if any member should find himself in a small minority and disposed to differ from the rest, he should consider the matter carefully, weigh the reasons for and against his view, and remember that he may be wrong; that if, on so doing, he can honestly bring himself to concur in the view of the majority, albeit hesitatingly or reluctantly, he should do so, but if he cannot do so consistently with the oath he has taken and he cannot bring the others round to his point of view, then it is his duty to differ and for want of agreement there will be no verdict.

LORD DENNING

6 How would I start to describe the positive achievements of our society? I should count it a gain wherever rational judgment rather than emotion or rigid dogmatism determined public decisions; and also a gain whenever the narrow self-interest of individuals or local groups gave way to an acceptance of the common interests of a larger community. My criterion for social advance would be the accessibility, for everyone in our community, of the means to develop their innate capabilities.

G. M. CARSTAIRS: *This Island Now*

7 His abilities were his mastery of the irrational factors in politics, his insight into the weaknesses of his opponents, his gift for simplification, his sense of timing, his willingness to take risks. An opportunist entirely without principle, he showed considerable consistency and an astonishing power of will in pursuing his aims. Cynical and calculating in the exploitation of his powers as a showman, he retained an unshaken belief in his historic role and in himself as a creature of destiny.

ALAN BULLOCK: *Hitler, a Study in Tyranny*

8 The densely developed centres of towns and cities naturally generate a great deal of movement. But they have become so embedded and constricted in vast expanses of surrounding development that movement within them and to them is understandably difficult. This is particularly the case with motor traffic, much of which is attracted in from other parts of the town or from outside the town altogether and which has to filter through streets and localities with which it has no concern whatsoever. The power of town centres as

generators and attractors of traffic seems not to have been fully understood, and mistaken reliance has been placed on ring roads for the relief of central congestion when in fact much of the traffic has business in the central area and is not divertible to places outside that district.

Traffic in Towns (Buchanan Report)

9   Throughout ancient and medieval times Britain occupied a position on the verge of the known world. Since there was nothing beyond, every impulse of private adventure and national expansion on the part of the islanders had to expand itself upon Europe. Yet old Europe was no longer malleable stuff and could take no impress of British language and customs, even from the most vigorous efforts of young England, as the barren close of the Hundred Years' War had very clearly shown. And now the gate of return that way was bolted and barred by the rise of the great continental monarchies, so that Englishmen seemed shut in upon themselves, doomed for ever to an insular and provincial existence, sighing in old manor-houses for the spacious days of Harry the Fifth.

G.C.E. O Level.

10   During the past year planning application has been made to build holiday villages in many parts of Wales. Experience shows that speculative development of this type in nearly every case entails a change in land usage and frequently a loss of agricultural land. The population of the holiday village will usually be greater than the residential population, thereby dominating and fundamentally changing the character of the area and throwing the whole community out of balance. Many problems will arise due to such factors as the increase in cars and the inadequacy of the existing road systems, the inability of public services to cope with the influx of people, and, finally, a threat to an existing way of life which the local people seldom relish being forced upon them. Whatever benefits that may accrue will only be of a short term nature: in the longer term the loss of the characteristics of the area will probably have an adverse effect on their livelihood and way of life.

COUNCIL FOR THE PROTECTION OF RURAL WALES: *Report*, 1963

Chapter 6

Abstraction II

'There is no branch of detective science which is so important and so much neglected as the art of tracing footsteps.'

Sherlock Holmes

In Chapter 3 we covered the first stages of abstraction, the selection of the important points and their writing down as notes. You will have noticed, though, that in many of the examples it was difficult to separate the one or two main points from the other points in the passage, often because these other points were important, but not quite as important as those finally selected. In most cases where a summary is necessary, you will find that you can divide the points made into three groups: main points, subsidiary points, and comparatively unimportant points.

Main points are obviously the most important, as we saw in Chapter 3, and they will vary in number according to the length and nature of the material. They form the framework of the passage, the main line of statement or argument.

Subsidiary points are also important, but less so than those we have selected as main points. Usually they add to the meaning of a main point, or they develop it in a particular direction.

Comparatively unimportant points are those we can afford to reject when we are giving a condensed or brief version. They will often include illustrations of all kinds, and sometimes material which interested the writer or speaker, but which was not properly part of the main topic.

When we have to make a *Summary*, therefore, we shall always leave out the third group, the comparatively unimportant points, as they are the ones which may be most easily sacrificed. On the other hand, we shall always include the main points, as they are essential to any summary. Whether or not we include the subsidiary points will depend upon the situation, that is upon the length of the summary we are making, but usually we shall be concerned with summaries which will include both main and subsidiary points. This means that abstraction for summarising is really a process of selecting the two groups mentioned, main points and subsidiary points, leaving the third group which we are not going to use. Our notes must accordingly show main and subsidiary points and must indicate which are which.

The process is exactly the same when we are making notes for other purposes. We may make notes, for example, from a History or Geography textbook in order to learn the points for an examination, and to use them later for revision.

Examples of pupils' work

Make brief notes for a summary of the following passage, indicating clearly which are the main points and which are the subsidiary points that you would include.

The tendency to dispense with men and intelligence is held to go far beyond the consumer gadgets. The unmanned missile is about to replace the old-fashioned hand-operated bomber. In the near future, according to enthusiasts, unmanned missiles will take flight to intercept other unmanned missiles which will prevent these from intercepting other automated missiles. The operation will be handled under contract by IBM. If the globe were larger or the explosions smaller the prospect would be not unattractive. The machines having taken over, men would all be non-combatants. The charm of war has always been greatest for those whose role was to guide it from a certain distance.

These visions of the triumph of the machine can be multiplied endlessly. We do not take them seriously for we do not really believe that we are being replaced, and our instinct is sound. If there is a competition between man and machine, man is winning it – not for at least two centuries has his position been so strong as compared with the apparatus with which he works.

And the fact that this is the age of ascendant man, not triumphant machine, has practical consequences. If machines are the decisive thing, then the social arrangements by which we increase our physical plant and equipment will be of first importance. But if it is men that count, then our first concern must be with arrangements for conserving and developing personal talents. It will be these on which progress will depend. Should it happen, moreover, that for reasons of antiquated design our society does well in supplying itself with machines and badly in providing itself with highly improved manpower, there would be cause for concern. There is such cause, for that precisely is our situation.

J. K. GALBRAITH: *The Liberal Hour*

In the light of the work you have done so far, consider how the following typical answers could be improved. Notice particularly the different ways in which the notes are arranged.

a   *Main points:*
1 Unmanned missiles taking over from hand-operated war weapons.
2 Men would no longer directly participate in any war.
3 Despite this change, it must be emphasised that man still has complete control over his machines.
4 This proves that man has become more powerful through the ingenuity of his inventions.
5 Cause for alarm only if highly improved manpower compares unfavourably with machines.

Subsidiary points:
1 War operations concerning unmanned missiles will be handled by IBM.
2 The charm of war is greatest for those who conduct it from afar off.
3 Globe too small and missiles too powerful to make unmanned warfare attractive.
4 Man's position over machine is the strongest it has been for 200 years.
5 If machines become more powerful than man, our social life will have to be re-arranged.
6 Personal development must be our No. 1 concern.

b   *Men supposedly being replaced by machines.* Unmanned missile replaces manned. These being developed for every aspect of warfare. Unfortunately world is too small and explosions too big.
   This is not actually true. Man is winning the battle with machines. He rightly takes little notice of them.
   We must concern ourselves with the situation. Our society is supplying itself well with machines and badly with manpower. We are increasing equipment, physical plant, etc., not developing personal talents.

c   1 Tendency to dispense with men and rely on machines goes beyond consumer gadgets (unmanned missiles replace manned bombers; if globe smaller – good, men being non-combatants).
   2 Man does not believe he is being replaced – true (not for two hundred years has man's position been so strong compared with machines).

3 Progress relies on the increase of plant and equipment being of first importance, or the development of personal talent.

4 Man is ascendant but antiquated set up of society fails to develop manpower (just provides itself with more and more machines).

5 This is a cause for concern.

d ENCROACHMENT OF MACHINES INTO MAN'S TERRITORY. Example of automated missiles taking over from old bombers.
WE DO NOT BELIEVE THAT WE ARE BEING REPLACED BY MACHINES. SOCIAL ARRANGEMENTS DEPEND ON WHETHER IT IS MAN OR MACHINE THAT COUNTS. If machines count most, then develop and improve equipment. If man counts most then develop personal abilities because PROGRESS WILL DEPEND ON THESE. If society does well in machines but badly in manpower then there is cause for concern. THERE IS CAUSE BECAUSE THIS IS WHAT IS HAPPENING.

Now write your own notes, avoiding all the mistakes you have detected.

Layout of Notes

The purpose of making notes is to remind ourselves of the points in the original passage which we are going to use either when revising for an examination or as the basis for a summary. They must be as brief as possible, bearing this purpose in mind, but we now realise that our notes will cover two kinds of points, main and subsidiary, and that we need to distinguish clearly between them. We can best do this by setting out our notes in this way:

1 Main point
    (*a*) Subsidiary point
    (*b*) Subsidiary point
    (*c*) Subsidiary point
2 Main point
3 Main point
    (*a*) Subsidiary point
4 Main point
    (*a*) Subsidiary point
    (*b*) Subsidiary point

You must be prepared for the fact that the number of subsidiary points attached to any one main point will vary from none to three, though in exceptional cases there may be more than three. Using this method, the notes from *b* of the worked example above would become:

1   Men supposedly being replaced by machines.
   (*a*) Unmanned missile replaces manned. These being developed for every aspect of warfare.
   (*b*) Unfortunately world is too small and explosions too big.
2   This is not actually true.
   (*a*) Man is winning the battle with machines. He rightly takes little notice of them.
3   We must concern ourselves with the situation.
   (*a*) Our society is supplying itself well with machines and badly with manpower.
   (*b*) We are increasing equipment, physical plant, etc., not developing personal talents.

Good layout does not improve the quality of the notes, of course, but it does make them easier to read and to understand.

Exercise A

Write down in note-form the main and subsidiary points which you would include in a summary of each of the following passages. The number of *main* points you should look for is given in brackets at the end of each passage.

1   There is hardly any limit to the pleasure, excitement and profit of studying history. But one difficulty meets us at the very beginning of our study – where shall we begin? For the story of our world has been going on for thousands of years without any interrruptions or breaks. So we must just break into the story at some point which suits us, and pick up the threads of the story as we go along. About a hundred years ago, in the middle of the 19th century, Britain and the world were so completely different from what they are today that a hundred years ago is a convenient point from which to start to explain how the world has become what it now is. Let us begin by comparing daily life a hundred years ago with daily life today and by explaining how the startling changes came about.

c. h. c. blount: *The Last Hundred Years*   (1 main point)

2   It has often been said that motor racing, like war, speeds up technical progress. This is entirely true, for many of the refinements built into any production car are a direct result of lessons learned on the tracks. A car which, in the hands of the private owner, would

perhaps motor for thousands of miles without trouble, might retire within minutes of starting its first race, because of a structural or mechanical failure. The suspected parts are stripped down, modified, and an improved version goes into the passenger car.

Motor racing relies absolutely on the component and accessory manufacturers who support the sport, sending their own technicians to help prepare the cars and watch over them at the actual event. Their word is gospel, and their advice is accepted without reserve. It is, of course, true that the component and accessory manufacturers advertise the successes of their products in the event of victory, but it is scant return for the effort and money which they pour into the sport in the form of free equipment or supplies, starting and successes bonuses to the drivers and teams, and technical knowledge.

PETER MILLER: *From Start to Finish* (2 main points)

3   The viruses, as a group, cannot be seen at all even with the aid of the most powerful microscope which uses visible light. They are, in fact, so small as to be beyond the resolving power of the best lenses, and for this reason are frequently known as the 'ultramicroscopic viruses'. This extremely minute size is therefore one characteristic, but there are others; we have mentioned the fact that bacteria can be grown artificially on nutrient media such as agar, upon which they form colonies visible to the eye. Now one fundamental fact about the viruses is that no one has ever yet succeeded in growing a virus or causing it to multiply upon an artificial medium of any sort in a laboratory. In other words, viruses can only grow and multiply inside a *living cell*, and here perhaps we have their most important and significant characteristic. Another interesting point is that only viruses causing disease have been described; no free living or non-parasitic viruses are definitely known, and this is hardly surprising when it is realised that the symptoms of the diseases they cause are almost the only way we have to know that they exist at all. They may therefore be what are called 'obligate parasites', which means that they are incapable of existing independently.

You should therefore conceive of the virus as an extremely minute disease agent which cannot be seen even by the aid of a microscope and which can only multiply itself when inside a living cell.

K. M. SMITH: *Beyond the Microscope* (3 main points)

4   The penalty for going to an unskilled hairdresser can be worse than merely looking a fright. Particularly where dyeing or permanent-waving are concerned, real skill – and knowledge of the complex

chemicals used – are very important today if injury is to be avoided.

The colouring of hair is becoming more popular and accounts for nearly a quarter of the money spent in salons these days. Both permanent dyes (usually called tints) and temporary rinses can be made from potentially dangerous chemicals. The safe vegetable colourings like henna, camomile, and so on, have largely been abandoned, and the more attractive alternatives are usually coal-tar derivatives which can cause allergies, or even poisoning. For this reason, a good hairdresser will want to try out a little of the dye on a small patch of your skin, to see whether, in the course of a day or two, it produces any irritation or rash. If no test is done, the hairdresser may want you to sign a chit exonerating him if the dye does in fact cause you any harm – and this might take the form not only of skin disease, but loss of hair or even temporary partial blindness.

Coal-tar derivatives are not the only offenders. Metallic dyes (the sort that require daily application for a week) carry similar hazards.

Only a few people react unfavourably to these dyes; but some people who are at first unaffected by them become sensitive later, so the patch test needs to be done every time. But the patch test itself, regularly repeated, occasionally causes sensitivity!

Careless permanent waving is another source of trouble, causing hair to become brittle and break off. Although the basic cause might be in something other than the waving itself (for instance, previous over-bleaching, or even illness that has temporarily weakened the hair), a good hairdresser will recognise that the hair is not fit to be waved and recommend you to wait. If, on the other hand, hair that had been in good condition became lank and lifeless after permanent waving, the hairdresser could almost certainly be blamed for maltreating it. The problem is, of course, proving what has happened – and a remedy may be impossible. Hence the importance, in this field more than most, of avoiding catastrophe by checking on the hairdresser's qualifications beforehand.

ELIZABETH GUNDREY: *At Your Service*   (3 main points)

5   Look at the charges of the judges, at the resolutions of the grand juries, at the reports of public officers, and at the reports of voluntary associations. All tell the same sad and ignominious story. Take the reports of the inspector of prisons. In the House of Correction at Hertford, of seven hundred prisoners half could not read at all; only eight could read and write well. Of eight thousand prisoners who had passed through Maidstone Gaol only fifty could read and write well.

Turn from the registers of prisoners to the registers of marriages. You will find that about a hundred and thirty thousand couples were married in the year 1844. More than forty thousand of the bridegrooms and more than sixty thousand of the brides did not sign their names, but made their marks. Nearly one-third of the men, and nearly one-half of the women, who are in the prime of life, who are to be the parents of the Englishmen of the next generation, cannot write their own names. Remember, too, that though people who cannot write their own names must be grossly ignorant, people may write their own names, and yet have very little knowledge. Tens of thousands who were able to write their own names had, in all probability, received only the wretched education of a common day school. We know what such a school often is: a room crusted with filth, without light, without air, and with a heap of fuel in one corner and a brood of chickens in the other; the only machinery of instruction a dog-eared spelling book and a broken slate; the masters the refuse of all other callings – discarded footmen, ruined pedlars; men who cannot work a sum in the rule of three; men who cannot write a common letter without blunders; men who do not know whether the earth is a sphere or a cube; men who do not know whether Jerusalem is in Asia or America. And to such men, men to whom none of us would entrust the key of his cellar, we have entrusted the mind of the growing generation, and with the mind of the rising generation, the freedom, the happiness, the glory of our country.

(3 main points)

T. B. MACAULAY: Speech in the House of Commons, 18 April 1847

Exercise B

Write down in note form the main and subsidiary points which you would include in a summary of each of the following passages:

1   The railways of Britain just grew. Once Parliament had given permission for the establishment of a line, made rules for the protection of property on route, ordered fences to be put up and safe level-crossings installed, the fledgling company was all alone. A poor and inefficient one might spend seven years laying 51 miles of track, as the Eastern Counties did. A rich and well-run concern, like the London to Birmingham, could grow and expand until, as the London and North-Western Railway, it virtually controlled the midlands. Only in the 1844 Act, which guaranteed third-class passengers a seated and covered journey once a day at a penny a mile, did the government interfere in railway affairs. Otherwise, it gave not a penny towards

railway building, nor took any part in the running of companies. Men like Hudson were allowed to swallow up their smaller neighbours or bully them into co-operation; unprofitable lines went bankrupt or limped along with ancient engines and inferior rails. The result was a haphazard system with frequent duplication of lines leading to cut-throat competition. Nevertheless by 1852 the basis of our present-day network was in existence, with two routes to the north, London connected with the south coast and the G.W.R. snaking into Devon and Wales.

This astonishing achievement in a mere twenty years was not produced without teething troubles. The battle of the gauges, although the most famous, was in some ways quiet compared with some lesser-known railway disturbances. In them a new type of general appeared, the railway manager, a man just as determined to conquer with rails as the warrior of old had been to conquer with soldiers.

L. E. SNELLGROVE: *From ' Rocket' to Railcar*

2   The problem of how to move the work and not the man was solved by the assembly-line method which Ford copied from the meat-packing stations in the United States. The men, the tools and the car parts were spaced out in a line, arranged in the order in which they would be needed. The partly completed car moved slowly along this line, each man doing his job as it came by. The job might be very simple. One man might fit a screw in place, another put the nut on it, and a third tighten it with a spanner. A door panel might be put in place by a workman and screwed down by his neighbour. And all this time the car was moving slowly between the lines of men, usually at a rate of 45 inches a minute. This movement was sometimes mechanical and sometimes caused by gravity, that is, by rolling the car down a slope. If a job had to be done under a car a man stood in a special trench and the car rolled above his head. By this means a mere frame at one end of the assembly line came off the other end as a completed machine, ready to be driven away. Even small parts can be assembled in this way, for they are slid by wire from one bench to the next. This manufacturing scheme is called 'mass production'. It is tremendously fast and 60 cars an hour can be built by one assembly line. Neither does it need skilled men because it is easy to teach a man his own small task.

This, then, was the secret magic which Henry Ford used to make millions of cars. There were many jokes about it. It was said that if a man dropped his spanner sixteen cars went by without a certain bolt, that soon Ford would produce yellow cars to be sold in bunches like bananas, or that the latest Ford car was being sold with no doors but a tin opener to cut your own. The Ford jokes became part of American life. Everybody tried to make up a new one and in the end a 'Ford Joke Book' was printed.

L. E. SNELLGROVE: *From Steam Carts to Minicars*

3   In the Second World War the aeroplane spelt the end of large, shell-firing battleships. Britain possessed the most formidable ships of their sort the world has ever seen, the 'King George V' Class. Each was 740 feet long, 103 feet wide with a gross tonnage of 44,500 tons and no less than 14,000 tons of armour plating. Ten fourteen-inch guns, four to a turret, 16 five-inch guns and 80 smaller weapons comprised gun-power without equal at sea. The cost of these warships was immense; the very electric firing control system to fire off the guns cost £213,000. Yet in December 1941 one of them, the *Prince of Wales* was sunk by Japanese aircraft off Singapore. Older kinds of ships, such as the *Hood, Barham* and *Royal Oak* were easily destroyed by gunfire or torpedoes. It was apparent that the large battleship of the future would need to fire aircraft, not shells; in other words it would need to be an aircraft carrier.

The Americans understood this during the war because their sea fights with the Japanese were contests between aircraft sent from carriers. For instance, in the 1942 battles of the Coral Sea and Midway Island no ships came within gun range. At Leyte Gulf in 1944 the Japanese admitted defeat when their four aircraft-carriers were sunk. The distance between opponents in sea fights, starting at nil in battles like Salamis, has gradually lengthened from yards to miles and from a few miles to hundreds, until today a ship can fire a rocket missile, or an aircraft, across continents.

L. E. SNELLGROVE: *From Coracles to Cunarders*

4   On purely physical grounds, there is very little doubt that some form of exercise, adapted to the needs of the individual, is beneficial. The real argument for exercise, however, is not that terrible things will happen to you if you don't take it, but that it is enjoyable for its own sake, and the best antidote for brooding and worrying. Jane Austen's heroines used to take a walk 'in order to recover their spirits'. Walking out of doors supplies novel stimuli for you to perceive and react to, starts new trains of thought, and the muscular activity itself can often lift one's mood. In many games you are forced to attend and

react to a quick succession of stimuli, so that you are quite unable to think of anything but the immediate present, thus relieving you of any current worries or obsessions.

Exercise does not have to be in the form of strenuous competitive games and sports. Not everyone has an aptitude for athletics, and some probably avoid team games because they have never been good at them, or because they learned to dislike them at school. The range of sports and active recreations is wide, however, including such relatively mild activities as walking, swimming, tennis, badminton, golf, dancing, skating, etc., so that everyone should be able to find some form of exercise suited to his tastes and interests, which will take him away from his studies, and preferably into the open air, for at least one or two half days each week.

A habit of regular exercise is also desirable because, in the long run, the inactive tend to become overweight. This is, perhaps, a greater consideration in middle age than in youth. It seems that since the human body is adapted for activity, the sedentary almost inevitably eat more than they require. The mechanisms which regulate the intake of food allow an intake sufficient for a good deal of activity. Hence you must choose between activity, obesity, or, if you are determined enough to restrict your diet, feelings of semi-starvation.

HARRY MADDOX: *How to Study*

5 Corporal punishment has fallen generally into disfavour lately because of the growing awareness of the temptation to indulge sadistic impulses. But the danger is small in the case of most parents, and this corrective for the normal rule-breaking of youth actually fits in very well with the general scheme of life. Nature teaches its lessons by inflicting physical discomfort on those who do what is not good for them, and no parent, however well-meaning, can prevent hot iron from burning the child who touches it, or a dog from biting the youthful bully who torments it. Social life, generally speaking, is based on the same principles; if you break its rules or make yourself offensive to others, you will get hurt in one way or another. Man is a social animal and his child has to be one too, quite soon in life. The upbringing of the young should be a preparation for adult life, and it is just as well that quite early they should learn in a simple fashion the painful fact that if they do not consider other people in their actions other people will make it unpleasant for them.

It is reasonable to suppose that in their reaction to this form of social training children are the same now as in earlier times, and that we are no more likely to have a nation of neurotic wrecks through corporal punishment of the young than were the Tudor Kings. Indeed, it seems probable that children have been very much the same – internally if not outwardly – in all ages. If as embryos they pass through the physical evolutionary stages of man, is it not likely that after birth they pass through the mental and social evolutionary stages? It does not satisfy the sentiments to regard them as young savages, but this exasperated epithet of the goaded adult is very near the truth.

A. E. JONES: *Juvenile Delinquency and the Law*

6   Egyptian ships could have voyaged successfully only in the relatively calm waters of the Mediterranean or the Red Sea; an Atlantic storm would have destroyed them. Consequently, when an Egyptian king, ruling much later than Queen Hatshepsut, wished the coast of Africa explored he hired Phoenician sailors and Phoenician-keeled ships. In 600 B.C. they are said to have sailed around Africa from east to west, taking three years and stopping for long periods to grow food. Their voyage was coast hugging, which is more dangerous than deep-sea travel because of shoals and hidden rocks, but it showed that the Phoenicians were evolving a sea-going vessel destined one day to conquer the oceans. As this happened, ships divided into two types, for whilst some voyaged for trade others did so to fight. Designed for different tasks, the war-galley and the merchant ship soon went their separate ways.

For war a ship needed to be fast and manœuvrable. This was not possible, relying on the wind, so the warship, though equipped with a sail, became primarily an oared vessel, powered by a hundred or more muscular men, its steering paddles swept from side to side by a steersman who sat in a large covered seat called an hedolion. Naturally it had no guns so it could only inflict damage by ramming. This led to the keel being extended forward beyond the bows and sharpened into a copper-sheathed beak just below water-level. Such rams were buttressed by long beams which ran the length of the hull to help cushion the jar when a collision occurred, for without them the warcraft must have crumpled under the impact. In fact it is doubtful whether ramming was ever as popular as is supposed; boarding and capture were more usual tactics, especially in the open sea.

L. E. SNELLGROVE: *From Coracles to Cunarders*

7   Jet engines are possible because of a law first discovered in 1680 by Isaac Newton, a great English scientist. After carefully observing various movements he came to the conclusion that 'to every action

63

there is an equal and positive reaction'. This may sound rather difficult to understand, but many examples from everyday life prove
Newton to be right. A firehose is pushed back by the force of the water
rushing out of it; a swimmer kicks backwards to propel himself
forward. Nor is it necessary for these objects to push against anything.
A rocket in outer space has nothing to push against yet it travels at
thousands of miles per hour. Newton himself proved his law when he
constructed a special carriage which was driven by a jet of steam from
a boiler.

The jet engine obtains its power by forcing air out behind it. This
air enters the motor and is compressed by heating and movement of
various types. This heating and compression cause it to leave the rear
nozzle much faster than it came in. By such very simple methods are
our great jetliners able to speed at over 500 m.p.h.

Whittle compressed and speeded up the air by using a turbine which
spins the air, but the turbo-jet is not the only type of jet engine. The
simplest is the ram-jet in which the air is compressed by the very force
with which it comes through the inlet-hole, into the burning chamber.
This depends upon the speed at which the plane is travelling and
consequently such an engine cannot operate at low speeds; it has to
be carried to a certain speed by another aircraft or use an auxiliary
motor for take-off. On the other hand, the greater its speed the more
the air is compressed and the faster it leaves the plane. Speed makes
more speed with this type of jet propulsion, and because there are
fewer moving parts to break up under stress it is capable of higher
speeds than the turbo-jet.

L. E. SNELLGROVE: *From Kitty Hawk to Outer Space*

8   While the misbehaviour of the young was so often in the past
dealt with informally, nowadays the socially correct thing is to bring
it before the juvenile court. So the official figures of Juvenile Delinquency now include what once was Domestic Naughtiness. In the
general gloom cast by these figures it has almost escaped notice that
the child professional criminal, who used to be the most frequent
juvenile visitor to the police courts, has very nearly disappeared. He
belonged to a period when children of poor homes, either through
death or want in the family, were frequently turned adrift at an early
age and by economic pressure were forced into crime. What Oliver
Twist found in Fagin's kitchen could not be discovered in London
now. The habitual child offender whom the modern juvenile court
meets comes often from a bad home, it is true, but he is not turned out

of it in these times; he is not half starved or half naked. Theft is not his living; he does not steal from necessity, but for the luxuries of childhood which his parents cannot or will not buy him and have not taught him to do without. His trouble is not really economic but moral, as is shown by the fact that other children living round him in similar financial circumstances remain honest. He is not often nowadays deliberately encouraged in crime by his parents, but they are either lazy, shiftless, drunken, immoral, mentally deficient, indifferent, or just well-meaningly ignorant and make no effective attempt to control his natural propensities. Fifty years ago children of such parents tended to become professionally criminal equally with those who were turned out of their homes. Enforced schooling has brought with it a restriction on the time available for illicit activities, and, with the disappearance of the vilest slums, there hardly remains a neighbourhood where, as once used to be the case, social approval of wrongdoing is so universal as to make a young inhabitant turn to crime as naturally as a public schoolboy turns to cricket.

A. E. JONES: *Juvenile Delinquency and the Law*

9 Exploration in the Arctic Circle still offers countless opportunities for fresh discoveries, but it is an adventure not to be undertaken lightly. As an occupation it is more lonely and remote than anything else in the world, and at any moment the traveller must be prepared to encounter hazard and difficulty which call for all his skill and enterprise. Nevertheless, such enterprise will be carried on as long as there are uninvestigated areas to attract the daring and as long as the quest for knowledge inspires mankind.

Investigations have shown that the Arctic zone is rich in mineral deposits, but even if these deposits were themselves of little value, the economic importance of the Arctic would not be appreciably lessened. For it is generally agreed that 'weather is made in the north' and, as the success or failure of the harvests all over the world is largely determined by the weather, it follows that agriculture, and all those industrial and commercial activities dependent upon it, must be considerably affected by the accuracy of the daily weather reports. Modern meteorologists regard the conditions prevailing in the Arctic as of first-rate importance in helping them to arrive at accurate results in their forecasts.

Yet, apart from any economic or other practical considerations, there is a strange fascination about this vast unconquered region of stern northern beauty. Those who have once entered the vast polar

regions like to speak of their inexpressible beauty, the charm of the yellow sun and dazzling ice-packs, the everlasting snows, and the unmapped land where one never knows what lies ahead: it may be a gigantic glacier, which reflects a beam of sunlight over its frozen expanse, or some wonderful, fantastically-shaped cliff, which makes an unfading impression on the memory. It may even be an iceberg, stately and terrifying, moving on its relentless way, for the Arctic is the birthplace of the great icebergs which threaten navigation.
Cambridge: G.C.E. O Level

10   Radical changes in the way of life of the population have had, and will continue to have, many repercussions on the educational system. Three of these changes have a direct connection with it. They are: the greater ability of the parents to support a lengthy education for their children, the greater freedom of the married woman to take up paid employment, and the earlier incidence of marriage for an increasing number of girls. The other three are more concerned with the nature of the society in which children grow up. They are: the larger proportion of old people that society has to support, the smaller age-range of children within the family, thus limiting a boy's or girl's intimate circle to his or her own contemporaries, and the comparative rarity of both births and deaths within the family.

It seems clear that most families can now support a longer school education than formerly. Families are smaller. They are started earlier in the parents' life; and about four-fifths of all children are born in the first ten years of married life. These facts taken together are significant. Lack of money used to make it necessary for manual workers to put their children to work as early as possible. The father reached his peak earning capacity in early manhood; each additional child meant an increased cost on a fixed income until the older children could go to work to relieve the family exchequer. To this economic force working against any education longer than the minimum may be added a psychological one. Older children are more likely to get attention when there are no younger ones to distract the parents' notice. Consequently, it was not until the days of generally small families that manual workers and their wives could look at education for their children in the same sort of perspective as non-manual workers. The manual worker of today normally has a family whose numbers do not constitute an excessive burden on his income. Moreover his wife is probably able to supplement the family income when the children are older.

This diagnosis is corroborated by the fact that children in large families tend to have a shorter education than those in small families. Among National Service recruits the proportion who had left school at 15 rises with each additional member in the family, no matter what occupation group the father belongs to. In recent years, the State has made some provision towards the cost of supporting a large family, but it is hardly yet sufficient to give equality of opportunity to members of large families.

Joint Matriculation Board: G.C.E. O Level

Point of view

Most of the summaries you will be asked to make in school, and in examinations, will be what can be called neutral; this means that they are not for a particular audience, or from a particular point of view, and that your own opinions and attitudes must be kept out. Your aim is to give an objective account, though condensed, of what the author said. This neutral type of summary is obviously important and much used in daily life, as when a brief account of a new industrial process is needed. We can imagine such a summary being biased in favour of, or against, the adoption of the process, but this would make it a bad summary if what was asked for was a straightforward account of the process.

There are many occasions in daily life, however, when a neutral summary is not given, or asked for, often rightly, sometimes wrongly. If a friend asks for a summary of a film you have seen, you will give an account based on your own recollections, dictated largely by your likes and dislikes, but also bearing in mind what you know of your friend's preferences and attitudes. At the same time, he will be making allowances for what he knows from past experience to be the differences in opinion in your respective judgments of films in general. This, incidentally, is the kind of approach we should make to newspaper critics.

In the same way, summaries of politicians' speeches may well vary from newspaper to newspaper, depending on the political attitude of the paper. There will be no distortion of what the politician said, provided the paper is a reputable one, but the process of abstraction, the selection of important and the rejection of unimportant points, may be so varied as to lead to very different reports of the same speech.

For another example we may refer back to the managing director's report mentioned near the beginning of Chapter 3 (page 19). Let

67

us suppose that in one of the detailed reports from heads of departments there was the statement that Machinist Williams had complained that the tea-break was not long enough for him to finish his mug of tea without gulping it down. The managing director may well have decided that this item was unimportant and not included it in his report to the board of directors, though we may hope that he would nevertheless have referred it to the welfare officer. But there are circumstances in which Machinist Williams's complaint would be the most important point in the managing director's report to the board. What do you think they are?

Compare these two newspaper accounts of the same incident:

TRAIN HOLD-UP

(*a*) *The Guardian*

Eight masked men staged a train robbery yesterday near West Drayton, Middlesex, but a railway ganger working nearby forced them to drop three of the four cash boxes they had grabbed from the guard's van.

The train – the 9.5 a.m. Paddington to Cheltenham – was approaching West Drayton when masked men burst into the van and overpowered the guard, Mr George Manning. They pulled the communication cord and as the train came to a halt they threw out four cash boxes believed to contain about £8,000 for railwaymen's pay.

Others of the gang were waiting near the track with a car and a van. As the raiders carried the boxes to the vehicles a railway ganger, Mr Joseph Sexton, shouted and chased them. They dropped three boxes before reaching the van with the remaining one which held £768.

(*b*) *The Daily Mail*

Train bandits riding a Paddington express missed a £20,000 payroll haul yesterday – by two seconds. They pulled the communication cord two seconds too late. The train stopped 200 yards past the spot where the rest of the gang were waiting with the getaway van. And they escaped with only £790.

For they panicked when they were chased by railway ganger Mr Joe Sexton and dropped three of the four payroll boxes they had thrown from the guard's van.

The train was the 9.5 a.m. Paddington–Cheltenham diesel express.

Four bandits boarded the train with 300 other passengers before it left London.

As it approached the gang's rendezvous spot at West Drayton, Middlesex, the bandits:

PULLED the communication cord.

BROKE INTO the guard's van, overpowered the guard, 50-year-old Mr George Manning, and forced him to lie on the floor.

CUT the chains on four metal-bound strong-boxes containing the railmen's wages, and tipped the boxes down the embankment when the train stopped.

But the two-second error in pulling the cord left them a 200-yard run across soggy ground to their van.

Mr Sexton's party of plate-layers, 300 yards down the track, stopped work and hurried to see why the train had halted.

The bandits, all wearing nylon stocking masks, were afraid the railwaymen would cut them off.

As Mr Sexton ran after them they abandoned two of the wages boxes and staggered on with the other two.

Almost exhausted, they dropped another box just a few yards from their van. It contained £4,000.

In the fourth box was only a fraction of the haul they hoped for.

The first gives a straightforward, brief account of what happened, and is therefore a good example of a neutral report. The second is based on the same facts, but it is written to emphasize the dramatic nature of the crime and what newspapers call the 'human interest'.

You should remember that any summary you make should be neutral, a faithful, condensed account of what the author wrote, without any additional comment from you, unless you are specifically asked to do something different, or unless the situation demands a different kind of summary.

Exercise C

1 Make notes for a summary of the following passage from the point of view of:

(a) an athlete;

(b) an overweight and lazy middle-aged office worker.

Is exercise good or can it be harmful? Some people, particularly those who are in poor physical condition after years of an inactive urban life, are afraid of the effects of exercise and wish to avoid unnecessary strain and effort. They think that exercise will only increase bodily wear and tear, and tell apocryphal stories of hale and hearty old men whose only exercise consists in helping to carry the coffins of their more energetic friends.

At the other extreme are those who think that natural selection, over thousands of years, has fitted the human body for strenuous activity in agriculture, hunting and war; and that those who live inactive sedentary lives in modern cities accumulate body-fat, lose muscular tone, and often worry excessively. In other words, muscles will atrophy unless they are used, and general bodily decay will be the result of inactivity and lack of exercise. There is, in fact, some medical evidence which suggests that those in sedentary occupations are less healthy than those in more active work. Bus conductors on double-decker buses are less likely to get coronary heart disease than the drivers. Walking postmen get less severe heart disease than postal office workers. Abnormalities of the heart in general are less common among active than among sedentary workers.

HARRY MADDOX: *How to Study*

2 Make notes of the *facts* contained in this advertisement:
Twice as many people bought room heaters in 1963. Many of them young marrieds setting up home for the first time. Why? First, because solid fuel room heaters are the *only* appliances that combine the cheerfulness of an open fire with high heating efficiency. They offer the cheer and liveliness of real fires, behind glass panels as big as television screens. And because they are enclosed, they are highly efficient. Some can run four or five radiators (50 sq. ft. of heating surface), a towel rail, and hot water – from the fireplace in your living room.

Second, the running costs of these systems are so low that many young couples can now afford to enjoy *proper heating earlier in life*. A modern room heater, like the Queen Ten-Four shown above, could make your living room a charming, welcoming place. Why not investigate, and send in the coupon at the bottom of this advertisement?

National Coal Board Housewarming Plan

3 Make notes for a summary to be used as advertising copy by a large record company:
By now all but the most ostrich-like have recognised the existence of the twentieth century – with nearly two-thirds of it gone, it is perhaps as well. The names of contemporary statesmen, scientists, writers, painters are household words. But this is hardly true of the world of

music, where for many 'classical' music ends with Tchaikovsky, if not Beethoven, and 'modern' music means only the latest eruption of Tin Pan Alley.

This is understandable. One cannot gain an appreciation of twentieth-century music by reading about it, although books can provide a guide to intelligent listening. Unfortunately the opportunities for hearing twentieth-century music are not plentiful. The BBC does its bit, but rarely on the channels of the masses. The annual Promenade Concerts regularly introduce new works, but few of us can go to the Proms., and those provincial concert-halls which have not yet been converted to bingo parlours tend to play safe in the choice of programmes. Gramophone records are potentially the greatest educational force in music, but here, too, the companies play safe. While recordings of the 'Nutcracker Suite' proliferate – 65 at the last count! – modern music is neglected, particularly on the cheaper labels that are the staple fare of the music lover of slender means. Yet records are a vital necessity in this sphere. Modern music has, in general, moved away from the 'pictures in sound' of the nineteenth century romantic composers, and often experimented with unfamiliar and complex patterns of notes. Such works need to be listened to again and again, just as the works of Picasso and Eliot need more than a cursory glance if they are to yield up their meanings.

Topic 12

4 Makes notes for a summary of the following passage by a teenager who was involved in one of the incidents mentioned and who feels he is not to blame:

Sentences like those passed at Clacton yesterday are one answer, and without doubt a necessary answer, to the hooliganism which plagues a small portion of our young people today. But the real answer, by common consent, must be found further back. There are too many of the young who seem unable to find a peaceful and contented place in our society. Undisciplined louts run wild in Clacton at a public holiday and try to smash up the place; a puzzled chief constable in Birmingham invites the recalcitrants to a parley and sees the proceedings break up in chaos. Why should these things be? Here is an affluent society which has lavished upon its children benefits that, even in this century, would have seemed beyond the dreams of youthful avarice. Yet some of them cannot make terms with their time.

Many would say that what we lightly assume should be the seda-
tive influence is itself the provocative. In the age of Dickens and
Lord Shaftesbury the young of the industrial proletariat, worn out
with 12, 14, even 16 hours of daily labour in the mines and the
factories, dropped into bed at last far too exhausted for any possibility of mischief – or for much chance of survival. Today the wheel
has come full circle. Our boys and girls, taken straight from school
into employment for short hours at high wages, come into a world that
offers little after working hours to spend those wages on – or rather,
little that will absorb the ebullient energy of youth which once spent
itself in sweated labour.

Television, bingo, all the sedentary pleasures, fail to satisfy the
insistent demand of the developing sinews. Playing fields in an ever
more crowded island are never adequate to the need. A contracted
empire denies the scope for adventure that an earlier age took for
granted. But the energy is there and we have to live with it and use it.
It must have outlets. It must have control as well. Discipline is
required; and all experience declares that youth leans upon wise
discipline, and is grateful for it in the end – whether in the family, in
the school, in the regiment, or in the workshop. Yet also more could be
done to offer to the young, along with the unprecedented leisure the
new affluence has created, better education in use of leisure and better
opportunities for enjoying it.

The Daily Telegraph, 28 April 1964

5   Some light-hearted material to finish the chapter. Provide in
note-form the serious instructions to be found in this piece of writing:

Stopping and Mowing – instructions that should have come with my
motor-mower.

Adjustment of blades. There is a hairsbreadth adjustment on this
machine, between the position where it just brushes the top of the
grass and the one where it digs great gashes in the earth. Practise with
a new electric light switch. If you can find a position where the light
just flickers between 'on' and 'off' you'll be able to wangle these
blades. Remember that they are finely, not to say neurotically adjusted. Quite a small pebble will wrench the blades out of shape. You
will know when this has happened when they either make a frightful
clanging noise or won't go round at all. The people for whom we make
our proper mowers do not have pebbles on their lawns, let alone the
small metal fire engines, dolls' boots, plastic alphabets, nails, and
spoons that litter yours.

Operation. It is only possible to operate this machine at a steady trot. At ordinary walking pace it will stall. And remember, the clutch is not a gradual affair like the one on a car. The instant you engage it the machine will rush away, with or without you. So it's no good trying to cut round those silly little circular rosebeds you have. This machine only mows in a dead straight line.

PAUL JENNINGS: *The Jenguin Pennings*

Chapter 7

Giving a Title II

There is nothing to be added to what was said about titles in Chapter 4. This chapter will therefore repeat the rules, give another example and provide further practice with increasingly complex material.

Rules

1   The title should give an accurate indication, as fully as possible, of the main topic of the passage.

2   The student's attitude and opinions must not influence his choice of title. He is concerned with what the author of the original passage wrote, and not with his own reactions to it, except on rare and special occasions (see Chapter 6, 'Point of View', pages 67–73).

3   The title should be a serious one, and not misleading, sensational, ambiguous, obscure, deliberately mystifying or whimsical.

4   The title should generally be restricted to a maximum of eight words. A one-word title will rarely be adequate.

Examples of pupils' work

Africa is a land of contrasts. In some of the deserts it rains once in five years: in the swamps it rains 300 days every year. The people too are contrasted. In fact, there are no *African* people as such, and there is no race indigenous to Africa – they have *all* come from somewhere else. There are boundaries between countries, but they have resulted mainly from European conquest and discovery and bear little relation to the physical barriers of the Sahara, the tropical forests, the mountains and the great river valleys.

The ways of life of Africans are naturally dependent on the physical features of their environment – rainfall, vegetation, type of soil, altitude. These determine their diet, and, to a large extent, their habits. The cattle-people live in the dry savannah country which extends from Dakar to the Sudan and South Africa. The forest-dwellers live in a relatively small area on the West Coast and in the Congo Basin, and cultivate root vegetables such as yams and sweet potatoes. The grain-eaters grow sorghum, millet and maize in the border between savannah and forest, but the tsetse fly – carrier of sleeping sickness – makes life unhealthy for both men and animals. It is only in the mountains of Kenya, Rwanda, and Burundi that both cattle *and* crops can survive.

Topic 10

Misleading titles suggested for this extract were:
    The Surviving Land.
    Introduction to Africa.
    Africa and its Statistics.
    Geographical Africa.

Vague titles included:
    A Continent of Continents.
    The Face of Africa.
    Africa and the Africans.
    Life in Africa.

One whimsical title is worth considering:
    The Dark Continent: Several Shades of Grey.

How successful do you think this is?

Among the good answers were:
    Contrasts in Africa.
    The Dark Continent and its Contrasts.
    Some Contrasts of Africa.
    Africa: Main Contrasts.

And the most popular:
    The Contrasts of Africa. (given four times)
    Africa – Land of Contrasts. (given eight times)

In this case we agree with the decision of the majority.

Exercise A

Give a suitable title for each of the following passages:

1   Mr Pickwick's apartments in Goswell Street, although on a limited scale, were not only of a very neat and comfortable description, but peculiarly adapted for the residence of a man of his genius and observation. His sitting-room was the first-floor front, his bedroom the second-floor front; and thus, whether he were sitting at his desk in his parlour, or standing before the dressing-glass in his dormitory, he had an equal opportunity of contemplating human nature in all the numerous phases it exhibits, in that not more populous than popular thoroughfare. His landlady, Mrs Bardell – the relict and

sole executrix of a deceased custom-house officer – was a comely woman of bustling manners and agreeable appearance, with a natural genius for cooking, improved by study and long practice, into an exquisite talent. There were no children, no servants, no fowls. The only other inmates of the house were a large man and a small boy; the first a lodger, the second a production of Mrs Bardell's. The large man was always home precisely at ten o'clock at night, at which hour he regularly condensed himself into the limits of a dwarfish French bedstead in the back parlour; and the infantine sports and gymnastic exercises of Master Bardell were exclusively confined to the neighbouring pavements and gutters. Cleanliness and quiet reigned throughout the house: and in it Mr Pickwick's will was law.
CHARLES DICKENS: *The Pickwick Papers*

2 A defeated army was falling back through the mountains from Espinosa. Such was its condition that an ignorant observer would find it easier to guess that it had been defeated than that it had been an army. The twenty thousand men of whom it was composed were strung out along twenty miles of road. At the head came such of the cavalry as were fortunate enough still to have horses to ride; they felt safer there than in their proper place covering the retreat. Next came the infantry, in groups, in herds, or in ones or twos. Their white Bourbon uniforms were now in strips and tatters, and their skin, blue with disease and cold, showed through the rents. Perhaps half of them still retained their muskets, and of these perhaps a quarter had bayonets as well. Here and there little groups still displayed some soldierly bearing, and marched steadily beneath the cased regimental colours, but these groups were few, for most of the colours had been lost at Espinosa.

The long column of misery tended continually to grow longer, as the more robust struggled farther forward and the weaker fell farther behind. There were enough weaklings in all conscience; even in summer the men had been badly clothed, and even in victory insufficiently fed, and now it was winter, and Espinosa had been fought and lost, and the route of the retreat lay away from the fertile plains and up into the inhospitable mountains, already covered with snow.
Welsh Joint Education Committee: G.C.E. O Level

3 Advertising assaults not only our eyes and ears but also our pockets. Its critics point out that in this country 1·6 per cent of national income is spent on advertising and that this advertising actually raises the cost of products. When a housewife buys a pound of flour,

5 per cent of what she pays goes to some advertiser or other, even if she has not bothered to ask the shopkeeper for a particular brand. If she buys a named brand of aspirin, up to 29 per cent of what she pays may represent the cost of advertising the name.

These amounts seem a great deal to pay for the questionable benefits of advertising, but there are a few things to be said in its favour. Although some things cost more because of advertising, other things cost less. Newspapers, magazines, commercial radio and television all carry advertisements, and the money received from the advertisers helps to lower the cost of production. In this way we get information and entertainment at lower prices than would otherwise have to be charged, and so what we lose on the swings we gain on the roundabouts. Apart from this very important consideration, advertising to some extent ensures that a product will maintain its quality. It also gives rise to competition among manufacturers, which benefits the customer by offering him a wider choice. Competition may even succeed, in some cases, in reversing the influence of advertising and causing a reduction in price.
Cambridge: G.C.E. O Level

4 Religion has a further important function to play in relation to contemporary science. It keeps technology under control. Here I think we should bear a distinction in mind between two types of science. The science of dead matter has almost reached the end of a cycle, the science of living matter is still in its early stages. Ahead stretch limitless possibilities including the possibility of commanding the secret of life itself. Mary Shelley's Frankenstein monster may well within a few generations be translated from fiction into fact. How is this knowledge to be used? We shall look in vain for guidance on this question to the vague although widely diffused· benevolence and goodwill which for so many people today constitutes their only principle for ordering life. But the Christian religion, precisely because it has a view of human nature, because it can essay an answer to the question 'What is man?', possesses ordering power. The Christian view that man is not absolute master of his own fate, but holds his life and body on trust for other purposes, evokes little response in an era which places a supreme value on personal emancipation, and has provided man with the means of its achievement. But the technology which promised a paradise now shows signs of delivering a hell. Against the tyranny of scientific techniques, the emancipated man finds himself defenceless, having rejected the Christian view of human

nature, which if it places limits on man's independence by stressing that he is the user not the proprietor of life, also preserves his human-ity, by erecting barriers beyond which technology cannot pass.
NORMAN ST JOHN-STEVAS: 'Science and Faith' in *Science and Society*

5   A staff of twenty report the meetings of the Commons, and perhaps five Standing Committees which meet three mornings weekly from 10.30 a.m. to 1 p.m. Capable of speeds of over 200 words a minute, the 'Hansard' team are among the fastest shorthand writers in the United Kingdom. Editor, deputy editor and two assis-sant editors deal with about 130,000 words a day (the size of two aver-age novels) transcribed by the parliamentary reporters, plus several thousand words of the Standing Committees.

The 'Hansard' reporters begin at 2.30 p.m., each taking notes for ten minutes in turn up to 8.30 p.m., when the turn is halved to five minutes. Immediately a reporter has finished his turn, he leaves the gallery and dictates his notes to a typist in the 'Hansard' rooms and edits the transcription – correcting grammatical slips and obvious errors. A Member of Parliament can read through the report and make minor alterations, but he cannot alter the substance of his speech.

After the report has passed through the editorial hands it goes by special messenger to the Government printers in Pocock Street, Southwark, not far from Westminster, where it is set up in type, two columns to a page. The last batch of copy is sent to Pocock Street at about 11 p.m. Printing is completed at about 2 a.m., and shortly after-wards the Post Office collects copies for distribution to Members of Parliament in the London postal area by breakfast. Supplies are also available at H.M. Stationery Office shops at 9 a.m. Members may submit corrections to daily reports within five days, when the 'Han-sard' report is bound in volume form to become part of the history of Westminster.
S. R. CAMPION: *Press Gallery*

6   The estimate should say (and this is a vital thing to get in writing) what temperature the system is planned to give. A desirable standard is usually 65 F. for living-rooms, with the outside temperature at 32 F., and 1 to $1\frac{1}{2}$ air-change an hour. Obviously, to achieve this will mean more radiators and a bigger boiler in a draughty, north-facing, thin-walled bungalow than in a well-insulated, sheltered, compact terrace-house. Not only may the size of the radiators be crucial, but also their positioning: and an estimate should be accompanied by a floor plan showing where each is to go. Insulating the roof, to conserve

the heat, should be allowed for. Finally, the estimate should say what the annual running cost should average. All this a trained man is well able to calculate and there should be no risk that the system will fail to give the warmth you want. Provided that the estimate is full and detailed you can assess it by comparing it with studies in *Central Heating in Your Home*, an invaluable book described below; and, if there is any dispute later, the details in the estimate may well prove conclusive. The Institution of Heating and Ventilating Engineers say that in most cases when they are asked to give evidence that an installation is inadequate, their testimony does not help because the estimate the householder accepted was so vague. If there is no *proof*, in the estimate, that anything more than background or partial heating was to be provided, the householder cannot hope to win his case against the contractor. Further, the estimate should show wheth-er painting radiators, connecting up gas and electricity, making good of plaster, and work on flues are included or not. And it should specify the materials to be used – e.g. whether you should get chromium valve controls or only brass ones.

ELIZABETH GUNDREY: *At Your Service*

7   The only possible argument against the study of living authors is·the point that the student forgoes the perspective of the completed work, of the explication which later works may give to the implica-tions of the earlier. But this disadvantage, valid only for developing authors, seems small compared to the advantages we have in knowing the setting and the time and in the opportunities for personal acquain-tance and interrogation or at least correspondence. If many second-rate or even tenth-rate authors of the past are worth study, a first-rate or even second-rate author of our time is worth studying, too. It is usually lack of perception or timidity which makes academics reluctant to judge for themselves. They profess·to await the 'verdict of the ages', not realising that this is but the verdict of other critics and readers, including other professors. The whole supposed immunity of the literary historian to criticism and theory is thoroughly false, and that for a simple reason: every work of art is existing now, is directly accessible to observation, and is a solution of certain artistic problems whether it was composed yesterday or a thousand years ago. It cannot be analysed, characterised, or evaluated without a constant recourse to critical principles. 'The literary historian must be a critic even in order to be a historian.'

R. WELLEK and A. WARREN: *Theory of Literature*

8   The consultation ended in the men returning to the windlass, and
the pitman going down again, carrying the wine and some other small
matters with him. Then the other man came up. In the meantime,
under the surgeon's directions, some men brought a hurdle, on which
others made a thick bed of spare clothes covered with loose straw,
while he himself contrived some bandages and slings from shawls and
handkerchiefs. As these were made, they were hung upon an arm of
the pitman who had last come up, with instructions how to use them:
and as he stood, shown by the light he carried, leaning his powerful
loose hand upon one of the poles, and sometimes glancing down the
pit, and sometimes glancing round upon the people, he was not the
least conspicuous figure in the scene. It was dark now, and torches
were kindled.

It appeared from the little this man said to those about him, which
was quickly repeated all over the circle, that the lost man had fallen
upon a mass of crumpled rubbish with which the pit was half choked
up, and that his fall had been further broken by some jagged earth at
the side. He lay upon his back, with one arm doubled under him, and,
according to his own belief, had hardly stirred since he fell, except
that he had moved his free hand to a side-pocket, in which he remem-
bered to have some bread and meat (of which he had swallowed
crumbs), and had likewise scooped up a little water in it now and
then. He had come straight away from his work, on being written to,
and had walked the whole journey; and was on his way to Mr.
Bounderby's country house after dark, when he fell. He was crossing
that dangerous country at such a dangerous time, because he was
innocent of what was laid to his charge, and couldn't rest from
coming the nearest way to deliver himself up. The Old Hell Shaft, the
pitman said, with a curse upon it, was worthy of its bad name to the
last; for though Stephen could speak now, he believed it would soon
be found to have mangled the life out of him.

When all was ready, this man, still taking his last hurried charges
from his comrades and the surgeon after the windlass had begun to
lower him, disappeared into the pit. The rope went out as before, the
signal was made as before, and the windlass stopped. No man removed
his hand from it now. Every one waited with his grasp set, and his
body bent down to the work, ready to reverse and wind in. At length
the signal was given, and all the ring leaned forward.

For, now, the rope came in tightened and strained to its utmost as
it appeared, and the men turned heavily, and the windlass complained. It was scarcely endurable to look at the rope, and think of

its giving way. But, ring after ring was coiled upon the barrel of the windlass safely, and the connecting chains appeared, and finally the bucket, with the two men holding on at the sides – a sight to make the head swim, and oppress the heart – and tenderly supporting between them, slung and tied within, the figure of a poor, crushed, human creature.

CHARLES DICKENS: *Hard Times*

Exercise B

Give a suitable title for each of the passages in *Exercise B* of Chapter 6 (pages 59–67).

Chapter 8

Summary I

Notes on their own are of limited use. This chapter will begin with exercises to give practice in turning notes into a form in which they will be more useful. This is really composition work, and we solve problems like those it raises every time we talk at length. It is also the last aspect of summary work to be isolated for study; you are now able to make use of, together, all the skills practised separately so far in this book.

Reading is like looking through a telescope – the material studied may be clear at once, or it may need bringing into focus. No astronomer would be satisfied with the blurred image of a planet he was investigating, and he would adjust his telescope until the image became sharp. Very little writing makes a wholly clear impression straightaway: as readers we are too ignorant, or too tired, or too inattentive; but we can do something about the focus. Preceding chapters have shown how.

Any writing worth study needs reading carefully – twice. The perhaps vague impression gained on a first reading will be sharpened by a second, and many of the details which were indistinct then will become clear now. Such comprehension work done, we need to concentrate specially on areas that remain hazy. This is of course PARAPHRASE, and it will ensure that the whole of the passage being studied is in focus. At this stage its main features can be clearly pointed out – ABSTRACTION – and you should make written notes of them.

Now you have to write the summary. To try to do so direct from the passage itself will mean that, instead of condensing its meaning, you will find yourself copying its phrases – which is quotation, not summary. So put the passage away. From your notes alone write a careful composition – following the pattern of the ideas which they record, but shaping and joining the sentences as stylishly as if you were writing an essay. When you have finished, compare your draft with the original passage to ensure that you have not misrepresented it, or left out something important. Read over your draft carefully, to see if its style satisfies you. Give it a TITLE. And then, incorporating any revisions you may have made, write out the fair copy. For the

82

moment, the length at which you write is unimportant (as long as you leave nothing out); but it is never good style to use bafflegab, or to write in the barnacular.

Exercise A

1   Make notes on the following passage:

From the beginning, Henry Ford tried to produce cars swiftly and cheaply. He aimed to give the ordinary man a strong, reliable car which would be easy to drive and cheap to buy. His whole life was spent doing this. By 1909 he was selling 10,000 cars a year, something he had been told was impossible. His designs were of eight different types, each given an alphabetical name, such as Model A, Model B, and so on. Then he thought of an unusual scheme. He resolved to produce just one car and one car only. This would simplify construction because his factories would be able to concentrate on manufacturing a single set of parts. On the other hand, the customers would have no choice; as Henry Ford said, 'Any customer can have a car painted any colour he wants so long as it's black.' But though Ford himself might joke about the idea, his salesmen were not so happy. What if the buyers did not like that one model? Henry's reply was that he would be able to produce it so cheaply his customers would jump at the chance of such an inexpensive car. He was determined to put all his eggs in one basket. The Model T was the result.

L. E. SNELLGROVE: *From Steam Carts to Minicars*

2   Compare these 15-year-olds' summaries with each other, and with your notes (not with the original passage), using the questions below.

(i)   Henry Ford's lifelong plan was to build eight different types of cheap, reliable car which could also be easily driven. He changed his scheme, producing only one type of model, which simplified construction. There was no choice of model or colour, but Ford was confident that because of its cheapness it would sell.

(ii)   Ford's lifelong ambition was to produce a cheap, reliable and easily-driven car. He developed an unusual scheme, for that time. Instead of making eight types of car, as he had been doing till then, he decided to make just one model. This was the Model T. Contrary to his critics' opinion, Ford thought that this car would be popular because of its cheapness, and because people would not mind having no choice. He was right.

(*a*) Point out the distortion in the first sentence of (i).

(*b*) Rewrite the second sentence of (i), without introducing any new material, so that the *reason* for Ford's change becomes plain.

(*c*) Is the writer of (i) justified in leaving the salesmen out?

(*d*) (ii) includes several ideas not in the original passage, two of which alter its meaning. Which are they?

(*e*) Find the unimportant details which (ii) mentions.

(*f*) Most people would have stylistic criticisms of (ii), and would want to tidy it up. Would you?

(*g*) What reasons are there for thinking that both these summaries are too short?

3 (*a*) Criticise the following summary for distortion and omission.

   (*b*) Comment on the length of the last sentence.

   (*c*) What weaknesses in paraphrase can you find in the summary?

When Ford had reached the output of 10,000 cars a year, he wanted to make them swiftly and cheaply, of eight different types, all lettered in the alphabet. To reduce their price and increase production, he resolved to produce just one car and one car only, believing that his customers would jump at the chance of such an inexpensive car, and would not worry about not having a choice of model or colour.

4 With these three unsuccessful attempts in your mind, read the original passage carefully once more. Reconsider your notes. And now, *with only your notes in front of you*, write your own summary.

Exercise B

1 Make notes on this passage, and then discuss in class the problems raised in turning them into a piece of connected writing.

Cookery has always been a science, depending on natural laws such as those that determine the effects of applying a certain degree of heat for a certain period of time to a certain quantity of meat. But it has undoubtedly also become an art. In the Middle Ages men undertook long hunting expeditions and returned with enormous appetites; they had to school their stomachs to undergo long periods of fasting and concentrated bouts of feasting, and their first concern was with the quantity, rather than the quality, of their food. In later times, when feats of physical exertion and endurance were less often required of them, they became more interested in the preparation of their meals; their appetites were more readily appeased but needed stimulation.

The stimulation took various forms, including a wider choice of foods and greater variety in methods of presentation. Then cookery became an art.

Cambridge G.C.E. O Level

2   Write your own summary. (And ask yourself if it is long enough; if it distorts or adds to the original; if it is a smooth, well-linked and satisfying piece of writing.)

If you are still not satisfied with your skill in making notes into connected writing, try the following exercise.

Exercise C

1   Combine the sentences in each of the following groups, making *one* sentence of each group. Pay special attention to the linkage, and avoid if you can the use of 'and' as a joining word. You may re-arrange the order of the sentences within each group, but should include all the information given. (In the first group, some link words are suggested.)

  (i) Tidal waves are the result of earthquakes.
     Tidal waves travel at speeds of hundreds of miles an hour. (SO/HOWEVER/BUT/THEREFORE.)
     Warning of tidal waves can be given. (ALTHOUGH/ALSO/BECAUSE.) Earthquake Waves move at 15,000 miles an hour.

  (ii) In Leicestershire the Chief Constable has used special constables mounted on motor cycles.
     They have been used to assist the regular police.
     They patrol some stretches of road.
     The regular constabulary must continue to be mainly responsible for road traffic.
     Criminals often use motor-vehicles.

2   Combine each of the following groups of notes into a well-knit paragraph, making less important points properly subordinate.

(i) General stood on hill – overhung with trees – commanded uninterrupted view of battlefield – general remained all day – no rest or food – did not wish to miss chance for attack – sudden thrust at enemy weak point – cut enemy in two – overwhelm each part separately.

(ii) Snakes legless – expect them eat small animals, plants – not mobile – but not so – mostly live on fairly large animals – astonishing characteristics – sharp teeth, sloping towards throat – prey cannot easily escape – jaws can spread wide – many poisonous – drug, not overpower, victims.

3   The following is an extract from Lieutenant Bligh's log, after part of his crew on the *Bounty* had mutinied and he was cast adrift on the ocean with eighteen men in a small boat (28 April 1789).
Rewrite the extract in the form of a connected narrative.

11 May. – Our situation extremely dangerous – sea running over stern kept us bailing with all our strength.

14 May. – Suffered much from cold and shivering.

16 May. – Now starving. Night truly horrible.

17 May. – Some people solicited extra allowance, which I positively refused.

20 May. – Constant rain. Always bailing.

21 May. – At dawn some seemed half-dead from hunger but no one suffered from thirst.

22 May. – Dark dismal night. Our situation extremely calamitous.

4   Write a succinct statement of the service British Rail offer in this advertisement.

SIX QUESTIONS YOU OUGHT TO ASK BEFORE SENDING GOODS TO IRE-LAND. 1. Will they cross to Dublin or Belfast overnight? 2. Will they be carried 'door to door' – both sides of the Irish Sea? 3. Will they travel in specialised containers? 4. In special container ships (sailing regularly every night)? 5. Can the containers be sealed before they leave? 6. Are they really safe during transit? IF YOU DON'T GET 'YES' TO ALL SIX QUESTIONS, YOU'RE ASKING THE WRONG PEOPLE. TRY ASKING BRITISH RAIL.

5   From the following advertisement write a paragraph giving the important features of the Keymatic. You will need to make notes before you begin the connected writing.

Here are the features to look for when choosing a washing machine. Use this check list to help you compare the Keymatic with any other machine. 1. Absolutely no attention once you have switched it on. 2. Your hands never go near water – the washing can never drip on the floor. 3. Works from hot and cold taps, or cold tap alone – no special plumbing needed. 4. Tilted drum makes loading easy. 5. Takes a big family-size load – 8 lb dry weight. 6. Does not need a special low-suds washing powder. 7. *Eight* quite different programmes – right for every kind of wash – all easily selected by the Keyplate. 8. *Two* separate washing actions: gentle for delicates and vigorous for the big wash. 9. Every fabric gets the right spinning time.

10. Exact temperature control – right for every kind of wash. 11. Easy
H.P. terms, with a generous trade-in on your old machine. 12. Excellent servicing by Keymatic engineers.

Exercise D

1 Read the following extract until you are sure you understand it:
the third sentence needs special care. Then make notes on it.

Safety in the water is just as important as safety on the roads, and it
should be the business of every school to see that children are able to
look after themselves. Training must be based on what might generally be termed water ability and sound common sense. Water
safety is based on swimming ability but it has to be definite, demanding and, in a way, comprehensive. A person may be regarded as a
swimmer when he can do a length or two of a pool, but this is only a
start as far as survival tests are concerned. Swimming is an accepted
and pleasant part of holidays by the sea, and this often leads to difficulties. Many people venture in for the first time with little or no
knowledge of the degree of shelving of the sea bed, the possibility of
local currents or undertows, or even whether the tide is making or
ebbing. It is often assumed that since other people are bathing the
conditions are safe. This may not always be so. There are certain elementary rules which children should be taught. A shingle beach
usually slopes steeply; a heavy breaking wave near the shore is
dangerous; local authorities are prudent as regards bathing conditions. At many resorts some warning sign, usually a red flag, is displayed to indicate danger. It is well to accept this advice.
The Times Educational Supplement, 24 April 1964

2 Comment on these two summaries (again, use your notes, not the
passage); consider omissions, distortions, any undue borrowings
from the original, and style.

(i) Safety in the water is as important as safety on the roads, and
children have to be taught to look after themselves, because they like
to go where they have never been before, where there could be
undertows and dangerous currents. More people then come, and
assume the water is safe. There are a number of rules that people
should learn. Where there is a shingle beach, the sand slopes steeply,
and there are large breaking waves near the coast. Being able to swim
a length does not mean that one has knowledge of the sea.

(ii) Schools must ensure that children are competent in the water
by training them extensively in swimming, and by exercising sound

87

judgement. It is not enough to be able to swim. People swim at the seaside with ignorance of local conditions, taking safety on trust. Children should be taught to be observant, and to be alert to danger, and to take notice of warning signs erected by the authorities.

3   Re-read the original passage; check your notes. From your notes alone write your summary, revising it carefully, as in *Exercise B* 2.

Exercise E
This is designed to give you further practice in turning notes on a passage into a well-written summary. You will sometimes find that it helps to alter the order in which the original points are made, though never to distort their importance.

1   From the following passage, give as briefly as you can the author's opinion whether dogs and cats dream.

It is always a good thing to say that one does not know the answer to a question if that really is the case. Frankly, I don't know if dogs and cats dream, and I very much doubt if anyone else does.

We must always avoid, as far as possible, the temptation to endow animals with all the feelings, emotions and understanding of human beings. Personally I think that some kinds of animals have more intelligence than many authorities credit them with; but I also think it is a mistake to interpret animal behaviour in human terms unless one cannot account for some action or piece of behaviour in any other way. Having said this, I hope the connection with dreaming will be clear. We often say our dog is dreaming because it twitches and whines or yelps when asleep in a way that reminds us of the way it whines or yelps when awake and playing or hunting. We then suggest that the dog is 'dreaming' of a rat or an exciting walk. We cannot *know* this or prove it in the present state of our knowledge. However, I think it is fair to say that dogs and cats have very good memories for some things, and if their memories work in the same way as ours do then it is not impossible that they can call up in sleep a memory of some past experience. This is very near to dreaming, at all events.

MAXWELL KNIGHT: *Maxwell Knight Replies*

2   Write a short but comprehensive statement of the conditions for membership of the Club of Queer Trades.

The absolute condition of membership of the Club of Queer Trades lies in this, that the candidate must have invented the method by which he earns his living. It must be an entirely new trade. The exact definition of this requirement is given in the two principal rules. First, it must not be a mere application or variation of an existing trade. Thus, for instance, the club would not admit an insurance agent simply because, instead of insuring men's furniture against being burnt in a fire, he insured, let us say, their trousers against being torn by a mad dog. The principle is the same. Secondly, the trade must be a genuine commercial source of income, the support of its inventor. Thus the club would not receive a man simply because he chose to pass his days collecting broken sardine tins, unless he could derive a roaring trade in them.

G. K. CHESTERTON: *The Club of Queer Trades*

3 In a broadcast discussion-programme, the speaker was asked: 'Thrift has always been considered a virtue. In these days of Hire Purchase, does public opinion no longer consider this so?' Summarise his answer, in reported speech.

Frank Byers: 'I think this is a very difficult one, and I can't help feeling that the question is phrased in a sort of confusing way. After all, I don't think you want to be very hard on Hire Purchase. It's done a tremendous amount of good for newly-weds, for people who have children – who want to get a pram and can't afford to save up for it. I believe that Hire Purchase, within reasonable limits, has done a great deal for this country.

'And I don't think it necessarily does away with the idea of thrift. I can imagine quite a lot of people who start out in their married life with quite a lot of Hire Purchase, but not more than they can afford. As they get on and their wages increase, so they get to the position where they start saving. And they go on saving through various means.

'You can have Hire Purchase at certain times of your life. You can have thrift at others. And I believe that both these things are important.'

Any Questions?

4. Make notes on these passages, and then from your notes either speak or write connected summaries.

(*a*) We have all heard stories of the children who do their homework best in the company of a radio set tuned into the Light Programme or Radio Luxembourg. No less than their parents, children of today live in a world in which pop music is the background to all their actions. The radio at home is only switched off when the television programmes start, and then frequently the transistor set is switched on in another room, the same transistor which seems to be as necessary a part of a day out as food and drink. But perhaps the clearest indication of the popularity of pop music is to be seen in the sale of gramophone records. There do not appear to be many homes without a record player, and whereas the vast majority of pop records (the astronomical sales of which rise every year) used to be bought by the teenagers at work, an ever-increasing number is being sold to children of 12 years of age and upwards. It is a fact that young children (under 11), after one or two hearings, know all the words of the latest pop song. A pointer to their taste in music is provided in the BBC record programme *Children's Favourites.*

Pop Goes the Hymn Tune (Prism Pamphlet No. 14)

(*b*) Today we take for granted the cabinets of frozen food, dehydrated packets of soups, cake mixes and the great variety of tinned foods available in every town and village throughout the country. It is only recently that so much food has become available in these forms, and it is therefore not surprising that this has brought about changes in our eating habits. Less fish, citrus fruit and fresh vegetables are being bought, but the amounts of frozen and tinned foods purchased are constantly increasing.

Shops selling food have also changed; supermarkets and the serve-yourself type of shop are becoming increasingly popular. In these most of the food is prepacked in transparent paper and marked with the weight and price, and all the housewife has to do is to select the type and amount she requires.

The smaller shops where portions of cheese are cut or bacon is sliced while the customer waits are found less frequently, and it is seldom that one now finds small bakers' shops. Most of our bread today is baked in enormous factories and two-thirds of all bread bought is wrapped. The consumption of bread and cereal products has fallen over the past few years, while that of sugar has increased.

Providing the changes which are taking place do not reduce the nutritional value of the food we eat there will not be serious consequences. Whether the taste is as good is another matter.

ANNE ALLISON: *Running Your Home—food and entertaining*

Exercise F

Write connected summaries from your notes on the following passages, and provide each with a title:

1   The use of drugs in sport has hitherto been thought of as unsporting because their effect was to impair performance and the only way to use them was to administer them to an opponent. Poor Abraham Wood inadvertently drank liquid laudanum received from pretended friends while he was contesting a pedestrian contest with Captain Barclay Allardice in 1807 and shortly afterwards had to resign the match. More recent products have been found to have positive rather than negative effects on performance and a different situation has, therefore, arisen. No serious attempt has yet been made to regulate the use of drugs for positive assistance. Already caffeine is widely used by professional cyclists and Varidase was used by boxers in the Olympic Games in 1960 to minimise the effects of bruising. Other sportsmen take other drugs, some to stimulate, and some to relax or induce sleep between two strenuous efforts. Pharmaceutical research has been rapid and spectacular. The American Medical Association has estimated that amphetamine alone could improve the performance of runners by $1\frac{1}{2}$ per cent and swimmers by 1 per cent. As the use of drugs becomes more and more a part of daily life, so the governing bodies of sport will need to decide how to regulate their use.

P. C. MCINTOSH: *Sport in Society*

2   Since much of the American continent in summer suffers from excessively high temperatures, the air-conditioning or air-cooling of buildings has become very general, and this is spreading to the tropics. The question then is, what temperature should be aimed at, and what humidity? Mistakes were made in the early days of air-conditioning, and there were many cases of pneumonia caused by the excessive cooling of buildings when the difference between the temperature outside and the temperature inside was too great. Another trouble was the effect on appetite which has been experienced in the tropics. After a morning in a very hot office one went into an air-conditioned dining-room for lunch, and experiencing the zip caused by the difference in temperature one was tempted to swallow a couple of cocktails, perhaps have a pint of beer with lunch, and thoroughly enjoy one's food in the cool atmosphere, only to find that when one emerged outside afterwards there was a virtually complete collapse owing to the high temperature. It has now been realised that one secret of air-conditioning is that the contrasts must not be too great.

L. DUDLEY STAMP: *Applied Geography*

3   To the Editor of *The Guardian*:

Sir, I was very interested to read the letter by Mrs Anne Evans published on Friday, 31 July, in which it is suggested that all perishable foodstuffs should be date-stamped to avoid the sale of unsound commodities. This has been considered by the Association of Public Health Inspectors on several occasions, but there are certain difficulties in this suggestion.

Many perishable foodstuffs have varied shelf lives, and date-marking of production could easily create confusion in the mind of the purchaser when confronted with different commodities of various ages, all of which could be quite suitable for consumption.

The ultimate responsibility for ensuring that foodstuffs sold to the public are fit for consumption must rest with the retailer, who should see that stock is correctly rotated. Many retailers have introduced their own coding system indicating the date of delivery to their premises, as the manufacturers' coding is normally known only to themselves. When problems arise with perishable foods it is usually found that the retailer has been negligent in his stock control, and no amount of coding will overcome that.

Public health inspectors encourage individual stock coding and rotation systems among retailers, and many shopkeepers realise the advantages of such schemes. It is, however, unfortunately true that some shoppers completely upset a good retailer's rotation system by delving deeply into the display cabinet for the carton at the bottom of the pile.

Yours faithfully,

R. JOHNSON,

Secretary, The Association of Public Health Inspectors,

19 Grosvenor Place, London, S.W.1.

The Guardian, 11 August 1964

In the rest of this exercise, compare the number of words in your summary with the number of words used in the original.

4   The following letters were received by the BBC after a broadcast discussion about the standard of politeness and honesty now found in England. Construct one neat paragraph from the relevant points made in all of them.   (The letters contain 400 words.)

(i) *Shotgate, Essex*

If your team considers there has been an improvement in common politeness and honesty during this materialistic age of the last twenty years, then all I can say is GRRRR! I can also suggest that they travel regularly on the rush hour trains from Liverpool Street Station – *second class!*

A year ago – to preserve my natural sense of courtesy – I resigned from a pleasant position in London to dodge the travelling and the animalism exhibited in the anxiety of the ordinary travelling public to get aboard the first train out at any cost. The fact that others have been waiting a considerable time is ignored by the late arrivals, who edge and elbow their way in unless expelled by brute force. Heaven help anyone who shows the slightest consideration or courtesy! He is considered a fool and can be knocked down and trampled upon if necessary.

Talk to a great number of travellers about any form of moral or physical honesty, and your mild protests are laughed at as if you come from another world. They'll say in effect: 'If I don't take it, someone else will.'

W. A. TAYLOR

(ii) *Leicester*

Courtesy should begin in the home, and how often do we find it in the relationships between parents and children today?

Most children are ill-mannered, selfish little creatures, all because they have parents who will not take the trouble to teach them from early days the elementary principles of thankfulness and respect for their elders. Street scenes, and daily events in buses, and even at school, are sufficient to show the increasing decline of civility and good manners.

As for honesty, where does it prevail today? Ask the manager of any large store and he will tell you of the hundreds of pounds lost yearly in pilferages. British Railways and road haulage firms are at their wit's end to cope with the daily thefts.

GEORGE A. MORLEY

(iii) *Stockton-on-Tees, Co. Durham*

On the subject of common honesty, I was surprised that no member of the team mentioned present-day advertisers – or at any rate, some of them. What, for example, could be more dishonest than to describe a cigarette as 'cool', 'clean', 'fresh' and 'invigorating'?

JOAN E. ALLEN

(iv) *Hastings, Sussex*

The question about good manners reminded me of a remark made by an old French lady who was the Reverend Mother of a local convent. She said she liked travelling in England because 'the

Frenchman, he bow and smile; but the Englishman, he open the door'.

E. K. Tyrrell

5   Summarise the passage beginning 'Jet engines are possible . . .' on pages 63-64 above.   (The passage is 338 words long.)

Exercise G

In this exercise you will be asked to make summaries which need to be written from a different point of view from the original, or which draw on only part of it.

1   The story of newspapers as they now are begins at the end of the last century. During most of the century Britain's newspapers were written as though people's favourite reading was the full reports of speeches of statesmen, speeches often running into pages of closely-set type. Few pictures, little entertainment, much turgid prose. What the proprietors failed to see was the growth of a new readership, a new generation taught to read as a result of Lord Shaftesbury's Education Act, but not taught to read very well. They knew and could understand simple words, short sentences, short paragraphs. It was a generation repelled by what it regarded as the dullness of existing papers. And one young man who lived in Hampstead, London, an imaginative and impecunious young man, stumbled on a great discovery. A market was being ignored. This young man was Alfred Harmsworth, later Lord Northcliffe. He founded the *Daily Mail* in 1890 as the first halfpenny daily paper. It was an immediate and phenomenal success. Within ten years it reached a sale of a million copies a day. By 1929 it doubled that figure. It was written in simple language (indeed, some of its critics said it was written by people who couldn't write for people who couldn't read). It was clearly printed, pithy, well illustrated and easy to understand; its format and spirit of enterprise revolutionised newspapers in Great Britain. It ran campaigns which were successful in getting people to wear funny hats, eat wholemeal bread, grow sweet peas and take an interest in aviation. Northcliffe laid down the fundamental principle dominating modern journalism: 'Entertain, and never bore your readers.'
SIR LESLIE PLUMMER: *Inquiry* (Newspapers)

Briefly trace and explain the success of the *Daily Mail*.

2   *Berwick-upon-Tweed, Northumberland*
At 10.10 on the evening of Tuesday the 20th of August, 1963, what

appeared to be burning material was seen a number of times about half a mile off-shore and two miles north of Berwick. The honorary secretary decided to launch the life-boat *William and Mary Durham* at 10.30 p.m. to investigate. The tide was five hours ebb, the light wind was in the north-west and there was a moderate sea running in-shore. A search of the area where the lights were seen proved negative, so a wider area was covered with the aid of a searchlight and parachute flares, but again without result. At two o'clock the next morning the life-boat returned to harbour to check that the boat had not already come ashore and to warn the fishing fleet, which was about to put to sea, of the casualty and to co-ordinate any further efforts. The assistance of a helicopter was requested at first light. With the wind in the north-west and the ebb tide it was felt that the casualty might have carried south-east, and Holy Island lifeboat was asked to assist in the search. At 2.30 a.m. the life-boat put to sea again and searched south-east of Berwick light. Almost an hour later she found a 16-feet open boat, with a crew of two, five miles east by south of the light. A rope had fouled her propeller and the boat was towed into harbour. The boat had no navigation lights and her anchor rope was not long enough to reach the bottom. The life-boat was rehoused at 3.40 a.m. The assistance of the helicopter was not required.

The Lifeboat, December 1963

Although this account deals with an incident of a kind often reported in the Press, it is quite clearly written for a public with a special interest in every detail. What do you think that public is? Write the report which might have appeared in a good national newspaper.

3 Any time of the year is holiday-time at Weston-super-Mare, the big and friendly resort of South-west England. Delightfully situated on the shores of the Severn, with the green hills of Somerset rising in the background, Weston is famous for its wonderful, health-giving Atlantic air, mild climate and golden sands. All the family find plenty to see and do at this gay seaside town.

Weston is, too, an ideal centre for exploring the many West Country beauty spots, and, almost on the town's doorstep, are Glastonbury – reputed to be the site of the first Christian Church outside Palestine – Bath, Cheddar Gorge, Wells and Wookey Hole Caves.

It's easy to get to Weston. Express trains from London and Birmingham take only three hours, and through trains run from Lancashire and Yorkshire. From most parts of the country there are excellent train and coach services, and between Easter and October there are regular services of steamers from Wales.

Many people of all ages every year find renewed health in Weston's invigorating air and equable climate. As long ago as 1819, Mrs Piozzi, the friend of Dr Johnson, wrote 'the breezes here are most salubrious' and, about the same time, it is recorded 'a medical gentleman of celebrity sent 100 patients to Weston for the benefit of the air, only four of whom left the place without being benefited'. Members of the medical profession continue to send their patients, and the healthiness of its climate contributes in no small measure to Weston's growth.

Weston is spaciously built round a picturesque bay and, although it is protected from the North-east winds by wooded Worlebury Hill, it faces North America without land in between. On this Somerset coast the tide rises to a greater height than anywhere else in Britain, and it is believed that the extraordinary rise and fall of the tide, constantly diffusing ozone, is largely responsible for the outstanding health-giving properties of the air.

Weston-super-Mare Town Guide

Write one orderly paragraph containing the essential facts about Weston which are given in this extract from the Town Guide.

4   The ultra-modern motorship *Pole Star* ploughed north at full speed through a fog. Its radar suddenly revealed the aged S.S. *Santa Anita* ten miles away and headed south. The *Santa Anita*, lacking radar, was groping along at half speed with its foghorn bellowing. As it appeared to the *Pole Star* captain that the two ships were on parallel courses and could not collide, he went below for some much-needed sleep. Had he stayed at the radar, however, he would have seen that the *Pole Star* was headed across the *Santa Anita*'s course. Soon the *Pole Star* rammed and sank the older ship with some damage to its own bow. The *Santa Anita*'s owners sued. 'Our captain slowed to half speed and sounded his foghorn in accordance with the rules,' the *Santa Anita*'s owners contended, 'but your gadget-minded skipper negligently kept going at full speed until he rammed our ship. Therefore it's all your fault.'

'While our skipper might have been more careful, the "Santa Anita" captain is at fault for not sighting the "Pole Star" in time to get out of the way,' came the rejoinder. 'Both captains are to blame.

So we should no more have to pay for the loss of your ship than you should have to pay for smashing our ship's bow.' If you were the judge, would you make the *Pole Star* owners pay?

The *Pole Star* owners did have to pay. The court said that the *Santa Anita* captain had used due care. It blamed the captain of the *Pole Star* for not sticking by his radar and for 'merely guessing' that the other ship was steering a parallel course. 'What happened here,' it continued, 'demonstrates how radar may, when not properly used, increase the chances of collision. . . . It seems likely that the "Pole Star" would have proceeded more cautiously had she not been equipped with radar.'

You be the Judge

Summarise as briefly as you can: (*a*) the causes of the accident; (*b*) the legal arguments used by the rival owners; (*c*) the judgment in the case.

5 It may be useful to describe some recent experiments carried out by the BBC with the help of the Library Association and the Booksellers' and Publishers' Associations, which set out to estimate the numbers of people who wanted to borrow or buy some selected books before, during, and after they had been broadcast as serials, and compare the three results. The inquiries were conducted at sixty-five public libraries, having about half-a-million registered readers, and at bookshops in the same districts. The publishers concerned also kept careful records of fluctuations in sales.

The weekly demand in public libraries for Trollope's *The Last Chronicle of Barset*, which was broadcast as the Sunday night serial, increased by 60 per cent during the eleven-week period of the broadcasts. A similar increase appeared for Galsworthy's *The Silver Spoon*, which was read as 'A Book at Bedtime'. The library demand for Elizabeth Bowen's *The House in Paris*, which was read as a 'Woman's Hour' daily serial, increased three-fold. Six school broadcasts of dramatised extracts from *David Copperfield* produced a smaller but quite significant rise in borrowing. Cecil Day Lewis's translation of the *Aeneid* (in twelve dramatised parts) produced a demand for the book far exceeding that previously recorded for all other translations put together. These increased demands were fairly steady over the whole period of the broadcasts – there was no sudden rush at the beginning or at the end. Similar trends were reported by the booksellers and publishers.

The months following the broadcasts were critical to this inquiry because, if listeners regarded a broadcast version as a substitute for reading the original book, one would expect normal borrowing to decline after the broadcasts had ended. This inquiry showed that three months after the broadcasts the demand was still above normal, and in one instance nearly twice the normal figure. Another interesting finding was that the demand for other novels by these same authors also increased to about double the pre-broadcast figure.

JOSEPH TRENAMAN: *The Book World Today*

Outline clearly: (*a*) the purpose of the survey; (*b*) its findings.

6   Local taxation is raised by what we call *rates*. They are a very vexed point. They are always too high, never too low. Sometimes there is a rate of, let us say, thirty shillings in the pound. How can there possibly be? What does this mean?

The rate is first of all a tax levied by the local authority, but it is not based on income. It is based upon the rental which, theoretically, a house ought to bring. Originally, the rate was based on the rent that people did actually pay, or which they would have had to have paid if they had been renting the house they owned. However, there has been so much chopping and changing over rent today that this is no longer a practicable basis, so rental value is arrived at like this: the Inland Revenue has a corps of valuation officers, and these examine property and measure it up. They check its condition, see where it stands, its outlook, and compare it with other houses. Two houses may be very different. The first house may lack amenities – 'no bathroom, overlooks gasworks, two bedrooms, no hot water, frontage 23 feet'. The second may have many amenities: '90-foot frontage, overlooks golf-course, two-car garage, running water in bedrooms.' The amount of rent these two houses bring on an open market is obviously very different. The valuation officers decide what rent a house would fetch on a completely free market with a willing landlord and a willing tenant. They have their own way of arriving at the decision, but as it is a single corps run by the Inland Revenue as an agent of the central government, it does extend over the whole of the United Kingdom, so there ought at least to be justice done between a property in one area and a property in another.

S. E. FINER: *Inquiry* (Local Government)

Explain sympathetically, to a puzzled and aggrieved resident, the system on which his house has been assessed for rates.

7   The SPEAKER took the Chair at half past two o'clock.

LIEUT.-COL. CORDEAUX (Nottingham, Central, C.) asked the Minister of Power if he would give general directions in the public interest to the Electricity Council and the Gas Council not to demand repayment by house-holders of cash stolen from their electricity and gas meters unless satisfied that the money was stolen by the house-holders themselves.

MR PEYTON, Parliamentary Secretary Ministry of Power (Yeovil, C.): 'No. This is a matter best left to the discretion of the area boards.'

LIEUT.-COL. CORDEAUX: 'The householder has no say in the theft-resisting qualities of the meter, and has no control whatever over the frequency of clearances and therefore over the money likely to be in the meter. In these circumstances, is it not monstrous that any house-holder, whether rich or poor, should be required to make good the loss?'

MR PEYTON: 'The boards are entitled themselves to do what they can to ensure the security of money which belongs to them. If the boards are to carry the losses those losses have to be passed on, in the ultimate, to the customer.'

SIR BARNETT STROSS (Stoke-on-Trent, Central, Lab.): 'Is not this a strange doctrine?' (Cheers.) 'Surely if the householder has put his money away and has given it to the board, once it has gone into the meter that money is no longer legally the householder's; it belongs to the board. If it is stolen, surely the loss is the loss of the board and not of the householder who is now supposed to pay twice? That is a monstrous suggestion.'

MR PEYTON: 'That depends on the terms of the contract. Most boards stipulate expressly in their conditions of supply that, although the money belongs to the board after it has been put into the meter, the householder is, nevertheless, to be responsible for its custody.' (Opposition cries of 'Oh'.)

MR CARMICHAEL (Glasgow, Woodside, Lab.) said that in Scotland, if the householder could prove that he was in no way responsible for the meter having been broken into, the board was responsible for the cash.

MR PEYTON: 'I am not responsible for decisions of the court. This is a matter much better left to the discretion of the area boards who make every attempt to deal with it sympathetically, particularly in cases of hardship.'

The Times, 14 February 1964

In one paragraph each, summarise: (*a*) the request, with the reasons for it, which Lieut.-Col. Cordeaux is making; (*b*) Sir Barnett Stross's observations; (*c*) the Parliamentary Secretary's answers to both members. Use reported speech.

8 *Radio Times* and *TV Times* give the times at which BBC and Independent Television programmes are broadcast. They often give also, in such a way as to make you want to watch them, an outline of what the programmes will contain. If you study the current issues, you will notice a sharp difference between the outlines provided for informative or factual programmes (travel films, sports relays, documentaries, etc.) and for short stories or plays. What is it?

(*a*) Agree on two programmes of different kinds to watch or listen to, and then write outlines of them which might have appeared in the programme papers.

(*b*) Watch (or listen to) one instalment of a broadcast serial, and then provide a summary suitable to be printed in the announcement of the next.

(*c*) Give a brief indication of the content of one of these programmes for a friend who missed it.

*   *   *

So far in this book there has been no restriction on the number of words to be used in the summaries. This is because a word-limit seems to worry many people, and they spoil their first attempts by making them *too short*: in trying to be brief, they either leave out important ideas, or else fail to link their notes into a well-written summary.

Not all prose can be condensed to the same extent, as you will have discovered from *Exercise F* above. An extract from a speech or discussion, for instance, will probably reduce to fewer words than an extract of similar length from a writer arguing about the efficiency of the National Health Service. Again, a passage taken from a book intended to be read by non-specialists (and so full of examples and explanations) will be more readily shortened than a piece of technical writing meant for specialists.

And so when you are given – as from this point onwards in this book you will be – a limit on the number of words you may use in your summary, you should look on this as a help, and not as a cramping restriction. The number of words you are allowed will give you an idea of the amount of important material the extract to be summarised contains. If your first draft is much shorter than it needs to be, then you have left out something essential or not taken the space necessary to make your meaning quite clear. If it is too long, check your notes to see that they include nothing unimportant, and check your draft to see that they have been written up as economically as possible.

The following summary, made by a Fourth-former, will illustrate the point. It contains 116 words, which is 16 words above the set limit.

The first time the author visited Malaya he found that the white inhabitants, their conditions and pastimes had not changed in the last twenty-five years. They lived in isolation, but some were able to go to Singapore to visit their friends. All the newspapers the people received were six weeks old and therefore could never be up to date. The standard of communication became transformed by the air service which enabled a closer and more intimate association between home and alien lands. International news was obtained fresh from Fleet Street. This changed the whole outlook of British workers abroad, strengthening their connections with England, which they knew was much closer and more dear to them.

The first comment to make on this is that, since it is unsatisfactory as a piece of English writing, it is unsatisfactory as a summary. Can the writer *mean* that the white inhabitants of Malaya had not changed in twenty-five years; and what does he intend us to understand by 'their conditions'? After the plurals of the first sentence, it is a surprise to find in the second that 'they lived *in isolation*'. The last eight words of the third sentence are redundant. In the fourth, what exactly are 'alien lands'; and was it just *communication* that the air service transformed? Why should international news come from Fleet Street; and does 'fresh' receive the emphasis that it seems to need? In the final sentence, what does the opening 'this' refer back to; are the 'British workers abroad' the 'white inhabitants' who were mentioned before; and is it really clear why England should have become 'more dear'?

By taking more care over his final draft, the writer would have completed his summary well within the 100-word limit – and would still have had room to include the vital points (such as the link between the paragraphs) he has missed out. Here is the original passage:

When I first visited Malaya the lives the white men and their wives led there differed but little from what they had been twenty-five years before. They got home leave once in five years. They had besides a few weeks' leave every year. If they lived where the climate was exhausting they sought the fresh air of some hill-station not too far away; if, like some government servants, they lived where they might not see another white man for weeks on end, they went to Singapore so that they might consort for a time with their kind. *The Times*, when it arrived at a station up-country, in Borneo for instance, was six weeks old, and they were lucky if they received the Singapore paper in a fortnight.

Aviation has changed all that. Even before the war people who could afford it were able to spend even their short leave at home. Papers, illustrated weeklies, magazines reached them fresh from the press. In the old days Sarawak, say, or Selangor, were where they expected to spend their lives till it was time for them to retire on a pension; England was very far away, and when at long intervals they went back was increasingly strange to them; their real home, their intimate friends, were in the land in which the better part of their lives was spent. But with the rapidity of communication it remained an alien land, a temporary rather than a permanent habitation, which circumstances compelled them for a time to occupy. Their ties with the homeland, which before had insensibly loosened and sometimes broke asunder, remained fast. England, so to speak, was round the corner. They no longer felt cut off. It changed their whole outlook.

w. somerset maugham, *The Complete Short Stories* (Introduction to Vol. 3)

Write down any important points in this passage which are new to you, i.e. which were omitted from the summary of it. Then consider how far the words or phrases examined for reasons of style above are acceptable as condensed versions of material in the original passage. Finally, criticise the following summary, first for style, and then (paying particular attention to the words *in italics*) for accuracy in condensing.

Before *the arrival of aviation, colonial life* was very similar to what it had been 25 years previously. Leave home came every five years, but there was *an annual leave* which was spent either in the hills or in *a large town for the society*. Communications were appalling *and* 'The Times' was often up to six weeks old when it arrived in some places. With the arrival of aviation, there were a great number of changes. *Newspapers* arrived fresh from the press; even the shortest leave could be spent at home. England, which had previously seemed miles away, was now only a few hours' flight away. England now remained *their* home and their adopted land remained an alien country, *a temporary rather than permanent habitation.*

(129 words)

Neither summary, by the way, was given a title.

*   *   *

In summary writing, as in other arts, preparation and practice and advice have their place; but the time comes when it is necessary to show that all your training has had some effect. That time has come now. And the most useful final word is to remind you to continue using the method of summary writing which you have been rehearsing.

1   Read the passage till you understand it.
2   Make your notes on it, and check them carefully.
3   Put the passage away. Write your first draft from your notes alone.
    (It never pays to try short cuts: if you make a mistake in these early stages, no amount of patching later can put it right.)
4   Revise your draft in three ways:
    (*a*) Compare it with the passage for omissions and distortions;
    (*b*) check its length;
    (*c*) polish its style – especially sentence-structure.
5   Invent a title, put it at the head of your page, and then
6   Write your Fair Copy.

Exercise H
Summarise the following passages, taking special care to preserve the links between their main ideas. Give a title to each of your summaries, and keep within the suggested word limits.

1   Four hundred drug companies compete in one of the fiercest of modern rat races. About 150 companies make patent medicines – the cough cures and pick-me-ups that one can buy freely across the chemist's counter without prescription. The other firms specialize in drugs for the doctor, those which can be obtained only on prescription. Some big companies make both. The size of the firms varies from the back street herbalist to the giants like I.C.I., Glaxo and Beechams. Much of the UK market has been cornered by Continental and American firms; in fact US companies probably control about 50 per cent of the whole drug trade of the United Kingdom.

The large companies display a glistening picture of well-equipped laboratories and whiter-than-white-coated chemists. Some of the research they do is most impressive, so much so as to show clearly the potential of the industry. But much is wrong. A great deal of so-called research is in fact completely trivial pottering around in an attempt to introduce minor refinements which will put the firm's product one up on its rivals. The waste – not least of the gifted men and women involved – is staggering.

A second snag is the cost, particularly the cost to the taxpayer. The number of prescriptions under the National Health Service has been fairly constant year by year, but costs have mounted steadily, far more than the increase in the cost of living or the cost of raw materials. In 1949 the N.H.S. drug bill was £20 million; in 1961, it was £79 million; in 1962, with 13 million fewer prescriptions than the year before, the cost was £83 million, an average of 8s. 3d. per prescription. When pressed on this point, manufacturers talk of the cost of research, but since much of this research is merely wasteful competition there seems no reason why the consumer should foot the bill. Colossal profits are being made by the big firms.

Topic 11   (Limit: 50–75 words)

2   When I was younger, I liked to travel alone, especially on long journeys that were not holidays but had some connection with work. My reasons were various. I did not want to accept, as one has to accept the weather, the moods and whims of travelling companions; I did everything quickly myself, and hated hanging about for other people, particularly men. I believed that the solitary traveller sees and remembers more, is more sharply aware of new experience, than a man who is enjoying other people's company along the way.

At sixty, I no longer look forward to travelling alone. I can make more allowance for other people's moods and whims, and I am less impatient if I am kept waiting. On the other hand, though I am not afraid of solitude, which is the writer's natural element, I dislike more and more the peculiar isolation of the solitary traveller, that homeless and lost feeling which can strike all the harder when one is continually surrounded by people. These people may be wonderfully friendly, kind, hospitable, but they are strangers with whom nothing can be taken for granted, to whom so much always has to be explained. Even the barest acknowledgement of their hospitality demands nervous energy. You cannot talk your way out of a fit of depression, because you are either alone or with people who quite reasonably expect to entertain or enjoy being entertained.

                                              (Limit: 40–60 words)

J. B. PRIESTLEY and JACQUETTA HAWKES: *Journey Down a Rainbow*

3   Over and over again in science fiction we meet the idea of telepathy. A whole host of individuals with this strange gift are scattered
through an endless variety of stories. What is the truth about telepathy? The short answer is that we do not know; but what a lot of
people do not realise is why we do not know. To be an accepted scientific fact, any phenomenon has to fulfil two conditions. First, it must
be reproducible – we must be able to repeat it whenever we please.
Secondly, we must have some sort of explanation as to how it works –
this may be wrong, but it must fit the accepted scientific knowledge
of the time. We are prepared to do without either of these but not
both.

The difficulty about all the experiments so far carried out on telepathy is that neither of these conditions is satisfied; current scientific
thought gives us not the remotest idea of how telepathy might work,
and we cannot reproduce the experiments at will. And so there are
those who say that there is 'nothing in it'. This is an illogical attitude,
because all we have done is to define science in such a way that there
cannot be anything in it; it does not follow that telepathy does not
happen. I incline to the view that there is 'something in it', though not
perhaps as much as its devotees often claim. If we do ever prove the
existence of telepathy without any doubt, it may be possible to
develop this and related faculties; for the moment the case is not
proven.   (Limit: 40–60 words)
BILL WILLIAMS: 'Man in the Future': *The Listener*, 14 May 1964

4   One educational problem recurs constantly in every kind of
school. Pupils are absent when important parts of a syllabus are being
taught. Pupils transferred from other types of schools or from other
parts of the country frequently have to face subjects unfamiliar to
them, but already studied in some depth by their new fellow-pupils.
Others, particularly Sixth-formers, find that they need a subject in
addition to their prescribed course of study for a particular career.
Many pupils want to explore an interest in subjects well outside their
immediate time-table and lack a teacher.

Even in the most enlightened school with an ingeniously flexible
time-table these problems are capable of solution in only one way.
Teachers give up dinner-hours or stay after school in an attempt to
teach the additional material or to make up for ground-work lost.
Invariably, this is done either under pressure of time or in the face of
a real tiredness on the part of a teacher who has been hard at it all
day. An inevitable feature of this kind of teaching is that the teacher

concentrates on imparting the facts in sufficient measure for the pupil to cope with the immediate problem.

Teaching machines will ultimately solve these difficulties. As scientific aids, they are only in their infancy. Given another decade of further development of scientific techniques and technology proportionate to the progress made by science in the last decade, particularly in the application of cybernetics and computers, teaching machines will provide the biggest break-through in education since the discovery that white shows up on black.

Topic 13   (Limit: 70–90 words)

5   Summarise in not more than 50 words the reasons the writer gives for the 'physical decline of the west'.

The United States needs to call up seven men to obtain two soldiers; of the five who are rejected, three are turned down for physical reasons and two for mental disabilities. The Americans have been more assiduous than any other nation in devising fitness tests and applying them to their citizens, and so the lack of fitness of citizens of the United States is exposed for all to see. There is no reason to think, however, that other affluent societies in Britain or Western Europe are escaping the insidious flabbiness which has begun to characterise the United States.

There is no great mystery about the causes of the physical decline of the West. The decrease of casual exercise, coupled with indulgence in food and drink, more than offsets any physical toughening which may result from increased participation in sport. One hundred years ago everyone everywhere walked to work. Most people in the world still do. The modern city-dweller, however, does not.

Often he does not walk at all if he can avoid it. 'We are faced with a curious paradox,' writes Lewis Mumford; 'the new suburban form has now produced an anti-urban pattern. With the destruction of walking distances has gone the destruction of walking as a normal means of circulation: the motor-car has made it unsafe, and the extension of the suburb has made it impossible.' At places of work lifting and handling are reduced to a minimum by the service of machines; facilities for refreshment and often for recreation exist on the site, and architecture at home and at work eliminates climbing.

P. C. MCINTOSH: *Sport in Society*

6   Trace, in 60 to 80 words, the development of the Gillette blade from first idea to successful production.

King Gillette conceived the idea of the modern safety razor at the end of the 19th century. He came from a family of inventors, but his formal technical training was slight. While employed as a travelling salesman he produced several minor inventions. He met William Painter, the inventor of the modern bottle-cap, and it was he who started Gillette on the search which resulted in the invention of the safety razor by suggesting that Gillette should try to invent something which the consumer can use, throw away, and buy again. According to Gillette's own account of his invention, the idea for a razor with a cheap disposable blade came in a 'flash' one morning in 1895 while he was shaving. He rushed out to purchase some 'pieces of brass, some steel ribbon used for clock springs, a small hand vice and some files' and built his first safety razor. He filed a patent application and the patent was issued in 1904.

The idea and a crude model did not ensure the commercial success of the invention. For six years Gillette sought for ways of making a cheap blade from sheet steel that would harden and temper suitably for taking a keen edge. He had almost no knowledge of steel, yet he felt confident he would find a solution. The steel experts were not enthusiastic; from their experiences they thought it would prove to be impossible. Gillette's friends thought the idea was a joke and refused to give him financial assistance. He remarked several years later: 'But I didn't know how to quit. If I had been technically trained I would have quit or probably would never have begun. I was a dreamer who believed in the "gold at the foot of the rainbow" promise, and continued in the path where wise ones feared to tread, and that is the reason, and the only reason, why there is a Gillette razor today.' Gillette finally found men willing to risk capital, but it took another ingenious inventor to solve the problem of making the cheap blade. The company showed its first profits in 1906 and after that sales increased at an enormous rate. Individual inventors created the modern safety razor: King Gillette had the idea and built a crude model and Nickerson, by devices of a high order of ingenuity bordering closely on invention, converted it into the razor in use today.

J. JEWKES and others: *The Sources of Invention*

7 The railways were not built without opposition. Many ordinary people, with the natural conservative fear of new things, mistrusted the 'locomotive monster'; and those who depended for their living or prosperity on the canals, the turnpike roads, and coaching traffic

all feared they would lose much of their trade and opposed the passage of the Bills through Parliament.

The greatest and most expensive resistance came from landowners, who argued that their estates would be spoiled by the passage of a railway through any part of them. They demanded exorbitant prices for the land itself, and then asked for and obtained additional large sums for 'consequential damage'. One landowner obtained £120,000 for land worth £5,000. A few were honest enough to return part or, in at least one case, all of these undeserved gains when they found that the railway benefited their land rather than injured it; but the railways cost far more than they should have done, for this reason alone.

Some towns refused to allow the railways to pass through, and so the lines had to find an alternative route which was often longer and more expensive. Such hostility was encouraged by the attitude of the Press, which always seemed ready to publish any arguments, however silly, against the railways. In 1835 they were referring to 'the fatigue, the misery and danger of being dragged through the air at the rate of 20 m.p.h. all their lives at the mercy of a tin pipe or a copper boiler.' Articles foretold the parching of the meadows and the drying up of springs, the failure of cows to give milk, and the extinction of the horse. Houses, it was said, would be crushed by the embankments, and everybody except the people who had invested in the railways would be ruined. Finally, the readers were comforted with the reflection that probably the locomotives would not work, but would be too heavy to move.

Both supporters and opponents of railways produced medical opinions to strengthen their case. The latter quoted doctors who said that tunnels would produce colds, catarrhs, and consumption. The deafening noise, the gloom, the glare of the engine fire would have a bad effect on the nerves. High speed would injure the lungs, and plunging from darkness to light would cause great harm to the eyesight. On the other side were doctors who said that the speed and the swing of the train would equalise the circulation, improve the digestion, soothe the nerves, and ensure good sleep.

L. F. HOBLEY: *Living and Working*   (Limit: 80–100 words)

8   One of the peculiarities of the motor-car is that virtually everybody wants to have one. Here and there, exceptions no doubt exist, but for all practical purposes it can be assumed that every family that can afford a motor car – or thinks it can afford one – will buy one, new or second-hand. This means that it is possible to predict how many

cars there will be at different dates in the future by estimating how many families will have incomes that will bring them in to the car-affording category. And car-affording has worked itself down the pyramid of incomes until there is now an enormous group of them just coming into range. It is estimated that, in forty-six years' time, there will be four times as many cars in Britain as there are today. This is a very impressive figure – but the year 2010 is still very remote. What is much more frightening is that in 1980 – only sixteen years off – there will be three times as many cars as there are today. That is why I call it a national emergency. It will be on top of us almost before we can think what to do about it.

One consequence of this flood of cars is worth singling out for mention, since it will have a direct bearing on government policy. A majority of the voters in this country will soon be car-owners. More-over, a car-owner takes his car-owning seriously – it becomes one of the major interests of his life. The politicians will take notice of this. They will be anxious to please the motorist, and frightened of annoy-ing him. This may greatly complicate the problem, as it will make drastic action politically difficult if it appears likely to meet with opposition among car-owners. (Limit: 80–100 words)

SIR GEOFFREY CROWTHER: Preface to *Traffic in Towns* (Buchanan Report)

Exercise I

This exercise and the next ask for summaries of different kinds and of different lengths. But you should approach each piece of work in the orderly way you have practised, and should again provide titles and observe word-limits in your finished summaries.

1   Fifteen years ago life in Pittsburgh was almost unbearable. The smoke was appalling, tainting everything, so that there was little relish in living. Throughout the States it was known as 'The Smoky City', and when its name was mentioned people would screw up their faces in distaste. The smoke came not only from a myriad factories and foundries, but from houses with coal fires, trains with steam loco-motives, steam tugs and countless varied smoky machines. Almost all has now been eliminated. Fuels that made much smoke were banned by law, first in the city of Pittsburgh, then in the surrounding districts. There was naturally strong opposition. Some of the most vociferous came from laundry operators, who foresaw a serious drop in business, and sometimes insisted upon maintaining their own small belching

chimneys, partly as a protest of principle, partly because (presumably) even a little laundry chimney dirties a few shirts. The railroads, after a show of reluctance, agreed to convert their trains almost entirely to diesel; to their secret delight, I am told, for they had wanted to make the change for years but had been prevented because the custom of coal-producers was so important to them. Stern penalties were imposed upon those who violated the smoke laws, and remarkably soon the place began to look up.

Indeed, some of the effects of the reforms were miraculous. Pittsburgh now gets 60 per cent more sunshine than it used to, and 60 per cent less dust and soot falls on the city. It is warmer, too, for the old horrible pall sometimes reduced the temperature by as much as 10 degrees. The Chamber of Commerce claims that despite the forlorn rearguard actions of the laundrymen, Pittsburghers have saved themselves an annual 41 dollars per head in laundry bills. The city's air is now sharp and clean; it is queer, like examining a half-cleaned picture, to look about you now in Pittsburgh and see, defacing old buildings, degrading trees, clinging to crevices and corners, blackening bridges and staling factories, engriming all the shores of the Ohio River, the dingy sediment left behind by the smoke.

JAMES MORRIS: *Coast to Coast*

Explain in fewer than 40 words each: (*a*) why Pittsburgh used to be known as 'The Smoky City'; (*b*) what changes the smoke laws have brought to Pittsburgh.

2   Until 1832, when the practice was forbidden by law, boys were employed to sweep chimneys. The following interview with a good master comes from a Parliamentary Report of 1817.

'What mode do you adopt to get the boy to go up the chimney in the first instance?'

'We persuade him as well as we can; we generally practise him in one of our own chimneys first. One of the boys who knows the trade goes up behind him, and when he has practised it ten times, though some will require twenty times, they generally can manage it. The boy goes up with him to keep him from falling; after that the boy will manage to go up by himself, after going up and down several times with one under him; we do this because if he happens to make a slip he will be caught by the other.'

'Do you find many boys show repugnance to go up at first?'

'Yes, most of them.'

'And if they resist and reject, in what way do you force them up?'

'By telling them we must take them back again to their father and mother, and give them up again; and their parents are generally people who cannot maintain them.'

'So that they are afraid of going back for fear of being starved?'

'Yes, they go through a deal of hardship before they come to our trade.'

'Did you use any more violent means?'

'Sometimes a rod.'

'You are aware, of course, that those means being gentle or harsh must depend very much upon the character of the individual master?'

'It does.'

'Of course you must know that there are persons of harsh and cruel disposition; have you not often heard of masters treating their apprentices with great cruelty, particularly the little boys, in forcing them to go up those small flues, which the boys were unwilling to ascend?'

'Yes; I have forced up many a one myself.'

'By what means?'

'By threatenings, and by giving them a kick or a slap.'

Parliamentary Report, 1817

(*a*) Omitting everything else, and in not more than 50 words, describe the method of sweeping which the boys were taught.

(*b*) Write an attack on the practice of using boys to sweep chimneys, drawing your material from any evidence of cruelty in this extract.

3   The following blurb appears on the cover of the Penguin edition of *Animal Farm*. Although it incidentally summarises part of the novel, its main purpose is to make people who pick the book up in a shop want to buy a copy; and this purpose would not be served if it told too much of the story.

This biting satire upon dictatorship is the history of a revolution that went wrong – and of the excellent excuses that were forthcoming at every step for each perversion of the original doctrine.

The animals on a farm drive out their master and take over and administer the farm for themselves. The experiment is entirely successful, except for the unfortunate fact that someone has to take the deposed farmer's place. Leadership devolves almost automatically upon the pigs, who are on a higher intellectual level than the rest of the animals. Unhappily their character is not equal to their intelligence, and out of this fact springs the main development of the story.

The last chapter brings a dramatic change, which, as soon as it has happened, is seen to have been inevitable from the start.

(*a*) Write lively blurbs for two books you have recently read – one fiction and one non-fiction. Remember that blurbs aim to win readers for the book, and that space on a dust-jacket is very limited.

(*b*) In a Companion to English Literature, or similar work of reference, a reader would expect to find an outline summary of the whole book (and not of just a part, as in the blurb above). Write the article on *Animal Farm* to appear in a new *Encyclopaedia of Books*, and try not to exceed 200 words.

(*c*) Write articles of similar length about the books for which you provided blurbs in (*a*) above.

4 Consider these words written by an eminent Harley Street Medical Consultant: '. . . it is in the treatment of the minor ailments of existence, the tension left over after the office, the coiled inner spring of the housewife's end-of-day frustrations, that music can be confidently prescribed. There is no better tranquilliser that I know than Good Music.' This is but a fragment of the vast amount of medical opinion that has been expressed on the value of Good Music as the finest natural means to healthy effective relaxation of mind and body.

The understanding of Good Music – the ability to listen to it and enjoy its enriching influence – the knowledge which enables you to talk intelligently about it – these are tremendous social assets that at any time can give you an immense personal advantage in less well-endowed company. A taste for Good Music opens up new avenues of social advancement from which you and your family will benefit immeasurably.

Even in your business life – just as in social circles – you will find that at any moment the ability to discourse knowledgeably on the great musical works, on the master composers, or on contemporary artists and current performances will contribute noticeably to your standing, for a love of Good Music helps you to build the intellectual stature upon which business advancement largely depends.

No parents should deny young children the opportunity of growing up with a background of Good Music. Of course, through the various stages of their development they will require child music in their first years and 'Pop' music in their adolescence; but sooner or later they must and will demand the deeper satisfaction offered by the really great music of the world. To deny them the opportunity of acquiring a knowledge of and affection for Good Music is to prejudice their opportunities in later life.

There comes a time in all our lives when the normal daily claims on our time cease to exist. This is one occasion in particular where Good Music can be such a good friend. With an interest in Good Music there is no such thing as loneliness. It has been said more than once that 'all musical people seem happy' – and so it is. Good Music – like nothing else – can fill so well the wastes of spare time that often make retirement or loneliness so boring.

It is difficult to name another interest which can provide so much real pleasure and such intellectual enrichment on so small a capital investment. A reasonably good Record Player of modest price *and* a basic library of first class Classical Recordings can be acquired *for less than* £100. The initial outlay can be quite small as your basic library of records can be built up month by month as your circumstances permit, but the joys of listening to great composers and artists go on and on. Here indeed is an investment which you will never – ever – regret, an investment which will yield the most wonderful dividends of your life.

E.M.I. publicity

Write a summary (100 to 125 words) beginning 'There are six good reasons why anyone should learn to enjoy good music', and build your paragraph on that topic sentence.

5 Most of the new 'modernist' buildings are in reinforced concrete, or in brick covered with cement to simulate concrete, and have sheer white walls devoid of cornices or mouldings. Photographed, as they invariably are, immediately after completion in strong sunlight against a deep blue sky, they look very effective; but in our climate they soon look shabby and the cement covering is liable to 'craze' or crack, spoiling the appearance. Roofs are always flat, a method which facilitates planning, as a sloping roof involves a good deal of scheming for the architect; but a flat roof that is badly built is a constant source of trouble and has other disadvantages which seldom arise with the sloping type. Windows are very generously provided, often at the angles of the building; and small panes are never used. Excessive glass-area, however, involves much loss of heat in our cold climate, and that fact should be borne in mind. The interiors of these houses are invariably well-planned from a 'functional' and labour-saving aspect; an important point in their favour. The despised drawing-room of Edwardian days, with a separate dining-room, gives place to

one large all-purpose 'lounge', a feature which may satisfy gregarious people with no children, but which fails under the conditions of normal family life, where one member of the household, at least, often seeks some refuge from the never-ceasing radio in order to work or rest.

M. S. BRIGGS: *Architecture*

In 60 to 80 words describe the disadvantages of the modernist buildings detailed above.

6   Eric Leighton, aged 51, of Dinton, appeared at the West London Court on Wednesday on a charge of stealing plants from the Royal Botanic Gardens, Kew. He pleaded not guilty, and conducted his own defence.

Mr Humbolt, an official of the Royal Botanic Gardens, said in evidence that as a result of recent thefts from the rock garden a special watch had been kept. The accused was seen to approach a small group of liliaceous plants. After satisfying himself that he was not observed, he took a trowel from his coat pocket and dug up two bulbs.

Mr Evans (prosecuting): 'I understand that these were rare plants.'

Mr Humbolt: 'Yes, sir, very rare indeed.'

Mr Evans: 'Then why were they not kept in a greenhouse?'

Mr Humbolt: 'Because they would have died there.'

Mr Evans: 'Please continue.'

Mr Humbolt: 'On being questioned by one of the guardians, the accused admitted taking the bulbs, but maintained that as he had often donated plants to the Gardens he considered himself entitled to do so. Three other plants and various cuttings were found on his person.'

Mr Evans: 'What is a cutting?'

Mr Humbolt: 'A cutting is a small shoot or branch removed from the parent plant for the purpose of propagation. Whereas propagation by seed may not come true, plants propagated vegetatively, that is to say by means of cuttings or by divisions of . . .'

The Magistrate (to the accused): 'Do you admit taking these bulbs and cuttings? And if so, how do you attempt to justify your action? Have you anything to say?'

Leighton: 'I have indeed; a very great deal. As a regular donor to the Gardens, and as a ratepayer, I consider myself perfectly entitled to take plants and cuttings when I do so without damaging or unreasonably reducing the size of the plant. I am not the kind of man who would take the single egg from a nest. I consider that rare plants should be as widely distributed as . . .'

The Magistrate (interrupting – to Mr Humbolt): 'Has the accused given plants to the Gardens?'

Mr Humbolt: 'Yes, sir. On a number of occasions.'

The Magistrate (to Leighton): 'Whether or no you have from time to time presented plants to the Gardens, what you have committed is theft. Are you sorry for what you have done?'

Leighton: 'Not in the least. And I shall do it again.'

The Magistrate: 'Are you aware that I have the power to commit you to prison? Will you express regret for your very foolish action?'

Leighton: 'No – I will not.'

The Magistrate: 'Very well, then. I find you guilty and you will have to pay a fine of twenty pounds.'

Leighton: 'I shan't pay.'

The Magistrate: 'You may have seven days to pay. If you do not pay, then you will have to go to prison for two months.'

Leighton: 'I haven't the slightest intention of paying.'

The accused left the court. It was learned later that his wife had paid the fine.

WILFRID BLUNT: *Of Flowers and a Village*

Using reported speech, and in 100 to 120 words, write an interesting summary of this fictitious case.

7   On 2 November 1959 the first long-distance motor-way to be built in England was opened by the Ministry of Transport. The equivalent of a mountain two miles high (nearly sixteen million tons of soil) had been moved to lay this seventy-mile, six-lane carriageway, one hundred and thirty-two bridges constructed to carry roads over it, and one hundred miles of pipes laid to help drain it of water. In eighteen months its way had been carved from St Albans to within a few miles of Birmingham and a magnificent road created out of muddy confusion. It was a great engineering achievement, worthy to rank with Stephenson's building of the London to Birmingham Railway over a century before. The countless thousands of ignorant labourers who constructed that railway with pick and shovel and brute strength would surely have been proud of these later men, who toiled through one of the wettest summers for years, their strength aided by giant bulldozers, huge mechanical diggers and machines capable of laying 7 inches of concrete in one massive stream.

During the opening ceremony at Pepperstock Junction, the Minister said: 'This motor-way starts a new era in road travel. It is in keeping with the bold, exciting and scientific age in which we live.' Then he picked up a 'phone from a nearby car and ordered the County Police along the route to lift the barriers at the access fly-overs and let the waiting motorists on to the beautiful twin ribbon of tarmac. There was no lack of drivers to try out the new marvel. That November day saw 1,000 vehicles an hour passing in each direction and by 7 p.m. over 13,000 had used the motor-way; one garage sold 250 gallons of petrol in the first two hours. At every fly-over bridge crowds, many waving white handkerchiefs, watched the speeding traffic below and the wide roads were blocked by their parked cars. To add to the excitement helicopters twirled overhead, their pilots ready to report any accidents or stoppages to the patrolling police cars, for on such a speedway a stationary vehicle could spell danger.

There were plenty of breakdowns to report. Before night-fall nearly 100 calls for assistance had been received, both via the air patrols and by means of the emergency telephones spaced at intervals of a mile along the carriage-ways. Car after car was forced to take to the earth 'shoulders' at the side of the track. Rejoicing in the pleasure of speed, many drivers forgot that their often-ageing cars were in no condition for hours of mile-a-minute cruising. All sorts of mechanical faults developed. Engines became over-heated, clutches were burnt out, water boiled in radiators. Other drivers miscalculated the amount of fuel needed for high-speed travel and rolled to a halt with empty tanks. One car even lost its engine, which just fell out of the chassis!

L. E. SNELLGROVE: *From Steam Carts to Minicars*

(*a*) Give the advice which, on the evidence of this report, drivers need before embarking on motor-way travel. (35 to 50 words)

(*b*) From the astonishing or amusing details given above, write a paragraph (60 to 80 words) for the 'Curious Facts behind the News' feature of a weekly magazine.

8   If a forgery is to be successful, it must deceive both the art expert who will examine the style, brushwork and subject matter and the scientist who will test the paints, dyes and canvas. A modern canvas with its starch, alkali and bleach is easily identified even by a superficial examination, and yet an old canvas requires prolonged and careful scraping and boiling if all traces of its previous dressings are

to be removed. When it comes to the actual painting, there are more pitfalls for the unwary forger: he may be able to concoct *some* mixtures of the correct composition but the ingredients will of necessity be of modern manufacture and their very purity could betray him. Recipes for some of the old paints are still obtainable but the details are often omitted: 'oil' could mean olive oil, linseed oil, nut oil or even hempseed oil. The surface must be dried correctly: too little heat will leave the paint soft and too much will produce tell-tale cracks. The varnish presents further difficulties – several layers must be applied and dried in such a way as to produce *craquelure*, the hall-mark of an old painting and the bane of a forger's life. The best way of achieving it is to apply two layers of varnish with different rates of drying; the slower-drying lower layer causes the upper layer to crack, and then dirt – of the correct composition – is rubbed into the crevices.

The discovery of a painting apparently by an old master is regarded with the greatest suspicion until it has been subjected to very searching tests. First the art expert pronounces on the artistic merit, style of painting, use of colours, and the thousand-and-one characteristics of the supposed artist. The scientist then examines the hardness of the paints, sometimes with a pin but more usually with various solvents. The chemical composition of the paints – often determined by spectroscopic analysis – may help to fix the date of painting, or at least the earliest and latest possible dates. Microscopic examination of the fibres of the canvas will show if they have been scraped and an X-ray will expose the internal brushwork. The presence of an identifiable fingerprint may show that a certain artist touched the wet paint, although it does not prove that he painted it.

Topic 9

Write a summary of 75 to 90 words on 'How to Forge a Masterpiece'.

Exercise J

1   Did you know that most of the so-called 'guarantees' offered with gadgets, appliances, cars and the like actually take away from the purchaser more than they give? Have you realised that the small print on the back generally removes the protection which you would otherwise have and so more than compensates for the benefits given on the front? When you get a 'guarantee', do you read it to see whether it is one of the worthless and semi-fraudulent incentives offered to gullible purchasers? If the answer to any of these questions is no – then read on. You are in for a shock.

The first rule to remember is that when you buy anything new, the law gives you all sorts of protection.

The Sale of Goods Act implies terms into contracts of sale, specially for the protection of the buyer.

If goods are sold to you in breach of terms implied by law into your contract, you are in a powerful position. If the breach is a serious one which 'goes to the root of the contract', then you will be able to call the whole deal off. If the goods have been delivered to you, you will be able to insist that the seller takes them back. And if you have paid any money for them, you will be entitled to get that back. There has been a breach of condition.

On the other hand, if the goods are defective and need some adjustment or repair, then the chances are that there has been a 'breach of warranty'. This less serious breach will give you a right to damages, to put you in the same position as you would have been had the contract been carried out by the seller. In practice, this means that either he will have to put the goods into proper condition at no cost to you, or else you can get the job done and force him to pay.

These are only some of the rights which the law gives you, quite apart from any guarantee. Many first-class firms give no guarantee at all because they quite rightly point out that you have quite sufficient protection given to you by the law of the land. If, then, you are offered goods with a guarantee, the first thing you should do is to make quite sure that these rights are not taken away from you.

'This guarantee is given in substitution for all statutory and common law conditions and warranties whatsoever,' reads a typical example. When you see this or any similar clause in a document, beware! The chances are that the guarantee is worthless.

The only real advantage of a guarantee is that it gives you contractual rights as against the manufacturer with whom you have made no contract, as well as against the dealer from whom you bought the goods. If the dealer is reputable and substantial, the advantage is negligible – but if he is disreputable or financially shaky it may help you. On the other hand, in the absence of a guarantee, you can sue the manufacturer for damages for any injury caused to you or to others through a defect in the goods caused by negligence in their manufacture. But guarantees generally exclude this right, limiting you to rights specified in the documents – and specifically excluding liability for consequential loss – loss, that is, arising as a consequence of faulty manufacture.

EWAN MITCHELL: *All You Need to Know about the Law*

(*a*) In 20 words, explain why you should read a guarantee carefully before signing it.

(*b*) Outline clearly the protection given to the buyer by the Sale of Goods Act. (60 words)

(*c*) Describe, in 30 words, 'the only real advantage' a guarantee may have.

2   The following two opinions were expressed spontaneously during a broadcast discussion programme in reply to the question: 'More people are spending their holidays abroad. Is this to keep up with the Joneses?'

Isobel Barnett: I think in some circumstances it may be. I think there's a lot of kudos sometimes to be gained from talking about 'My holiday on the Costa Brava' or some such. But I don't think this is always so. I think very often there is a desire for certain sunshine, for a change of food, for a change of language around you, for a change of life.

The people I feel should not take a holiday abroad and who are desperately keeping up with the Joneses are those who go off to sit in Monte Carlo or Barcelona or somewhere, and who spend the whole time demanding ham and eggs, fish and chips and a good cup of tea.

Now, if that is their attitude, they will get all those very much better and more easily in all of Britain's seaside holiday resorts, and they'll just have to take their luck with the sun. But I think for other people there is this desire – which I think is a very good one, particularly for young people – to get away and see that life is different. Seeing different customs, learning about different standards, hearing different languages – all this, I think, helps to develop a better personality amongst the young.

Marghanita Laski: Keeping up with the Joneses isn't always such a dreadful thing to do. Often it's a very good thing to do. It's one of the ways we educate ourselves half the time. Say we go abroad because the Joneses do – there's still an enormous chance that it will be a great new pleasure and inspiration, something absolutely splendid. Our lives will be enriched, and we never would have gone if we hadn't been trying to keep up with the Joneses in the first place.

I know perfectly well that, when I was at college, I used to listen to the music of Bach – which I couldn't understand in the least – because people I admired and respected did. And then it became a major pleasure of life.

I don't think we ought to despise keeping up with the Joneses at all. If the Joneses do things that are worth doing, this is one of the ways that we all move upwards a bit. I don't give a damn if culture and going abroad and music and education all become prestige symbols. Out of the people who go in for these things just because they're prestige symbols, somebody is going to get something real and worthwhile out of them.

Any Questions?

Report the views of these two speakers, allowing yourself 40 words for each.

3   The eight letters below are a few of those received by the BBC after the programme just referred to.

Tipton, Staffordshire

I suggest the reason more people spend holidays abroad is because they know more today about other countries, through education, radio, television, and, not least, cheaper travel. Now, too, they have the necessary money, which formerly they did not possess.

As a by-product, they may gain a new respect for this country. For 'what know they of England, who only England know!'

LOUISA M. MAYBURY

Knighton, Leicester

Why all this fuss over holidays abroad? My answer is simple – let everyone spend their holidays according to their particular tastes and inclinations.

Going to a place just because others, with whom you wish to be on a level, have been there savours of imitative snobbishness.

For me, the British Isles holds everything that goes to make the perfect holiday.

Though one may attain a great age, I am sure there would remain many thousands of miles of unexplored beauty, in the confines of this island home of ours.

ERNEST VINCENT

Paris, France

Anyone who goes abroad for their summer holidays will not be keeping up with the Joneses, but will be just plain sensible.

Until three years ago I had never been abroad. I now live in France and spend three weeks every summer touring the Continent with my husband. In spite of the fact that the cost of living is generally higher than in England, we find hotel prices considerably lower, service is better and the food excellent.

Also I only need to pack *one* suitcase with *summer* clothes, instead of the usual three with an assortment of clothes for every season and the eternal *mac* strapped on top.

Added to this is the pleasure of knowing one can drive from point A to B on a good wide straight road, at whatever speed one pleases, and be able to estimate almost within ten minutes how long the journey will take.

MARGARET NICHOLLS

Freshwater, Isle of Wight

We go abroad for our holidays to enjoy a countryside free from litter, a complete change of diet, no radios in cafés and no transistors, a warm welcome from friendly people; the fun of meeting many nationalities and trying to understand one another; the joy of walking in the mountains away from crowds, the mountain flowers and above all, the mountain air which re-vitalises and rejuvenates us.

MOLLIE and ARTHUR CONDON

Glasgow

I have done five continental trips simply because the humble coach tours I do are no more expensive than a visit to the South of England would be. The hotels and attention are always good, company congenial, and after a long working life, I am now seeing places formerly only dreamed about, and spending my meagre savings thus.

No one is interested whether you come out of the 'top' drawer or not. I find you get what you give in friendship, have always been lucky in my travelling companions, and had wonderful holidays.

Perhaps the more affluent members of society *may* try the Jones' lark. I wouldn't know, and am quite content with my coach trips at 'off' season prices in September. Incidentally, I am now seventy-eight.

MRS B. POTTS

London, N.W.10

I once lived in a small Welsh village. There were twelve houses in our street, and eight Mrs Jones. I was always known as Mrs Jones, the English woman!

But in all honesty I don't believe we ever tried to keep up with each other.

D. JONES

Brampton, Huntingdon

I am reminded of an incident in Switzerland a couple of years ago.

Riding in a cable car up one of those famous mountains, an affected loud English voice was clearly heard by everyone saying: 'We can't stand the Swiss butter. We always bring margarine with us from London.'

LYNN SMITH

(*a*) Express as concisely as you can the main point made in each letter.

(*b*) Write one shapely paragraph summarising the relevant comments made in all the letters.

4   The author reveals the secrets of his boyhood money-making activities in the seaside swimming pools near Durban.

The system we had was to explore the shelves under the rocks with gaffs and the minute we felt something yield to yank it out before it could even get a hold on its own refuge; thus we would catch two or three octopuses and hide them in a basket. Then we would go bathing in the swimming bath along with the Johannesburgers. Next, an octopus would be surreptitiously introduced into the bath and one of us would shout to the bathers: 'Hey, people, look out, there's a big kind of animal in the water there, which sucks all the blood out of your veins.' Those of us who were in the water would simulate panic (*pour encourager les autres*) and soon the pool would be empty, with an ideal circus of spectators, ready set all round for the show to begin.

When we had cleared the pool we would begin a show that put all the snake-charming acts of the Indian jugglers in the shade: because, to an amateur, an octopus is a far more horrible, slimy, hideous, venomous-looking and altogether creepy monster than the most dangerous reptile.... When we had got the spectators agog we would dive in, all four of us, leaving the native lad on the edge to indicate where the octopus was if he shot away, out of range of our underwater vision. Sometimes he would squirt a cloud of ink at the start but the four of us would dive through it together, and he would soon be driven out of his cloud, retreating and trying to manufacture more ink as quickly as possible. In the end, by means of splashing and diving after him, we would corner him at the shallow end of the bath.

Whoever caught the octopus first would let it get a grip all over him with its feelers; then rising up from the waist-deep shallow water, he would pretend to struggle, scream, and howl: 'Help, help, it is strangling me and sucking all my blood!' We would pretend to be trying to help our comrade but to be terrified and unable to save him. Then we would tug at the tentacles, trying to detach the suckers, which gave kissing-like smacks as they were detached, in a manner guaranteed to turn the stomachs and send a quiver up the spines of the toughest Johannesburgers. They would see the skin blistered with red sucker-marks, which were quite painless, but looked nasty enough.

After that one of us would unscrew the bottle of red ink which each one of us carried, and we would roll about milling and yelling in the shallow water, as if in a welter of blood and foam: till the boy who had the octopus would turn it inside out. Though this operation requires practice and skill, and it gives a sickening 'plop', it paralysed the beast at once. We would then offer to repeat the show if, when the native boy had taken round the hat, the results were satisfactory.

ROY CAMPBELL: *Light on a Dark Horse*

(*a*) Explain this 'system' as though you were the leader of the group telling a newcomer how to take part in it. (60 to 75 words.)

(*b*) In 100 words describe the scene as one of the Johannesburgers would see it. (Why will your tone be very different from the author's, particularly at the end of the first paragraph? Why will you not mention all the facts, as he does?)

5   This is the opening of a television play.

The interior of a vitriol factory. The atmosphere is smoky, noisy and busy. Alcott, one of the men at work, leaves his job and pauses at the foot of a gangway which leads to the laboratory and offices above. He starts up the gangway, stops again and leans over the rail. His coughing is audible over the noise of the machinery. Eventually he recovers himself and makes for the door of the laboratory.

Inside the laboratory Charlie Bunting is intent on an experiment. In his shirt-sleeves, and wearing a rather makeshift respirator over his nose and mouth, he is stirring a liquid in a retort over a bunsen burner. The vitriol tanks can be seen through a glass wall behind him. Alcott lurches in, mopping his brow and coughing badly. Charlie turns quickly and pulls down his respirator as Alcott steadies himself against the bench.

CHARLIE: Alcott! What's the matter?

ALCOTT: I dunno, I . . . I feel summat fierce.

CHARLIE: Do you feel sick?

ALCOTT: It's like I got indigestion only a sight worse.

CHARLIE: You'd better go and see Dr Clavering.

ALCOTT: I daren't go now.

CHARLIE: You must.

ALCOTT: I can't go till . . . till the shift's over, or I'll get the sack. [*Turns*].

CHARLIE: You must go at once.

Charlie helps him towards the door, but Alcott collapses before he can reach it. Charlie crosses to the door and opens it.

CHARLIE: Mr Lomax! Mr Lomax! Livesey! Come on.

He returns to Alcott as Livesey and Jones come running in.

CHARLIE: Get that stool.

Jones pulls a laboratory stool from the bench and they sit Alcott on it.

LIVESEY: What's up with him?

CHARLIE: He's fainted.

Charlie goes for smelling-salts as Pullen and some workmen enter, standing just inside the door.

PULLEN: What's up with Alcott?

LIVESEY: Aye, the same old thing. That's the first sign. It's the fumes from them vitriol tanks.

JONES: It's this stinking factory, that's what it is.

CHARLIE: Where's Mr Lomax? Get him, will you, Pullen?

As Pullen turns to go, Lomax pushes in.

LOMAX: What's all this about?

CHARLIE: Alcott was taken ill.

LOMAX: Well, we don't declare half-holiday because a man's fainted. [*To the workmen.*] Get back to your work. Go on. [*They start to leave, muttering among themselves.*] Look sharp!

CHARLIE: Wait a minute, Lomax, this man is very ill. He must be looked after.

LOMAX: I'm only thinking of the rules, Mr Bunting; you know how strict Mr Thomson is.

CHARLIE: I'll see about Mr Thomson right away. [*He gets his jacket.*] You must get him out into the air. And when he comes to, take him down to Dr Clavering's surgery. [*He goes quickly.*]

LOMAX [*to the men*]: I said back to work. All right, Pullen, you get back to your desk. Livesey, Jones – pick him up.

Pullen goes. Livesey and Jones bend down to pick up Alcott.

JONES: Poor chap. He looks summat ghastly, don't he?

LOMAX: Don't chatter. Take him out and put him by the horse trough. Then get back to work.

They carry Alcott out of the laboratory. Lomax follows them along the gangway, and his expression is enough to drive the watching men back to work. From a close-up of Lomax's stern face

Mix to:

Jabez Thomson's Office. Smoke stacks and warehouses are visible through the window.

JABEZ[*with suppressed temper*]: I've told you before, Charlie, and I'll tell you again – I make the rules and I expect them to be abided by. You can't run a decent organisation if every Tom, Dick or Harry can walk in or out of my factory just as he pleases.

CHARLIE: Alcott fainted, sir. You know just what that means.

JABEZ: I know nothing of the sort. How do you know what's wrong with him?

CHARLIE: Because that's how it starts. Fainting and dyspepsia to begin with – and then paralysis.

JABEZ: You got all that nonsense from Dr Clavering, I suppose.

CHARLIE: It isn't nonsense. And it wouldn't happen if you gave the men respirators.

JABEZ: What do you expect me to do about Alcott?

CHARLIE: You must give him time to recover properly.

JABEZ: And how long do you think that will be?

CHARLIE: He should have a month's sick leave.

JABEZ: You're off your head, Charlie.

CHARLIE: One of these days, sir, you're going to have a strike on your hands.

JABEZ: Oh? And who's going to encourage my men to strike? Have you any idea on *that* subject? Now, you listen to me, young man. If my daughter wasn't set on marrying you, I'd have you out of this factory so fast. . .

CHARLIE: I should never have come here in the first place.

JABEZ: There's gratitude for you! Perhaps you've forgotten I only took you on because your dad and me are pals.

CHARLIE: I'm not allowed to forget it between the two of you.

JABEZ: And it's not as if you work very hard.

CHARLIE [*stung*]: Work? What else do I do from the moment I enter the laboratory till I leave late at night?

JABEZ: But you *like* working in the laboratory, so it isn't work, is it?

CHARLIE: It's the department I dislike the least. And I thought I saw some faint hope of doing good there.

JABEZ: Well, you've done a bit. I'll grant you that. [*He looks at a piece of material in his hand.*] This colour stays faster since you found that new fixing process.

CHARLIE: Oh, that was just accidental. Happened to hit on a process that turned out to be profitable to you.

JABEZ [*sarcastically*] : Oh, well that's champion, isn't it? Thanks very much. What else do you want me to do with my time and money, may I ask?

CHARLIE: I'm trying to find a way here to make the work less dangerous.

JABEZ: Isn't it enough to have the Factory Acts and Government Inspectors poking their noses around without having one of my own employees coddling the men? Dangerous! It was good enough for their fathers and it'll have to be good enough for them.

HAROLD BRIGHOUSE: *Vitriol*.

Suppose a friend came in at this point in the play, and asked what you had seen so far. You would give the essentials of the action in as few words as possible. What would you say? (Two paragraphs: 110 to 130 words each.)

6   The following passage is a deliberate parody of the typical soccer report written by some journalists. Such a writer, says Mr. Arlott, "for years graced our local paper with a report of the Rangers' weekly soccer match at a length limited only by his resistance to writer's cramp. He wrote under such *noms de plume* as 'Townite,' 'Old Player,' or even—clever stuff, this—'Regnar'. And his language is still preserved in the minds of every one of his football-following contemporaries."

The Rangers returned to conquering form at Maiden's Midden last Saturday in a 'D' Division clash with their old rivals from Blastingstoke. Unhappily for the club's exchequer, a cold wind reduced the attendance to a paucity to watch a rousing encounter.

Fortune favoured skipper Muxton in the spin of the coin and he elected to defend the Dunnikin end, thus gaining the advantage of the elements. The homesters were in fine fettle and at his first touch of the sphere Bugby sent over a tempting flag-kick and Popper, eluding the visiting pivot, crashed home a flying shot to put the red-and-whites in the ascendant.

Muxton was the hero of a valiant home defence which foiled the Blastingstoke endeavours, and Wilting, between the posts, was rarely troubled. Melver was prominent as the brains of the side and dished up a masterly pass for Bugby to leave the visiting custodian helpless with a rising drive. Just before the interval, Wilting hurled himself across his charge to repel a header from the Stoke leader and keep the opposing score-sheet blank at lemon-time.

Popper set the leather rolling for the second period and the team from the north were fortunate to receive the benefit of the official's judgment when Muggins was brought down heavily from behind with the blues' citadel at his mercy.

The home adherents voiced their disapproval in no uncertain manner when Rangers' opponents stooped to robust tactics and the offside game to thwart the wizardry of McIver. But those doughty forwards, Bugby and Popper, were not to be denied and, after a skilful display of criss-cross passing which left their adversaries standing, the home leader notched his second success with a searing shot.

The local favourites now demonstrated their superiority and the speedy Sixton rattled the framework with a rip-snorting effort. When the elusive McIver was unceremoniously grassed by the Stoke right-half, the man with the whistle pointed without hesitation to the fateful spot. Muxton made no mistake with the kick, which evaded the discomfited guardian's despairing dive.

Rangers dominated the ensuing exchanges and Popper crowned a grand display when he recorded his hat-trick with a cannon-ball which bulged the rigging behind the gallant Jones.

Rangers remained masters of the situation through the closing stages and at the final whistle trotted off worthy winners to a rousing ovation. The contest was admirably controlled by Mr Mathias (Mudton) and his two flag-men, Messrs Boiley (Slipton) and Slippey (Wartor).

JOHN ARLOTT: *The Observer*, 6 January 1963

In the national Press, space is more precious and style very different; but readers of the sports pages want all the important details there are room for. How much could you tell them about this match in three column-inches (about 80 words)?

7   The letter with which this extract begins was written to the Society for Psychical Research on 10 October 1876.

I had left my house, ten miles from London, in the morning as usual, and in the course of the day . . . attempting to cross the road, recently made muddy and slippery by the water cart, I fell, and was nearly run over by a carriage coming in the opopsite direction. The fall and the fright shook me considerably, but beyond that I was uninjured. On reaching home I found my wife waiting anxiously and this is what she related to me. She was occupied in the kitchen wiping a cup, which she suddenly dropped, exclaiming 'My God; he's hurt.' Mrs S., who was near her, heard the cry, and both agreed as to the details of time and so forth. I have often asked my wife why she cried out, but she is unable to explain the state of her feelings beyond saying 'I don't know why, I felt some great danger was near you.' These are simple facts, but other things more puzzling have happened in connection with the singular intuitions of my wife.

Obviously everything may have happened exactly as the letter describes and, in that case, it was either a coincidence or evidence of the direct knowledge by the wife either of the fact of her husband's danger or of his state of fear. But as evidence it is very unsatisfactory. There is no statement in the letter as to exactly how long had elapsed between the incident and the writing of the letter. The letter does, however, make clear that the time that had elapsed was considerable since the writer says that he has often discussed the matter with his wife. Any incident that remains unrecorded for a long time is liable to undergo changes in the memory by which it becomes more self-consistent and also more impressive as testimony to whatever explanation is accepted for it. This process is likely to be helped by frequent discussion. There is no indication of how close the coincidence was in time or of how the time was checked either by husband or wife. Coincidence in time is, moreover, the kind of thing that is liable to become more impressive during the course of prolonged remembering and discussing of the incident. There is no independent confirmation of either the husband's danger or the wife's cry; the fact that the husband said that Mrs S. said she heard the cry remains, of course, testimony by the husband. We have no means of guessing how likely it was that the accident to the husband and the wife's conviction of his danger merely occurred about the same time by accident; we should need to know how close was the coincidence in time, how often the wife had such intuitions and how often the perilous state of the London streets in 1876 put the husband in danger. It may have happened just as the letter says, and it may have been due to the wife's paranormal powers, but as evidence it is worth very little.

R. H. THOULESS: *Experimental Psychical Research*

(*a*) Using reported speech, summarise the coincidence recorded in the letter. (35 words.)

(*b*) Why does the author regard the husband's letter as 'very unsatisfactory' evidence for his wife's telepathic powers? (45 to 60 words.)

8 As everyone knows, the Average Family consists of four people – father, mother, daughter and son. They are easily recognisable – I

shall describe their physical appearance in a moment – but for particularly unobservant people let me say now that that Average Family will shortly be portrayed at its very best by its friends the politicians. Some time this year, or at the very latest next year, there will be a General Election. This means that the hoardings will be covered with posters issued by the rival political parties, and it may be safely prophesied that many of these posters will portray pictures of the Average Family. You will see them in various poses and against different backgrounds, though the most popular situation seems to have the Average Family striding along a hilly path with the bright morning sunshine of Socialism or Conservatism lighting the calm, confident, good-looking faces of all four members of the family.

It is not only the politicians who know the Average Family; the newspapers know them, the B.B.C. knows them, and all successful advertising agents know them better than they know themselves. All these rich and powerful organisations spend fabulous sums of money and work themselves into frenzies with no other purpose than to become better acquainted with the Average Family; to discover its slightest desires and then to gratify them. Indeed, it is largely due to these enthusiasts that we really know beyond possibility of doubt what the Average-Family is really like, for it is pictorially represented in the newspapers, morning and evening, every day throughout the year. Thus, we know, for instance, that it insists on having cereals for its breakfast. Here it may be mentioned that when it finds food to its taste, three-quarters of the family (that is, father and the children) make manifest their satisfaction by grinning their heads off. Mother Average does not herself generally participate, being occupied in dishing out the wonder food to her appreciative family; *her* transports of delight are reserved for detergents and soap substitutes.

Father Average is a tall, well-built, good-looking man; mother is a pretty smiling woman with a 24-inch waist; daughter, age fourteen, is slim and trim and will be a beauty when she grows up; while son, age eleven, rising twelve, is a sturdy chip off the old block, a fine lad. If you have ever met a family that did not conform to this pattern, if you have ever seen short, paunchy, bald men, lumpy women, pasty girls or weedy boys, be certain they never came from an Average Family. If you ask why Daughter Average should be two years older than her brother, I cannot tell you. It is not my duty to explain these things; I am merely giving you the facts as certified by observers who have devoted their lives to studying the subject.

The experts make out that the Average Family, though as mysterious as the Sphinx, is nevertheless as lasting as the Pyramids. But there is one mystery no expert has tried to explain, which is that every Average Family is convinced that it is absolutely unique.

BRIGID (aged 15): *Young Writers, Young Readers*, ed. Boris Ford

(*a*) Using your own words as far as possible, summarise the characteristics of the Average Family as it is described in paras. 2 and 3. (45 words)

(*b*) What do you think – from the evidence scattered throughout this passage – was the author's attitude to 'the Average Family'? (20 words)

9   The first of all English games is making money. That is an all absorbing game; and we knock each other down oftener in playing at that, than at football, or other roughest sport: and it is absolutely without purpose; no one who engages heartily in that game ever knows why. Ask a great money-maker what he wants to do with his money – he never knows. He doesn't make it to do anything with it. He gets it only that he *may* get it. 'What will you make of what you have got?' you ask. 'Well, I'll get more,' he says. Just as, at cricket, you get more runs. There's no use in the runs, but to get more of them than other people is the game. And there's no use in money, but to have more of it than other people is the game. So all that great foul city of London there – rattling, growling, smoking, stinking – a ghastly heap of fermenting brickwork, pouring out poison at every pore – you fancy it is a city of work? Not a street of it! It is a great city of play; very nasty play, and very hard play, but still play. It is only Lord's cricket ground without the turf: a huge billiard table without the cloth, and with pockets as deep as the bottomless pit; but mainly a billiard table, after all.

Well, the first great English game is this playing at counters. It differs from the rest in that it appears always to be producing money, while every other game is expensive. But it does not always produce money. There's a great difference between 'winning' money and 'making' it: a great difference between getting it out of another man's pocket into ours, or filling both.

JOHN RUSKIN: *Crown of Wild Olives*

(*a*) In 15 words explain what, according to this author, money-makers want to do with their money.

(*b*) Explain carefully why the author calls London a 'city of play'. (25 to 35 words)

(c) How does money-making differ from the other great English 'games'? (15 to 20 words)

10   Hitler was far from being a fool in military matters. He had read widely in military literature and he took an eager interest in such technical matters as the design of weapons. His gifts as a politician gave him notable advantages in war as well. He was a master of the psychological side, quick to see the value of surprise, bold in the risks he was prepared to take and receptive of unorthodox ideas. The decisive support he gave to the expansion of Germany's armoured forces, his adoption of Raeder's proposal for the occupation of Norway, and of Manstein's for the thrust through the Ardennes, have already been mentioned as illustration of these gifts. Nor was Hitler far from the truth when he argued that if he had listened to the High Command he would never have pushed through German rearmament at the pace he wanted, or have dared to take the risks which brought the German Army its sensational triumphs of 1940–1.

His faults as a military leader were equally obvious. He had too little respect for facts, he was obstinate and opinionated. His experience in the First World War, to which he attached undue importance, had been extremely limited. He had never commanded troops in the field or learned how to handle armies as a staff officer. He lacked the training to translate his grandiose conceptions into concrete terms of operations. The interest which he took in technical details, instead of compensating for these deficiencies, only made them clearer. He was far too interested in such matters as the precise thickness of the concrete covering a line of fortifications for a man whose job was to think clearly about the over-all pattern of war. Moreover, he allowed himself to become intoxicated with figures, with the crude numbers of men or of armaments production, which he delighted to repeat from memory without any attempt to criticise or analyse them.

ALAN BULLOCK: *Hitler, a Study in Tyranny*

These two paragraphs form part of the summing-up in a fascinating and very detailed biography of Adolf Hitler. Suppose the author drew on the substance of them for an encyclopaedia article on the same subject – he would need to be brief, and for copyright reasons he would have to find different words. What do you think he would write? (80 words)

11   'I'm going to write to the editor of every enlightened and influential newspaper in the Kingdom,' said Egbert, drawing a stack of notepaper towards him. 'I'm going to suggest that there should be a

sort of epistolary Truce during the festivities of Christmas and New Year. From the twenty-fourth of December to the third or fourth of January it shall be considered an offence against good sense and good feeling to write or expect any letter or communication that does not deal with the necessary events of the moment. Answers to invitations, arrangements about trains, and, of course, all the ordinary everyday affairs of business, sickness and so forth, these will be dealt with in the usual manner as something inevitable, a legitimate part of our daily life. But all the devastating accretions of correspondence, incident to the festive season, these should be swept away to give the season a chance of being really festive, a time of untroubled, unpunctuated peace and goodwill.'

'But you would have to make some acknowledgement of presents received,' objected Janetta; 'otherwise people would never know whether they had arrived safely.'

'Of course, I have thought of that,' said Egbert; 'every present that was sent off would be accompanied by a ticket bearing the date of dispatch and the signature of the sender, and some conventional hieroglyphic to show that it was intended to be a Christmas gift; there would be a counterfoil with space for the recipient's name and the date of arrival, and all you would have to do would be to sign and date the counterfoil, add a conventional hieroglyphic indicating heartfelt thanks and gratified surprise, put the thing into an envelope and post it.'

'It sounds delightfully simple,' said Janetta wistfully, 'but people would consider it too cut-and-dried, too perfunctory.'

'The present system of acknowledgement,' said Egbert, 'is just as perfunctory and conventional as the counterfoil business would be, only ten times more tiresome and brain-racking.'

'SAKI': 'Down Pens' (short story)

In 30 to 45 words, summarise Egbert's proposals for a new 'system of acknowledgement' and an 'epistolary Truce'.

12   The tone of this author's views on Christmas is very different from Egbert's.

Three things go by the name of Christmas. One is a religious festival. This is important and obligatory for Christians; but as it can be of no interest to anyone else, I shall naturally say no more about it here. The second (it has complex historical connections with the first, but we needn't go into them) is a popular holiday, an occasion for merry-making and hospitality. If it were my business to have a 'view' on this,

I should say that I much approve of merrymaking. But what I approve of much more is everybody minding his own business. I see no reason why I should volunteer views as to how other people should spend their own money in their own leisure among their own friends. It is highly probable that they want my advice on such matters as little as I want theirs. But the third thing called Christmas is unfortunately everyone's business.

I mean of course the commercial racket. The interchange of presents was a very small ingredient in the older English festivity. Mr Pickwick took a cod with him to Dingley Dell; the reformed Scrooge ordered a turkey for his clerk; lovers sent love gifts; toys and fruit were given to children. But the idea that not only all friends but even all acquaintances should give one another presents, or at least send one another cards, is quite modern and has been forced upon us by the shopkeepers. Neither of these circumstances is in itself a reason for condemning it. I condemn it on the following grounds.

(1)   It gives on the whole much more pain than pleasure. You have only to stay over Christmas with a family who seriously try to 'keep' it (in its third, or commercial aspect) in order to see that the thing is a nightmare. Long before 25 December everyone is worn out – physically worn out by weeks of daily struggle in overcrowded shops, mentally worn out by the effort to remember all the right recipients and to think out suitable gifts for them. They are in no trim for merrymaking; much less (if they should want to) to take part in a religious act. They look far more as if there had been a long illness in the house.

(2)   Most of it is involuntary. The modern rule is that anyone can force you to give him a present by sending you a quite unprovoked present of his own. It is almost a blackmail. Who has not heard the wail of despair, and indeed of resentment, when, at the last moment, just as everyone hoped that the nuisance was over for one more year, the unwanted gift from Mrs Busy (whom we hardly remember) flops unwelcomed through the letter-box, and back to the dreadful shops one of us has to go?

(3)   Things are given as presents which no mortal ever bought for himself – gaudy and useless gadgets, 'novelties' because no one was ever fool enough to make their like before. Have we really no better use for materials and for human skill and time than to spend them on all this rubbish?

(4)   The nuisance. For, after all, during the racket we still have all our ordinary and necessary shopping to do, and the racket trebles the labour of it.

We are told that the whole dreary business must go on because it is good for trade. It is in fact merely one annual symptom of that lunatic condition of our country, and indeed of the world, in which everyone lives by persuading everyone else to buy things. I don't know the way out. But can it really be my duty to buy and receive masses of junk every winter just to help the shopkeepers? If the worst comes to the worst I'd sooner give them money for nothing and write it off as a charity. For nothing? Why, better for nothing than for a nuisance.

c. s. lewis: in *The Twentieth Century*, December 1957

Summarise the author's observations in 80 to 100 words.

13   It is not only the readers of serials who need to be reminded of previous instalments; their authors need this help too. Dickens – who wrote many of his novels for serial publication – would usually sketch out each chapter in note form, and add memoranda for further possible ingredients to the left of the main notes. But sometimes Dickens wrote his notes *after* he had completed the chapter; and they must then have been intended to remind him of what had just happened, when he took up his pen to write the next instalment.

Below are printed Dickens's notes and, to the left, memoranda for Chapter IV of *David Copperfield*. Together these cover, in the order in which they are eventually told, all the incidents of the chapter – with one exception. If you have read the novel recently, you will quickly notice which has been left out.

Chapter IV
I fall into disgrace

Miss Murdstone	
Their religion	
Picture of all that, and its effect on Davy's life	Progress of his mother's weakness under the Murdstones
Cast off and getting sullen	Miss Murdstone
Query His books and reading?	Beats him
His offence, and confinement upstairs	Bites
Child's remembrance of the latter	Shut up and dismissed
Sent away	

(*a*) Using these notes, and adding the omitted incident, construct in class a good summary of the chapter. (Not more than about 200 words; but it is more important to tell the story of David's adventures well than to stick rigidly to this limit.)

(*b*) Read Dickens's sketch for Chapter VII, printed below; add to or alter it until it can form the basis for your own summary; and then write a synopsis of the whole chapter which would be useful to a reader about to begin the next instalment of *David Copperfield*, which opens with Chapter VIII. (120–150 words.)

Chapter VII

My First half at Salem House

School – His progress
        Steerforth's character
        Traddles. Ditto
        Mr Mell's poverty and mother, and dismissal
Visit from Mr Pegotty? Yes. And Steerforth

Summing up, and going home

(*c*) If it is not convenient to read *David Copperfield* now, choose another novel for this exercise. First, from prepared notes, build up a good summary of about 200 words in class. And then, after some discussion of notes made on another chapter, write your own synopsis of it.

14   The following were the two opening speeches made to a school Debating Society on the motion: 'This House deplores the waste of money being spent on Space Research.'

PETER THOMAS (*Proposer*): Before we can form a thorough and accurate idea of the points at issue, Mr Chairman, we must realise one fundamental fact: the reason any responsible citizen should deplore the appalling expenditure on space research is neither economic nor political – it is a moral one.

Space research is, of course, usually defended on the grounds that it is necessary for military reasons, or that it will ultimately produce immense economic returns, for instance by the discovery of fresh mineral resources on other planets. This is a strange argument. Last year more money was spent on space projects than on Health, Roads and Education put together. Surely it would make better sense to exploit the mineral resources, and perhaps the nutritional resources too, of the ocean, than to aim hopefully at the stars? The coal we buy now from mines only a few miles away is expensive enough; if we had to import it from many thousands of miles in space the cost would be (literally) astronomical.

The population of the world is now 3,135 million; and this figure is expected to double in thirty-five years. World famine is a very real danger. Men like Piccard and Cousteau have proved the feasibility of exploiting the marine depths at a fraction of the cost of the present programme of space research. Our schools are short of teachers. There is not enough room on our roads even to park the cars that want to use them, and when movement *is* possible it is highly dangerous. Hospitals are understaffed and under-equipped, unable to cope with routine admissions, much less the stream of emergency cases which come their way as a direct result of our inadequate roads. This situation needs immediate and drastic rectification. One obvious step is to divert much of the money now being blown to pieces in rocketry.

Let us look at the other argument: Britain needs to defend herself, and space research is a part of her defence. This argument invites comparison of Britain with other countries – Switzerland, for example. Switzerland devotes her revenues to the essential apparatus of domestic well-being, a condition without which no country is worth defending. Her roads, schools and hospitals shame Britain's. If she can do it, why cannot we? It is a sad comment that an organisation such as Oxfam should be forced to depend on voluntary workers and gifts. This situation becomes more horrifying when one considers that £10 million (a fraction of the sum spent in space) would feed two million children for a whole year. Without that money, all of those children will suffer. Without it, many of them will die. Without it, too, most of the world's population will continue to go hungry to their beds every night. Meanwhile, of course, we have our 'deterrent' and our satellites.

Mr Chairman, if we are blind to economic sense, are we deaf to human suffering? Space research is amusing in itself, but ludicrous in defence and positively culpable in its greed for money in the world's present state. No humane person can endorse Britain's appalling spending, and I am sure this House will prove its own integrity and responsibility by unanimously supporting this motion.

AVRIL PRICE (*Opposer*): Mr Chairman, I agree with the Proposer: space research does cost a lot of money. But so does all scientific research, and considering that it is still in the experimental stage the sum is not exorbitant.

The large expenditure on rocketry which the Proposer referred to, but did not quote, was misleading; only a proportion of it actually goes in space research, much the greater part goes on conventional defence –maintaining ships, army lorries, soldiers' boots. There is not much extra-terrestrial about any of those. In Britain, just as in Russia and the United States, it is impossible to disentangle precisely space costs from other aspects of the armaments budget. In each country, however, only a small proportion of the national expenditure is devoted to actual space research, and its abandonment would certainly not lead to the dramatic changes in housing, roads and hospitals that the Proposer asked you to believe. In fact, governments being what they are, even if space research was stopped at once, fresh ways would be found of spending the money at present used on it.

It has been argued that, if we abandoned rocketry, we could help under-developed countries. Does the Proposer not know that, exactly because we have the courage to go on with it in the face of attacks from ill-informed people like himself, it is the means of helping them – and indeed helping all the world? Let us see how this is so. Cancer can be cured by radiation, but many forms of radiation cannot yet be made on earth. They exist in space, but they fail to reach earth because the atmosphere screens them. Space research gives us the atellites which allow us to study these radiations out in space. It gives us, too, the conditions of travel under which medical scientists can study the functioning of the heart under conditions of reduced or zero gravity; this investigation may well lead to new methods of treating heart-disease, at present the greatest killer in the western world.

Further, satellites will feed back to earth information which will enable meteorologists to make accurate long-term weather forecasts – of enormous value to farmers, and likely to lead to improvements in harvests. Space research, in this case, leads directly to an increase in food production! Think, too, how much money and suffering advance notice of hurricanes and storms will save.

Some of these gifts to humanity from space research are still in the future; but we benefit greatly already. Satellites are now in use in television, and in a few years most transatlantic and transcontinental messages too will go (at low cost) via an orbiting satellite. The amenity of this system will be great, but the saving in cost will be great too.

I am sure that I have shown the value of space research, in these few examples. It would be possible to add to them. But there is one final question: is it even *possible* to discontinue space research? Surely it is not. So many people are now interested in it (we would not be debating this motion if they were not) that they would be unwilling to let a government drop it. What we want, of course, is not less research, but more – and more co-operation in it, too, between all the countries involved. This would both increase its usefulness and reduce its cost. It would also improve international relations. If space research ended the cold war, if it really made possible at last peace on earth, who would quibble about its cost?

Mr Chairman, I beg to oppose the motion.

Write a summary of these two speeches to appear in the Minutes of the debate. Use reported speech. (150 to 175 words for both.)

15 During the week-end of June 20th and 21st, 1936, in the New-town district of Montgomeryshire, events moved more like the scenario of an American screen melodrama than happenings on a British railway. The whole of England was swept by storms of great violence, but in these Welsh hills both rain and thunder were of an almost tropical intensity. Conditions were bad enough on the Saturday, when the river Severn overflowed and Newtown itself was flooded, but so far the railway had suffered no harm. Through this district the main line of the one time Cambrian railways, later part of the G.W.R., follows the Severn valley, and it carries a heavy holiday traffic to the Cambrian Coast resorts.

Late on the Sunday afternoon things were beginning to look ugly at Scafell, a hamlet some two miles west of Newtown. The tiny station here is one of the few in charge of a station-mistress, and the lady in question was the wife of a retired permanent-way man, ex-Ganger Haynes. At 6 p.m. the thunderstorms culminated in a terrific cloudburst in the hills south of the Severn valley, which caused the rivers to rise so rapidly that Haynes feared for the safety of the railway. It was not the Severn that seemed the most potential source of danger, but the Dulais river, which comes down from the very hills where the cloudburst had taken place. So, at the height of the storm, Haynes and his daughter went to keep watch at the bridge.

Just at the point where the Dulais enters the Severn it is crossed by the railway, running on a 20 ft. embankment, the foot of which is washed on the north side by the waters of the Severn. At that time the bridge over the Dulais river was a solid masonry structure with an arch of 25 ft. span. When Haynes and his daughter arrived on the scene the neighbouring fields were already flooded, and the little river, normally nothing more than a turbulent mountain stream, was a really terrifying sight. A great volume of water was sweeping down, carrying all before it; bushes along the banks were being torn up as if they were tender seedlings, and the force of this onrush was scouring out the banks and bringing great pressure on the abutments of the railway bridge.

Dulais Farmhouse, just on the Newtown side of the river, was completely marooned, the ground floor rooms being flooded to a depth of five or six feet; and in the hope of being able to help the unfortunate people there Haynes and his daughter crossed the railway bridge. They were hardly over when a still more unexpected thing happened. On the Scafell side of the Dulais river was a group of huge venerable elms; under the tremendous winds these were waving like so many reeds, when suddenly one of them was completely uprooted by the rush of water. By some extraordinary freak of wind and water it was borne down stream in a perfectly upright position, and a few seconds later had crashed into the railway bridge. It struck the parapet, which was at once destroyed; the tree rebounded, and was then dragged under the arch by the force of the current. Its passage ripped away the crown of the arch, and immediately the whole bridge collapsed. A curious point noted by Haynes was that the downstream side of the arch fell in first.

The telegraph wires were undamaged, and at once Haynes thought of the up mail, which had already left Aberystwyth. Between them and the telephone at Scafell station was a breach in the line 60 ft. long, across which the tracks were suspended in mid-air. The only thing to do was to go to Newtown and send warning from there. The storm was now if possible worse than ever, and yet, amid darkness almost of night, in torrents of rain and incessant thunder, Miss Haynes set out to walk two miles down the line to give the alarm. It was by no means certain that she could get through. The way might easily be barred by floods or another washaway; so Haynes attempted to get back to his home by way of the road, which runs parallel to the railway and about a quarter of a mile away. By going a short distance from the course of the river he was able to wade across the flooded fields, and eventually he got to the road. This also was under water, but he managed to cross the river. He was hardly over when this bridge too was swept away. All the time the mail train was getting nearer. There are no signals at Scafell, and the bridge is approached on a curve from a deep cutting; speed is usually 50 to 55 m.p.h. at this point, and travelling thus on a day of poor visibility the driver would never be able to see the breach in time. But when at last Haynes reached his home and telephoned through to Caersws, the next station open, he learned that his daughter had been in time and the train was stopped.

o. s. KNOCK: *Railways of Britain*

Tell the story as if you were Haynes. (Limit: 200 words.)

Chapter 9

Summary II

Although we have stressed that summaries should be as well written as possible, probably most of your attention has so far been given to making your versions accurate and of the right length. As you become older, however, and especially in examinations, something more than accuracy will be expected; your summaries will need to be fluent and polished as well.

You will be able to judge the importance of making this final revision if you study the notes, corrected draft and fair copy printed below. The method used was the one you have practised.

1   Read the passage till you understand it.
2   Make notes on it. Check them.
3   Ignoring the passage, write draft from notes alone. (No short-cuts!)
4   Revise the draft for:
    (*a*) distortions and omissions;
    (*b*) length;
    (*c*) style.
5   Invent a title.
6   Write your fair copy.

Here is the extract which a Fifth-Former had to condense.
Summarise in 110 *to* 120 *words:*
Whether we think of television as a first-class method of propaganda, whether it is used more in some countries for national education at all ages than in others, whether it pours out a non-stop or a controlled stream of entertainment, whether it brings plays, films, documentaries, all opening a new world of ideas, or those 'give-away' shows which award huge prizes for ridiculous antics, it is first and all the time something that affects the individual. We talk of audiences in millions, percentages and averages, but each programme is seen by separate people; by the miners who asked for a shift to be changed so that they could see television; the mysterious 'housewife' who may not correspond at all to the housewife of the survey; the teenager in the grip of enthusiasms; the child to whom everything is new and to whom the little figures moving on the lighted screen are really magic;

the elderly man whose arthritis meant that he would never again see a Rugby International or a Boat Race until one day he found, sitting by the fire, that they were wonderfully brought to him. It is on individuals that television has its effect, and as they make up the family and the families compose the nation, they are much more important than any columns of figures.

What does television do to all these different people? Does it, as is often suggested, dim and dull their faculties? Is it a 'family drug'? Are we becoming, as Lord Lucas of Chilworth once said, 'a glassy-eyed community of crystal-gazers'? Are we sitting in a cave, as Plato suggested in a different context, seeing only a procession of shadows instead of life? Will children not read, because they can see pictures? Do we give up activity and sit spellbound by the screen? And does television so infect everybody that the 'star' personality and the popular programme become the common talking-point and reduce conversation to last night's 'telly', while stifling all other ideas that might enter people's heads?

MARY CROZIER: *Broadcasting*

A very brief summary (not more than 25 words) could be made of the main points in this extract, but such a summary would rob the writer's argument of its force and emphasis. And although the limit of 110 to 120 words will allow these to be conveyed, it also raises the problem of how to deal with the many examples which the extract contains. Why cannot they simply be omitted?

When the Fifth-Former who did this work had made his notes, he found that two points occurring separately in paragraph 1 could be combined. His first draft was too long, but when he had revised it (for accuracy, length and style) he was comfortably within the limit. His alterations are printed above the words (*italicised*) which they modified or replaced; you should try to give the reason for each change. Even when he had finished, and was satisfied that it was as accurate as he could make it, his first draft did not read smoothly. Can you detect why?

Having invented a title, he was ready to write his fair copy; and, because of the care he had taken in revising his draft, he was able to concentrate on improving the fluency of his summary. Almost the only further changes he made were in word-order; but if you think that, since they are mostly slight, they are unimportant, compare the two versions by reading them aloud! Note, too, that the fair copy is a more impressive summary simply because it is better written.

NOTES

1st para. (1) TV works by impact of programme on individual
     (*a*) whether its role is propaganda
                  education;
     (*b*) whatever quantity of mere entertainment;
     (*c*) exciting/rubbishy shows balance.

    (2) Statistics about audience: but view as individuals
       whether unusual housewife;
           enthusiastic teenager;
           novelty for child;
           grateful old ex-sportsman.

    (3) Individuals affected. Therefore individual more important than statistics.

2nd para. (1) What *is* TV's effect?
        Tarnish wits?
        Dope family?
        Glassy-eyed starers?
        Pictures preferred to life?
        Children stop reading?
        'Star', programme only topics of conversation.

FIRST DRAFT + REVISIONS.

Television makes its effect on each individual in its audience, although
          are
we *have become* used to thinking of the audience's size and tastes. This is
    universally
true   Λ   whether *the country uses*
           is   -ist
television *for* propaganda or edu-
      -al   *whatever the proportion of*
cation, *or if* mere entertainment
shown is controlled or not, and whether
                stimulating
more programmes are *exciting* than absurd or not. It does not matter if
              untypical
the individual watching is *unusual,*
          absorbed
enthusiastic, *novelty-minded* or *an*
    grateful
old sportsman. This is more important than any statistics about the audience.

FAIR COPY

The Impact of Television.

Although we are used to thinking of the size or tastes of television audiences, it is on each individual in those audiences that programmes make their effect. This is true universally, whether the medium is propagandist or educational, however large the proportion of mere entertainment, and whatever the balance between stimulating and absurd programmes. It is true however untypical, enthusiastic, absorbed or grateful each individual in that audience is, and it is more important than any statistics.

What is television's effect? The effect of TV may be to dull people's alertness, or to spellbind families or lead them to watch too much, or to prefer pictures of life to life itself. It may stop children reading, *or spellbind us all.* The stars and *most* monopolise popular programmes may *become our* 116 *only topics of* conversation. (138 words.)

The effect of television, however, is not certain. It may dull people's alertness, spellbind families, or encourage excess viewing. We may prefer the pictures of life to life itself. Children may cease to read, and television stars and programmes monopolise our conversations. (119 words.)

Impact
The *Effect* of Television

No one would claim that the Fair Copy is perfect, and there will be things in it which you would change. But the writer understood his original, and preserved its structure in condensing it; and his summary reads well.

1   The author of *Animal Farm* drew his own gloomy but powerful picture of the future in *1984*. The very different predictions which follow are a scientist's estimate of life in the 1980s.

The most profound changes in the way of life of ordinary people during the next two decades are likely to hinge on great developments in electronic storage and transmission of 'information' of all kinds, whether it be laundry bills, parking fines, detective stories, business letters, or the Test Match score from Melbourne. Computers will certainly exert a great influence. Linked on a nation-wide and world-wide basis, they will not only take on much of the routine administrative work of business and government, but will also be communication centres and stores of information. 'Paper-work' may almost disappear, and with it the shorthand-typist.

By 1984 we shall not yet be really in the 'Age of Leisure'. The working week will be a little shorter and holidays longer, but with great tasks to be accomplished in reconstruction at home and abroad, and with more years devoted to education, we shall not be fully relaxed within 20 years, even though automation in offices and factories will have gone much further. It will be a 'middle-class' community, with fewer farm and factory workers and more in service industries, marketing and research. The middle-class home will be even more labour-saving, perhaps with mobile domestic robots to do the cleaning and the washing-up. Electronic equipment in the living room will give almost limitless access to information of all kinds: the newspaper as we know it may have disappeared, when people can simply dial for the news, racing results or stock exchange prices.

Amid this electronic cosiness, we may be more neurotic – accustomed to taking behaviour-influencing drugs more potent than the tranquillisers and pep-pills of today – perhaps more criminally inclined. In short, we may not be very happy, for all our rising standards of living and expectation of still longer life as medicine tackles the remaining diseases. On the other hand, we may have better clues to the requirements for happiness, as studies of the human brain advance and detailed explanations of human attitudes and behaviour emerge. Serious mental illness will be more susceptible to treatment. We shall also be more alert to the psychological motives and deficiencies of our political leaders; but they may find new and possibly dangerous techniques for manipulating the minds of the people.

For the individual in 1984 there will remain anxieties as he looks at the world around him through the electronic window in his living room. Will it be war or peace? That dreadful question will still hang over him, as conflicts flare up around the globe. There will be at least three people alive for every two today. Not only do they have to be fed, but they also need to build up the economic resources that will enable them to escape from a life that is commonly 'nasty, brutish and short'. The technical knowledge to bring about spectacular advances in these countries already exists; if the richer countries do not make sure that it is applied, they will find that the gap between them and the poorer nations will widen rather than narrow, and political and racial strife will intensify as a result.

NIGEL CALDER in *The Sunday Telegraph*, 30 August 1964

(*a*) Some of the suggestions here lend themselves to short, sensational (and very distorted) summary. Write the lively and startling account you might find in the *Daily Mirror* or *Daily Express*; and provide headlines. (Not more than 4 column-inches, about 100 words.)

(*b*) In the quality papers, rather more space would be given to these predictions; and their treatment would be very different. Report them for the *Daily Telegraph* or *Guardian* in about 150 words; and again provide headlines.

2   This is a transcript of part of a BBC 'Any Questions?' programme. The question being answered is: 'Is there too much licence in adver-

tising, and if so, what steps would the team take to correct it for the protection of the gullible public?'

CLIFFORD SELLY: I'm not sure that the public is all that gullible, but I suppose some of us do need protection from time to time against the more extravagant claims of some manufacturers.

I read about a school – in North London, I think – where the sixth-formers were being indoctrinated by their teachers in some of the perils of advertising. They were being taught to have a healthy contempt for some of the more extravagant claims that they read on the hoardings and see on commercial television.

This is the real answer, isn't it? If we can create in the young a healthy scepticism, we've nothing to fear from the advertisers. We shall keep them in their place, I'm sure.

MALCOLM MUGGERIDGE: Obviously, most advertising is lies, isn't it? I mean, if you were going to advertise – you know, recommend something to someone – it's almost certain that you'll exaggerate its qualities, and therefore 90 per cent of advertising is lies, very cleverly put out. I think this is a pretty deplorable state of affairs. In fact, I think really the effect of advertising on our society in every way, including stimulating a desire for things that people really haven't got, is one of its most pernicious elements.

It's one of the few, to me, rather pleasing aspects of a Communist country that there is no advertising, except of course of the régime, which is pretty boring. So I would say in answer to this question, 'Yes, there is far too much licence in advertising, and increasingly so.' But it's extremely difficult to see how, in a society of our kind, it's possible to protect the public against it.

About making them sceptical at school and so on . . . I'm very doubtful about the efficacy of that. The public is undoubtedly getting more and more gullible, as you can see from the nature of the advertising which is put out, despite the fact that more and more money is spent on education.

ISOBEL BARNETT: I can't agree with Malcolm Muggeridge on this. I mean, there's good advertising and there is bad advertising. Advertising may mislead once; it shouldn't, if the public are as sensible as I think they are, mislead more than once. You may buy something once on its advertising: if the product is not up to standard you don't go back for more.

But again, one of the facets of our society is cut-throat competition, and for one product to compete against another they have got to advertise and they have got to sell more, and through selling more reduce the price. And so, while I think that some advertising is distressingly misleading, I think it is very quickly found out by those who buy the product and never buy it again.

And I imagine – I know very little about advertising and nothing about big business – but I imagine that if you were spending large amounts on advertising, it is only worth doing if you consider that your product is good and that people will come back for more, because you're not going to make a profit on one sale. You're only going to make a profit on continued sales.

So if you're going to spend a large amount on advertising, you must be convinced that people are coming back for more.

CLIFFORD SELLY: I don't think we want to try and put the advertising industry in a straightjacket. Occasionally they come up with great flashes of humour and originality, I think. I certainly have a soft spot for the sort of Barnum and Bailey touches.

There's a fabulous occasion I remember from the days of my youth on Merseyside when a fairly large ship got stuck in the Mersey. They tried getting one or two tugs out to move this boat but nothing seemed able to shift it.

Then a local advertising man had a brilliant idea. It was in the early days of flying, early days of advertising, and it was still considered quite a remarkable thing to send an aircraft up with a bit of a windsock behind it, towing a slogan. Well, he got a plane up into the air above this boat with the memorable slogan, 'Beecham's will shift it'.

MARGHANITA LASKI: I'm not at all convinced yet that there really is a relation between the selling of goods and the prosperity of the society and advertising, because Malcolm's wrong in supposing that it's only in Communist societies that advertisements are banned.

I've just come back from a week in Holland . . . no posters on the road at all, a very prosperous country, quite as prosperous as our own.

Cross over into Belgium . . . this tawdry advertising, immediately a sense of frustration, defeat, depression and garish society.

There's no advertising in Norway: advertising only on special little poster sites in cities in Switzerland. All these countries are as prosperous as our own.

And I don't think you're at all right, Isobel, in supposing that when manufacturers advertise they really have faith and trust in their goods. What they are doing half the time is keeping up with each other.

It's a rat-race, a phoney, false, inflated, artificial industry that has almost nothing to do with us and our choices, and it is a matter of fact, that no goods of any quality are ever advertised – they don't need to be.

MALCOLM MUGGERIDGE: The answer to Isobel, really, is detergent advertising. Everybody knows these detergents are exactly the same product, same chemical composition. Now millions are spent on advertising them. It is a total and utter waste, and the claims that are made for these identical substances have to become more and more extravagant, have to become more and more untrue. The whole effect on society of this idiotic activity, putting over on people things which are palpably false, cannot but in my opinion be bad.

Using reported speech, summarise this discussion in a number of well-written, well-linked paragraphs. (Limit: 125–150 words.)

3   Newgate in the 18th Century was what we should now call a maximum-security prison. Below is a description of an escape from it by Jack Sheppard, a famous prison-breaker of the time. As the extract begins, there are two hours of daylight left.

First of all he escaped from his handcuffs by means of the nail which he had kept concealed in his stocking. He clenched this nail firmly between his teeth and using it with practised dexterity he picked the lock. Then using the same nail he opened the immense padlock which secured the chain round his ankles to the staple in the floor. He was now free to hop about the cell but, although he found a weak link in the chain which fastened his ankles together, he was unable to squeeze his feet through the thick iron collars which encircled his ankles and to which the ends of the broken chain were still attached. Taking off his stockings, he used them to bind up the links of the chain round his legs.

He had already decided that the only possible way of getting out of the prison was by climbing up the chimney into the room above and from there making his way on to the roof. The narrowness of the barred window ruled out any chance of escape by that means, and although he could, he knew, break open the door of his cell, having done so he would still be on the same floor of the prison.

Having already poked his head up the chimney, he knew that across the flue about six feet above the level of the floor was a thick square iron bar the ends of which were buried into the brickwork of the chimney on either side. This had obviously been built into the chimney to prevent prisoners escaping by squeezing up the flue, as Jack intended to do. There was nothing to do then but to pull down the chimney brick by brick. So, setting to work with the broken link he scratched away at the mortar joints until he had at last worked one brick loose. He soon had a pile of bricks and mortar at this feet, and the thick iron bar in his hands. Taking the bar with him, he clambered up the chimney and, using the end of it as a battering ram, he smashed his way through into the room above.

This was a rectangular room measuring about twenty feet by ten feet, known as the Red Room, which had not been entered or used since 1716 when some rebels had been imprisoned there. Dust lay thick on the floor, but Jack noticed nothing for it was by now pitch dark. From now on he was working in complete darkness. He felt his way round the cell to the door, and with expert sensitive fingers he felt around its edges for the lock box. Within a quarter of an hour, he had bent aside the plate covering the lock box, picked the lock and forced back the bolt. The door creaked open on its rusty hinges and Jack walked out into the passage.

He turned left past the staircase and came to another locked door, the door to the chapel. This door appeared to have no lock and it was bolted on the far side by a bolt which he could not budge. It seemed very quiet in this part of the prison and he decided to take the risk of battering a hole in the brickwork beside the door. He knocked and rammed the wall, making a frightening noise in the darkness, but no one heard him, and soon he had made a hole large enough to get his arm through. He felt for the bolt on the far side and pulled it back. He passed through into the chapel.

The chapel, which he knew only too well, was on the top floor of the prison, and there was another door at its far side leading to the passage which gave access to the roof. He tried for more than half an hour to pick the lock, but his instruments were crude and the lock a strong one. Eventually, changing his tactics, he was able with his iron bar to lever the lock box far enough aside and to pick the lock from the inside. The door rattled on its hinges and pushing it open he hurried along the passage to the door at the far end. When he touched it, his heart fell. The immense iron plated lock box was clamped to the door by iron hoops and beneath the lock box an enormous bolt was fastened into its socket by a hasp secured by a strong padlock. The door itself was strengthened by four vast metal fillets.

Beyond this door was the roof. He was nearly free. But he was tired out and to break through this fifth door, heavier and better secured than any of the others, in complete darkness and without proper tools, seemed even to him impossible. For a moment he hesitated, wondering. He heard the clock bells of St Sepulchre's Church chiming eight o'clock. The thought that he had come so far in five hours put new hope into him. Deciding that the lock could not be picked and the bolt could not be forced he concentrated on the colossal metal fillet to which they were both attached. He managed to force his iron bar into a position in which he could use it as a lever and then, applying to the end of his lever his frenzied and scarcely human strength, he wrenched it from the door. The lock and the bolt were torn away with it.

He pulled the massive door open and walked along the corridor towards the roof. The door at the end of the corridor was bolted only on the inside, so having found the bolt he shot it back and came out gratefully on to the roof and into the fresh and sweet night air.

CHRISTOPHER HIBBERT: *The Road to Tyburn*

(*a*) Describe Sheppard's escape-route as interestingly as you can in 175 words.

(*b*) Basing your suggestions on Sheppard's escape, recommend to the Governor of the prison some ways in which its security could be improved. (Limit: 60 words.)

4　Summarise this passage in not more than 100 words. It can be done well in 80 words. Give a title.

Television, it is often said, is an intimate medium for watching in intimate, familial surroundings. This is to a large extent true (as it is, incidentally, of radio). Television is also a visual medium, and this means that if it does not have necessarily to convey its meaning largely or entirely in visual terms, it does at least have to keep the eyes occupied, because if the eyes wander the minds wander too. Both of these qualities are in themselves mixed blessings, and moreover each complicates the problems which arise from the other. The first means that quiet, intimate scenes are in general better suited to television than expansive rhetorical scenes. Effects can of course be graded, as they can on radio, by varying the distance of the speaker from the microphone and camera, but here the visual nature of the medium steps in to complicate matters. If you hold an actor in close-up while he soliloquises you are likely – unless the actor commands a quite exceptional degree of personal magnetism – to find your audience's attention drifting because one face in close-up for some length of time is not all that interesting to watch. Equally, if you move your actor far enough away for the big demonstrative moments he is likely on the normal home screen to be so small and insignificant-looking that again he cannot magnetise attention. And if you do everything in medium shot it will just look dull anyway.

But put like that, this argument seems to suggest that all drama should be impossible on television. This obviously is not true, but what it really resolves itself into is more than anything a matter of timing. Television must be able to mix up close, medium, and long shots, to move cameras around a lot or have a lot happening in front of them. Most stage-plays offer possibilities of all these things, but as it were in slow motion; they dwell in moods that television should ideally just touch on, they take time to make transitions which television can do in a flash. There is hardly a stage play written of which the author, once properly schooled in television techniques, could not equally well convey the essence for television in an hour.

JOHN RUSSELL TAYLOR in *Shakespeare: a Celebration*

5 The Archbishop of Canterbury received this letter, dated 30 August 1942, from the President of the Board of Trade, the Rt. Hon. Hugh Dalton.

My dear Temple,

I hope I am not overstepping the boundary line between Church and State in a proposal I want to put before you.

Two of our hardest problems at the Board of Trade, in trying to keep the nation adequately clothed, are women's hats and stockings. Hats are bound to become scarcer and scarcer; so much so that we do not even put them on the ration, but hope that women, and men too, will largely give up wearing them. Though there is a better supply of stockings, much labour and material would be saved if more women would go stockingless.

But convention yields ground slowly, and it would help me very much if you felt able to announce that women could, without impropriety, come hatless and stockingless to church. I do not, of course suggest that you should say that I had asked you to make such an announcement. This would not only be inappropriate, but might create prejudice. I observe, however, that many individual churches already show notices that women may attend uncovered, and I therefore hope that you might, perhaps, feel able yourself to take the action I have suggested.

Yours sincerely,

HUGH DALTON

To the President of the Board of Trade.　　　　　　*Lambeth Palace,*
London, S.E.1.
15 October 1942.

My dear Dalton,

I had the opportunity of discussing with the Bishops the question which you put to me in the summer. We did not think any difficulty could arise in practice concerning women's stockings. It is usually quite impossible to tell whether they are wearing any or not! But it was agreed that I should take steps to put out a statement to the effect that women should not hesitate to come into Church with their heads uncovered and I hoped that no bar to their doing so would be found when they came.

Yours sincerely,
WILLIAM CANTUAR

The Statement

Questions are frequently asked in these days concerning the old customary rule that women should not enter a Church building with their heads uncovered. The scriptural authority behind this rule is St Paul's regulation, but this required that they should be veiled. That has long ago fallen out of use, and after consultation with the Bishops generally, we wish it to be known that no woman or girl should hesitate to enter a Church uncovered, nor should any objection to their doing so be raised.

WILLIAM CANTUAR
CYRIL EBOR

WILLIAM TEMPLE: *Some Lambeth Letters* 1942–1944

Summarise this correspondence, and the statement issued by the Archbishops of Canterbury and York, in not more than 100 words. Use reported speech.

6　It was not until the present century that the vitamins were isolated and their importance to health fully appreciated. Vitamins are substances which play an essential part in the chemical processes of the body. Though required only in minute amounts, their absence from the diet for prolonged periods results in illness which is often serious and sometimes fatal. But it must be strongly emphasised that vitamin deficiency occurs only when some item of food is greatly restricted for a considerable time, and the condition almost never affects normal people who take a varied diet. Thus additional vitamins in tablet, capsule, or liquid form are rarely necessary except possibly during pregnancy. Similarly, there is no good evidence that extra vitamins increase bodily resistance to common ailments.

A vitamin deficiency disease which caused much sickness and loss of life among sailors in bygone days is scurvy. This condition, characterised by debility, anaemia, and bleeding from the gums and into the skin and internal organs, is due to lack of vitamin C – found in fruit and vegetables or their juices. On long unbroken voyages scurvy often killed more men than the naval battles they had set out to fight, and for this reason a fleet whenever possible sought land at least once every ten weeks in order to preserve the health of the crews. The gravity of the problem was well illustrated by Lord Anson's voyage round the world in 1740, when in three months almost three-quarters of the expedition's crew died from scurvy.

Yet as early as 1564, Dutch seafarers had found that they could avoid scurvy if they took supplies of citrus fruit with them on their travels. But others learned slowly, and it was not until 1752 that James Lind, a naval surgeon, drew the attention of the Lords of the Admiralty to the preventive and curative value in scurvy of fresh fruit and vegetables – items rarely found in the naval diet of the times. Another of the enlightened was the famous Captain James Cook, who between 1772 and 1775 travelled 60,000 miles with the loss of only one of his crew from scurvy. His secret was a 'potable broth', concocted from vegetable extracts and lemon juice, which he gave to his men at regular intervals.

Despite such reminders and examples, the Admiralty did not act until 1795 when it was decreed that all naval vessels should henceforth carry supplies of lemon juice. When this was done scurvy became a forgotten disease among those who once knew it so well; and the result was equivalent to doubling the fighting strength of the Navy. Incredibly, in the face of evidence of this kind, a dietary cause of scurvy was still not accepted universally until early in the twentieth century, when experimental observations established beyond all possible doubt that scurvy was due to lack of a substance present in fruit and vegetables. Later this was named vitamin C and isolated in pure form.

DAVID MARGERSON: *Medicine Today*

Write a summary in not more than 120 words, and provide a title.

7　This stormy scene is the climax of the television play, *Fiddlers Four*.

Interior of a large meeting hall. On the rostrum sits Alcorn, Smithson and Verity. Among the audience Lucy Verity, Walter Montgomery and Jim Pilling can be recognised.

BAMFORD: And so, without further ado or ceremony I give you our trusted friend, a man whose name is known throughout this town as a truly progressive force – Alderman Verity.

There is scattered applause as Bamford sits down and Verity rises.

VERITY: Good evening, friends and neighbours. You know why we are gathered here tonight, and you know I'm a man who comes straight to the heart of the matter. Like most of you I was born and raised in Carrington, and I've seen it grow from a sleepy little village to the manufacturing town it is today, and in this whole blessed town there's not a recreation ground, there's not a park, there's not so much as a blade of grass. Now, can any one of you deny we need one? Where do we have for our little children to play? They have nothing but the streets to run in. Are the streets good enough for them? Do they not have a right to something better than that? To play on the soft grass and breathe fresh air? And you, their mothers and fathers, don't you have a right to take a stroll on a summer evening or a Sunday afternoon, and fancy yourselves in the country? Of course you do! And that's why you're here. We want your support to carry through a plan to build a recreation ground here in Carrington. We can't do it without there's a big force of public opinion at our backs; that's the way you can help!

WALTER [*rising*]: You won't lack our support, Mr Verity, if you've a practical plan.

VERITY: I'm glad of your support, Mr Montgomery, but nothing is ever practical to some folk if it means putting up the rates.

WALTER: The rates have to be considered, Mr Verity.

The crowd murmurs agreement.

VERITY: A healthy town pays best, Mr Montgomery. Consider the purses of the ratepayers, and then consider the danger to little children playing in the streets and ask your religion which consideration weighs the heaviest.

WALTER: Really, sir! There can't be two sides to such a question.

VERITY: There'll be two sides right enough.

PILLING [*getting to his feet*]: You'll be excusing a man like me saying a word, I hope. . . .

VERITY: We wish to hear from everyone, Mr Pilling.

PILLING: I'm thinking it's more houses we need, in Carrington, sir. Folks can't thrive cramped up the way we are. I'm a gardener, sir, and

I can't get garden stuff to grow proper, in this air, so what chance has children?

VERITY: Then surely, man, a recreation ground is just the thing?

PILLING: Aye, but houses first, sir.

VERITY: You may think it odd to hear me say anything against houses, Mr Pilling – being in the building trade myself . . . but I've got some facts and figures here that speak for themselves. *Alcorn stretches across and gives Verity a slip of paper.* Thank you, Mr Alcorn. [*Looking at paper.*] Now! In the last year alone, eleven children have been killed in our streets, and another twenty-eight injured. Consider a moment, ladies and gentlemen, eleven innocent children killed! Would that have happened if we'd had a recreation ground?

A workman rises.

MAN: I'll support you, Mr Verity, but there's summat I'd like to know.

VERITY: Speak freely. This is an informal meeting.

MAN: I don't see where you'd build this playground. There isn't an inch of ground that isn't built on within two miles of town.

VERITY: I'm aware of that.

PILLING: A recreation ground two miles off wouldn't be much use.

VERITY: It'll not be five minutes from your door, sir.

MAN: Then you'll have to burrow for it or hang it in the air.

Laughter from crowd.

VERITY: The land we have in view is built on at present.

PILLING: Lot of good that'll do, turning people out of house and home to make a playing field, when houses are so scarce and all.

WALTER: To my mind, it's housing that's most urgent here.

VERITY: We'll get neither without we're helped. We want the help of . every man who'll say a word for us.

WALTER: But to pull down houses . . .

VERITY: We shan't pull down many.

PILLING: It'll be a small ground then.

VERITY: About ten acres.

MAN: You'll have to pull down streets and streets of houses to get ten acres.

VERITY: We shall pull down just five. No more and no less.

MAN: Five houses!

WALTER: Five houses, Verity?

VERITY: Yes, five houses, I said.

WALTER: Then you're thinking . . . oh, but that's ridiculous. The Polygon's the only place that applies to.

VERITY: And why shouldn't I be thinking of the Polygon?

WALTER: But the Polygon is . . .

VERITY: Yes, Mr Montgomery?

WALTER: It's my home.

VERITY: Yes, it's the home of the leisured and privileged classes of this town. It's five big houses with a tennis court in the middle and a great big garden behind each, and it's bang in the middle of town. You've got great gates to it marked 'Private', and someone to watch them and see none of the common herd get in to soil your sacred air by breathing it in their vulgar lungs.

WALTER: You put things a bit violently.

VERITY: I feel violently. Have you the right to monopolise this air? It's a shame and a scandal for the land to be wasted on you, and it's not going to be wasted much longer!

Walter is about to reply, changes his mind, and walks from the hall.

HAROLD BRIGHOUSE: *Fiddlers Four*

Write a summary (up to 250 words) which would give someone who had missed the play an idea of the tensions, disagreements and passions shown in this scene. Provide a title.

8   Man's view of the universe has been enormously expanded during the years since the close of the second world war, primarily because of the new techniques of radio astronomy and the space probe. It was, however, the introduction of the great optical telescopes which led to the major revolution in our ideas about the size and organisation of the cosmos. Until about forty years ago we still believed that the system of stars visible in the sky on any clear night, and known as the Milky Way, was confined in space and itself represented the totality of the universe. Even so short a time ago we believed that the Sun, the Earth, and the attendant planets were situated at the centre of this system of stars, and that the Sun was a typical star and seemed bright because it was close to us. The stars appeared faint, not because they were small and insignificant, but because they were at great distances. Nevertheless we believed that we were privileged to be situated in the centre of this assembly. It was estimated that there were many thousands of millions of stars in this Milky Way system and they were believed to be distributed in an approximately spherical enclosure of a size such that it would take a ray of light travelling 186,000 miles a second a few thousand years to traverse it. These ideas have been changed completely.

The investigations which were carried out by the American astronomers in the few years after 1920 following the opening of the 100-inch telescope on Mount Wilson showed that this egocentric view was wrong; that, in fact, the stars of the Milky Way are arranged in a disc of extent such that a ray of light would take a hundred thousand years to traverse the distance separating the extremities of the stars and that the system was asymmetrical. If one could remove oneself from the Milky Way system and look back on it through a large telescope, then the stars would appear to be arranged in a flattened disc with the stars concentrated in spirals radiating from the central hub like a giant octopus. It was realised too that the Sun, far from being at the centre of this disc of stars, was situated in an unfavourable position somewhere near the edge of the disc.

We know that this Milky Way system of local galaxy contains about one hundred thousand million stars. The Earth is a planet of the Sun's family, 93 million miles away. The most distant planet in our solar system, Pluto, is a few thousand million miles distant, so far away that the light from the Sun takes about six and a half hours on its journey towards the planet Pluto. These distances, which are still just conceivable in terrestrial terms, are minute compared with the distance which separates our solar family from the nearest star in space. In order to describe these distances it is convenient to use the expression known as the 'light year', which is the distance which a ray of light travels during the course of a year. The speed of light is 186,000 miles per second; the light from the Sun takes eight minutes on its journey, therefore the Sun is at a distance of eight light minutes. The light from Pluto takes six and a half hours on its journey to Earth so Pluto is six and a half light hours away. On the other hand the nearest star is enormously more distant, so far away that the light from it takes four and a half years on its journey.

SIR BERNARD LOVELL: *The Exploration of Outer Space*
In 100 words, summarise the changes in man's view of the universe described above, and provide a title.

9   Deer, stench, paradise; fascinate, square, disease; silly, enamel, pretty, complexion. The history of these words would be enough to show that words, like people, go up and down in the world. Like people, too, they die: bifarious, gripple, snudge, fubsy, plook, anythingarian have all passed away. And as with words, so with whole languages. The following account of some ways in which languages change was written for 'the general reader': so it is full of examples, and is generous in explanation.

It is only during the past few centuries that English has become the universal language in Cornwall. Formerly there was a Cornish language, a Celtic language related to Welsh, but this was gradually displaced by English, and finally died out. The last known native speaker of Cornish was an old lady who died in 1777.

The disappearance of Cornish, as a matter of fact, is just one example of a long-term historical trend, in which the whole group of languages called Celtic have retreated before Germanic and Romance languages (like English and French). In the time of Julius Caesar, Celtic languages were spoken over large areas of western Europe, including the whole of the British Isles and France, and parts of Spain, Italy, and southern Germany. Today, the surviving Celtic languages are spoken only by small minorities on the Atlantic seaboard, and are having great difficulties in holding their own, despite intensive efforts by some of their speakers to maintain their traditional language and culture.

Perhaps the most tenacious and vigorous of the Celtic languages is Welsh: there are still country districts in Wales where many children do not understand English, and where many adults pretend not to; and out of a population of two and a half million, nearly three-quarters of a million can still speak Welsh. But even Welsh is in retreat: between 1900 and 1950, the proportion of the inhabitants of Wales who could speak Welsh fell from about 50 per cent to under 30 per cent; the proportion who could speak *only* Welsh fell from about 15 per cent to under 2 per cent. It is difficult to see how even strong national feeling and a genuine love of Welsh traditions can hope to reverse this trend, as long as England and Wales form a single economic and political unit and the Welsh language is in direct competition with English.

This is one way in which a language becomes dead: it dwindles away until finally nobody speaks it at all. But a language can become dead in another way. Nobody today speaks classical Latin as spoken by Julius Caesar, or classical Greek as spoken by Pericles, so classical Latin and classical Greek are dead languages. But, although dead, they have not *died*: they have changed into something else. People still speak Greek as a living language, and this language is simply a changed form of the language spoken in the Athens of Pericles. The people who live in Rome today speak a language that has developed by a process of continuous change out of the language spoken in Rome in the time of Julius Caesar, though modern Italian developed out of the everyday language of the ancient Roman market place and of the common soldier, rather than out of the upper class literary Latin that Caesar wrote.

In fact all living languages change, though the rate of change varies from time to time, and from language to language. The modern Icelander, for example, does not find it very difficult to read the medieval Icelandic Sagas, because the rate of change in Icelandic has always been slow ever since the country was colonised by Norwegians a thousand years ago and Icelandic history began. But an Englishman without special training will find an English document of the year 1300 very difficult to understand; and an English document of the year 900 will seem to him to be written in a foreign language, which he may conclude (mistakenly) to have no connexion with modern English.

c. l. barber: *The Story of Language*

(*a*) Write a short accurate statement (not more than 35 words) of the two ways in which living languages may die out. Take care that it would be intelligible to someone who had not read the passage.

(*b*) Limiting your material to what is in this extract, write in 120 words the most interesting account you can of the changes in language which the author deals with. You will have space to include some examples, and may find the last paragraph best used first.

10   There are a good many inconveniences attached to the simple act of going to a theatre. The greatest of these is usually the play itself, and on this most critics rightly concentrate. In an empty week, however, I have been pondering those minor irritations, peas under the mattress, that ought to be removed if playgoing is to take its proper place among life's softer options.

One such pea, in London at least, is the difficulty of finding out what theatre is housing the play you want to see. The list of attractions used by West End managers to advertise their wares in the newspapers is primarily a list of theatres, not of plays. If your choice is *Divorce Me, Darling*, you may have to run through the names of forty playhouses, before finding what you want. In New York you would simply look under 'D', and there, after *Dig My Gallows Deep* and before *Dreyfus and Son*, it would be, followed by the name and address of the theatre. The London system harks back to the days of the actor-managers, when you went to the Lyceum to see Irving without caring very much what you were going to see him in. Nowadays, when the play and not the playhouse is the thing, the New York arrangement is clearly more sensible.

Having identified the theatre, you next have to get there. Here London has the advantage of both Paris and New York, expecially if you travel by taxi. Seen from the air round curtain-time, Broadway resembles a war of caterpillars; rows of cabs, minutely jerking forward, clog the whole area. In Paris, of course, all taxis vanish from the streets for half an hour before the curtain goes up. You occasionally catch sight of one roaring out to keep a date with destiny or dinner at Courbevoie, but the chance of its stopping is remote; the most you can expect is a tragic shrug from the driver as he flashes by, the slave of fate or his stomach.

Assuming you arrive at the theatre, you must then dispose of your coat. You will almost certainly be wearing one. Indoor drama thrives only in cold weather; few people in hot climates would be foolish enough to spend a whole evening indoors with neither wine nor words on their lips. The cloakrooms of most London theatres are mere holes in the wall, wardrobes occupied by five hundred coats and one human being. Berlin and Moscow are the only cities known to me that have solved the garment-reclaiming problem. At the Schill-Theater in Berlin there are two long walls of cloakrooms in the foyer, staffed by twenty attendants, and the same is true of the Moscow Art.

The scandal of London theatre programmes is notorious and seemingly incurable. Whenever I watch British audiences happily paying sixpence for eight pages of text, six of which are devoted to advertisements, a quotation from Brecht leaps to my mind: 'I can see their divine patience, but where is their divine fury?' In Paris, at the very least, you get a little booklet for your money; and in New York you get a rather larger booklet for nothing. *Playbill*, the Broadway programme, is published and edited by a private company. It is in fact a forty-page weekly magazine, with critical articles on international drama, and full biographies of the author, director, and actors. The only London theatre to have taken even a tentative step in this direction is the Westminster, where the programmes tell you not only who the actors are but where you last saw them. Unfortunately, in many of the plays produced at this theatre the information is not encouraging.

Interval amenities vary from capital to capital. In New York (as in Paris) I tend to doze, drugged by the heat: the reviving draughts that sweep across London Theatres are unknown in these upholstered ovens. The New Yorkers themselves, forbidden liquor in theatres, obey laconic commands to 'get your orange drinks, get your refreshing orange drinks'. The French make unhurried bee-lines for the

longest, best-stocked theatre bars on earth. Meanwhile the Englishman is barking his elbows in a tiny, thronged snuggery where warm
gin is dispensed by surly, glaring, female teetotallers.

The final hazard of London playgoing is the playing of the National
Anthem, during which we stand to attention, while gloves, scarves,
and programmes fall unregarded to the floor. This compulsive display
of patriotism (unknown outside Britain and the Commonwealth) is
today almost classifiable as a game. People with at least one hand on
the exit-door when the drum-roll begins are held to be exempt from
standing through Dr Bull's little melody. The rest may stay rooted to
the spot, staring vaingloriously at the curtain; if they move, some
forfeit is payable.

KENNETH TYNAN: 'The Hazards of Playgoing' in *Miscellany*
Summarise the 'good many inconveniences attached to the simple
act of going to a theatre'. (Limit: 150–175 words.)

11   A school discussion about religion was tape-recorded, and what
follows is a transcript of part of it. The teacher speaks first.

*Well, you've credited God with some nice characteristics, and you fit in with
all this that he can judge. Do you think that God judges nations as well as
individuals?*

Yes (majority).

Do you believe then that wars are God's judgement on a nation?

Yes – no (half and half).

Wasn't it in a story about Judah that God threatened a famine
because the people were so disagreeable?

*In the last chapters of the Bible it does say that God judges a nation for idolatry
and so on. You – or people like you – have often asked me why does God allow wars.*

Well, he causes a war when the world is overcrowded! When there
are too many people coming into the world, he has to have a war to
get rid of some of them.

No. . . .

You think war then is a nice way of killing off the surplus population?

I don't think war is anything to do with God.

*I think God gave man a certain independence and freedom, and that's where
wars come in. You see, if God didn't allow men to have wars, then they would
have no freedom, and they would have to do all good. It would probably be good
for them, but it wouldn't be what they themselves did.*

I think war is just greed. People have some land, and then they want
more and more and more and so on. I don't think God has anything
to do with war.

So you feel that man is responsible for his own wars?
Yes.
Just like atom bombs and things. You feel that this is our responsibility?
Yes.
Do you feel that it might be better for us if God stopped us doing these things, but he doesn't because of our freedom?
No, I don't think it would be better, because man wouldn't be able to decide for himself whether he wanted to believe in God or whether he wanted to reject God.
What do the rest of you think about that?
Well, I don't agree when they go making atom bombs and dropping them around.
But it is a human decision to do that – a human being decided to act in that way.
Yes, but you could say that it isn't fair when God lets one man shoot an arrow and it shoots another man dead, right back through the ages.
That is the freedom of man – God doesn't want that.
These people should think when they make these atom bombs that they're only going to kill people.
Well, it's a very, very grave problem, isn't it?
Yes, my parents went to some of the Nuclear Disarmament meetings and the man said it was up to some of the younger folk to do something because it would be them would be living, and it was up to them to stop them being made.
That's interesting. On the whole do you prefer to be made to be good or do you prefer to be allowed to be bad if you want?
I'd rather be bad (majority).
And are you prepared to take the consequences of being bad?
Yes (majority).
Well, it would be ever so dull with everybody being good and cheerful and so on. It changes the routine if somebody is bad once in a while.
You like a good row, do you?
I like a good argument.
Well, what do you think then is the value of Evil? You've got vice, and sin, and all sorts of personal failings, haven't you? Do you think this is of any real value? Joan?
Well, I don't think that serious crime is of value, but just the odd row, or a little lie between friends, I think changes the same routine of being good all the time.

You have to be a bit cheeky to get on anyway.

That's interesting – what do you mean by that, Carole?

Well . . . these films stars and so on, they say lies to get on in the world, and if they didn't say them they wouldn't get on.

Attract attention in that way, d'you mean?

Well, you couldn't really call that evil . . .

What – telling lies?

Well, not all their get-ups and publicity, because that's near enough accepted.

You would say then that the accepted standard for the people you know is that an occasional lie doesn't matter and a bit of cheek is a good idea?

It depends on the person.

You mustn't be too perfect.

You mean that you mustn't be any better than anybody else? So this is the pattern, is it? This thing called the force of public opinion, which says you can tell occasional lies, and be cheeky if you can get away with it, draw attention to yourselves somehow – must get on, get plenty of lolly?

No – you seem to have got the wrong idea of it.

Well, explain.

It's horribly difficult – but it would be so monotonous if everybody was good all the time – and sometimes good comes out of evil.

HAROLD LOUKES, ed. *About Religion*

In this discussion, as in most others, some of the important topics raised are not developed and some of the red herrings get discussed. Often, too, a short answer to a comprehensive question implies a very important point (look again, for examples, at the beginning of the transcript).

In not more than 100 words, write the neatest summary you can of the discussion.

12   If you want to collect classical records, there are three ways of going about it. You can buy full-price records in the shops; or you can buy cheap records through record clubs; or, in one case we found, by post from a magazine publisher. We have investigated cheap classical records of all these kinds.

How does a 'cheap' record come to be available? There are three main reasons. The record may be a new performance by little-known artists; it may be an older performance by well-known artists, which has already earned its keep as a full-price record; or it may be a record made from an imported or slightly sub-standard tape. Sometimes, however, it may be a new performance by well-known artists.

Cheap classical records first came from record clubs about ten years ago. A 12 inch long-playing record from a record company costs at least £1.25, while one from a record club costs many pennies less. Later, the record companies issued their own series of cheap records, in addition to their full-price ones. A full-price 12 inch long-playing classical record now usually costs at least £1.88, while most 'cheap' ones – whether from record companies or record clubs – cost about £1.00, and some cost as little as 45p.

We have assessed 12 inch classical long-playing records only, and we set out to answer three main questions. Is it worth joining a record club? Or is it better to buy cheap records from the record companies in the shops? And is it possible to build a good collection by buying cheap records only?

We chose the available recordings of sixteen well-known orchestral works in the standard repertoire, and asked a panel of four people (two critics, a composer and an orchestral player) to assess each of the 205 records for the quality of recording and for the standard of performance. The panel were not told the names of the labels or performers.

To assess the recording, the panel took into account both the qualities of the original tape (instrumental balance, volume, brilliance and range of tone) and those of the record they actually listened to (surface noise, pre- or post-echo, joins in the tape). To assess the performance, the panel took into account the fidelity to the score (tempi, expression, phrasing, orchestral balance) and the final impression.

The labels with the best recording quality for the works we assessed were Encore, Fontana Big and Masters of Art, Heliodor, HMV Concert Classics, and the *Readers' Digest*. The labels with the poorest recording quality were Atlas, Classics Club, Delta, Fidelio and Summit. The RCA Camden records also had poor recording quality, but this was explained as being from old recordings of historical and musical interest.

The panel made some specific criticisms. For example, the Saga Beethoven Piano Concerto No. 5 had bars 415–422 of the Finale 'slotted in from another recording', while the very similar Classics Club version had the original recording of this passage – 'and a proper mess the pianist makes of it!' The Classics Club Dvorak Symphony No. 9 had 'studio noise'. The Summit Grieg Piano Concerto had a 'bathroom acoustic'. In the Fidelio Schubert Symphony No. 8 the instruments were not distinct – 'clarinet sounds like oboe, oboe sounds like cor anglais, etc.' The Fidelio Nutcracker Suite sounded 'remote and muffled'; and the first note of the Sugar Plum Fairy Dance and of the Reedpipe Dance were missing.

The labels with the best standard of performance for the works we assessed were Ace of Clubs, Encore, Fontana Masters of Art, Philips, RCA Camden, and Supraphon. The labels with the least satisfactory performances were Atlas, Classics Club, Embassy and Saga. Again the panel made some specific criticisms. For example, the *Readers' Digest* Beethoven Symphonies had a good orchestra but unusual tempi and cold interpretations. The HMV Concert Classics Beethoven Symphony No. 3 had a lifeless second movement. The MK Beethoven Symphony No. 9 had a fair performance, but the last movement was sung in Russian. One Ace of Clubs Grieg Piano Concerto had a 'gingerly, mannered solo performance with altered chords and peculiar phrasing'. The Classics Club Schubert Symphony No. 8 had 'much the fastest performance of the first movement I've ever heard'.

Nearly all the orchestras, conductors and soloists on the records we assessed were well known. But a few of the record companies and record clubs gave their performers names which our panel hadn't heard of, and some of them were invented. And in some cases an identical performance appeared on different labels. The record company labels with performers whose names our panel hadn't heard of were Atlas, Embassy, Fidelio and Summit. None of these labels indicated that the names of the performers were not what they seemed. But the Classics Club, which had several imaginary performers, did at least say so.

The problem of identical performances on different labels was very confusing. In some cases several labels shared a performance and attributed it to the same performers. But in other cases several labels shared a performance and attributed it to different performers. Thus, Saga and Classics Club had the same performance of Beethoven Symphony No. 3; Fidelio and Summit had the same performance of Beethoven Symphony No. 9 (and this was the same performance as the one shared by Saga and Classics Club); Delta, Fidelio and Saga had the same performance of Dvořák's Symphony No. 9; Fidelio and Summit had the same performances of Grieg Piano Concerto, of Mendelssohn Violin Concerto, and of Schubert Symphony No. 8; and Atlas and Fidelio had the same performance of Tchaikovsky's Symphony No. 6.

If you want a record from a record company, you can just buy it from a shop. You can look at the sleeve notes and hear it played, and you know what it costs. With record clubs it's more complicated.

None of the three record clubs we investigated had a subscription or membership fee; the condition of membership was that you bought a certain number of records a year from lists chosen by the club. Each club had a special introductory offer, discounts for large purchases, and other special offers. With Classics Club and Concert Hall Record Club, it was not always easy to know how much you were paying for each record.

Record Clubs may be useful for people who want to collect records but don't know much about music and can't go shopping. The clubs we assessed have some good recordings of standard works and in some cases they also offer recordings of rare works. But life is much simpler if you don't join a record club, for they have complications (though the World Record Club had fewer than the other two). Getting records by post from a club may be useful, but there are firms that sell record company records by post. You can get a wider choice among record company records, and the records we assessed – which were all orchestral works from the standard repertoire – were generally cheaper, better recorded and better performed than the record club records. And other labels – MK, Saga, and Supraphon – had several rare works in their lists.

The records we tested from Concert Hall and World Record Club were not particularly good value for money. After the initial special offer, Concert Hall records cost at least £1.05 each and World Record Club records cost at least 98p each (both excluding postage). Neither of these clubs had enough first-rate performances on the records we assessed to make it worth paying these prices. Concert Hall claimed that their records gave 'a saving of a full 30 per cent of what you normally expect to pay', but we found that they cost nearly 50 per cent more than you need pay for some other cheap recordings.

The records from Classics Club were cheaper. Classics Club claimed that their records cost 'less than half the price you would be charged in record shops', but we found some of them as cheap on other labels.

The very cheap labels had generally poor recordings or performances – Atlas 45p; Delta 63p; Embassy 75p; Fidelio 50p; Saga 63p and Summit 45p.

In general the best value for money among the records of standard orchestral works which we assessed was from Ace of Clubs, Encore, Fontana Masters of Art, Heliodor, HMV Concert Classics, Philips, RCA Camden and Supraphon. Some MK records were also good value for money.

We found that you can build a good collection of standard orchestral works by buying cheap records only. *Which?* August 1964. [*Note*: We have decimalised the prices quoted in this article, but we have not attempted to bring them up to current equivalent levels.]

(*a*) As sub-editor of a national newspaper, you have only 4 column inches to report the main findings of this survey. Provide the 120 words your space allows, and write a head line.

A few days later, the paper's music critic discussed the report. In what main ways would his article differ from the sub-editor's?

(*b*) Write the summaries of this article which might appear in: (i) the Staff Magazine of a large store selling full-price LPs; (ii) the magazine issued for members by a Record Club not included in the survey. (Not more than 200 words each.) Provide headlines.

(*c*) Using only information drawn from the article, write a brief account (200 words) of the origins of record clubs, and the advantages and snags of membership.

13   In the following short story, John Appleby – now Assistant Commissioner of Police – talks about one of his cases:

'It all began', Appleby said, 'with a Professor writing a learned article called *Shakespeare's Stage Blood*. He wasn't starting a theory that the Bard came of a long line of actors. He was simply showing from a study of the old texts that the Elizabethan theatre was a thoroughly gory place.'

The Vicar nodded. ' "Carnal, bloody and unnatural acts",' he quoted cheerfully. ' "Accidental judgements, casual slaughters, death put on by cunning and forced cause ——".'

'Quite so. But the relevant point was this: when *X* drew his dagger or rapier on the stage of the Globe and appeared to stab *Y*, what in fact he did stab was a concealed bladder, full of some sort of red paint. The stuff spurted out all over the place, and gave an engaging impression of a neatly severed artery.'

'Messy. One hopes it came out in the wash.'

'No doubt it did. But the immediate effect was terrific. All concerned simply wallowed in this bogus blood, and the audience got no end of a thrill. Now, no sooner had the Professor published his discovery than it greatly took the fancy of a chap called Cherry, who was the moving spirit of a group of amateur players at Nessfield. Most of his company belonged to the staff of the University there, and this blood-bath business apparently gave very general pleasure to all. It was felt that something should be done to put this discovery about

Shakespeare's stage into practice. So Cherry decided that the next play should be *Julius Caesar*.'

The Vicar chuckled. ' "Stoop, Romans, stoop, and let us bathe our hands in Caesar's blood." '

'Precisely. "Up to the elbows, and besmear our swords." Contemplating that scene, Cherry, you may say, simply saw red. As it happened, I was visiting a friend of some consequence in those parts, and he took me along to the performance. For some reason that I didn't gather, it was quite an occasion, and we sat among a whole gaggle of the local nobs, all doing Cherry and his friends proud.

'They played uncommonly well. The scene in the Senate House built up some first-rate suspense, and when at length the conspirators had edged round Caesar and isolated him beside Pompey's statue, the audience was as keyed up as ever I've seen it at a professional production. Then Casca gave his signal, and that dignified group of noble Romans closed in like a rugger scrum, and had a high old time stabbing and hacking for all they were worth. You wouldn't have believed, Vicar, that most of them were Doctors of Philosophy and Readers in Ancient Hebrew and such like. And the gore! It exceeded all expectations. Every one of the conspirators – Brutus, Cassius, Casca, Decius, Cinna, and the rest ——'

'Ligarius, Trebonius, and Metellus.' The Vicar rubbed his hands in mild self-congratulation. 'Once learnt, one doesn't forget these things.'

'They were all dripping some beastly stuff supplied, I imagine, by the Department of Chemistry. And the rest of the scene went with a swing – Mark Antony's "Cry Havoc" speech and all. It was only when Antony and the servant of Octavius started to bear away the body that things went wrong. You see, it *was* a body. Caesar had been stabbed through the heart.'

The Vicar looked serious, but his memory did not fail him. ' "Imperious Caesar, dead and turned to clay " – eh? What an uncommonly disconcerting business.'

Appleby nodded. 'It was clearly *my* business, whether disconcerting or not. Scotland Yard was in the stalls, and Scotland Yard had to step into the limelight. So I got my august friend to announce my presence in due form, and there and then I took charge. Within half an hour I felt like concluding myself to be at grips with the perfect murder.

'Caesar – I needn't drag up those people's real names – had been an unpopular figure about the place. He was a mathematician with a boring habit of pestering his colleagues with insoluble problems.

He and Cassius had had a tremendous row over something entirely technical; Brutus was believed to be his bitter rival for the next Fellowship of some important scientific society; and Casca was convinced that he had done him out of a job.'

'Ah!' The Vicar was impressed. 'There looks to have been quite a field. But I put my money on Casca. "See what a rent the envious Casca made." '

'These things might be far from very substantial motives for murder. But they hinted an atmosphere which might nurse bad blood – *real* blood, you may say. And now think of the actual melée. There's nothing like a crowd of amateurs for doing that sort of thing in a really whole-hearted way, and for a conspirator meaning actual homicide this bit of stage assassination was ideal cover.

'And all I had to go on was a bunch of confused statements by these people – that, and eight daggers; seven of them trick daggers of the sort that disappear up the sheath, and one of an authentic and deadly kind. The seven were dripping this beastly red muck; the eighth —— '

'A nasty contrast, indeed.' The Vicar was sober. ' "And as he plucked his cursed steel away, mark how the blood of Caesar followed it." Would there be fingerprints?'

'I hadn't much hope from them – and so I was the more pleased when I suddenly had an idea. I gathered the cast together; told them I believed I knew who was responsible; and announced that I was going to have them enact the scene over again, with myself as Caesar.'

'My dear fellow, wasn't that rather risky? If the crime had been the work, say, of a homicidal maniac, this second chance —— '

'There were to be no daggers this time, and no disgusting red paint. Even so, I got well thumped, for those people's zest for violence wasn't to be exhausted by the mere spectacle of a murdered colleague. They found the re-enacting thoroughly enjoyable. And I don't doubt that, at the end of it, they were extremely disappointed when I simply told them to go home.'

'To go home!'

'Certainly. For all I'd wanted to do, you see, was to *count* – to count the conspirators. And my memory proved right. Eight daggers made one too many.

'It's true that there are eight conspirators, and you completed my own list quite correctly. But Trebonius' job, you may recall, is to get Antony out of the way; and so he isn't concerned in the killing.

Caesar, in fact, had killed himself. For distressing reasons into which I needn't enter, his life was no longer of any use to him; and it had pleased him to exploit the occasion of his own suicide to set his colleagues, and the world in general, a final little problem.'

'My dear Appleby, this is a very shocking story. Suppose that one of those unfortunate conspirators had actually been suspected of murder.'

'Nothing would have pleased Caesar more. He was a thoroughly malicious fellow – and, like the real Caesar, a good deal of an exhibitionist. He liked staging that sensation for all the important citizens of Nessfield. And had Casca or Cassius been brought to trial, he would have been delighted. He had even left with a crony a letter addressed to the Home Secretary and telling the whole story. It was to be posted ——'

'Only in the event of a criminal trial?'

'Only in the event of somebody having been hanged.'

MICHAEL INNES: 'Imperious Cæsar', in *Appleby Talking*

(*a*) Outline the hypothesis on which you think Appleby was working when he asked the cast to re-enact the murder. (It was based on more than just the number of daggers.)

(*b*) Compose the letter which 'Caesar' left behind him. (It will show, by tone as well as detail, his dislike for others in the cast, and will include the condition on which it is to be posted.)

(*c*) The Vicar keeps a careful diary. In 100 words, write the entry which records the above conversation, and the heading he gave it.

14   I. The following report was published in *The Times* of 28 December 1959.

Pork Chops at the South Pole
American Welcome for Soviet Expedition

Wellington, 27 Dec. The Soviet Antarctic expedition, on arrival at the South Pole yesterday, were given a meal of cereals, eggs, pork chops and fried potatoes cooked by a member of the American party at the American polar research station, Mr Ted Miller, of Kentucky.

The Russians are expected to stay at the station for two days before starting the final stage – via the Sovietskaya base at the Pole of Inaccessibility to the Soviet coastal station at Lazarev in Queen Maud Land – of their 3,700 miles trans-Antarctic trek.

The Leader of the Soviet expedition, Mr Alexander Dralkin, in a message received today at the United States Antarctic commander's

Christchurch headquarters, said: 'Our sincere thanks for your kind message in connection with our arrival at the South Pole station. We found here very warm hospitality from the members of the station.'

The American Antarctic commander, Rear-Admiral David Tyree, had sent a message to the Russians, when they were a few hours from the Pole, assuring them that the American party would extend the hospitality of the station and give any service the Russians might require that was within the station's capability.

The Soviet expedition is the fourth to reach the South Pole overland. The Soviet news agency Tass said yesterday that the expedition did not try to break any records. It stopped about every seventy miles to make scientific observations for a meridional cross-section of the ice covering the continent, and to cross areas never before trodden by men. Reuter.

II. The following notes were made in his private diary by a British observer attached to the American base, who is to give a talk on the expedition to your school Geographical Society.

Dec. 25. Russians expected tomorrow. Much excitement in station.

> Understand Tyree has wirelessed a welcome. Ted Miller says he'll put on a slap-up meal. 'Southern hospitality!' (Ted comes from Kentucky.)

Dec. 26. Russians arrived, under Alexander Dralkin. In good shape.

> Apparently they've not rushed it — seventy mile stretches. Language difficulties tricky but Americans and Russians doing their best – very friendly atmosphere. Russian equipment fantastic! Beautifully kept too. Yanks wide-eyed. Tyree made pretty speech. Said they were new boys to the Pole compared with Dralkin and his team. 'Sparks' busy with radio messages of welcome and thanks to and fro across Antarctica. Ted Miller excelled himself. All out of tins, too! Russians amused and pleased; produced vodka. Merry reunion. Ah well! Takes all sorts to make a world, even at the South Pole. Must get on with official report.

(i) Write the relevant part of the British observer's talk to your Geographical Society (in not more than 350 words), based on the Reuter report in I and the notes in II. Give the title of the talk.

(ii) Then write a paragraph of not more than 50 words based on the Reuter report, suitable for inclusion in the News in Brief section of a daily newspaper. Provide a headline.

15. There cannot be any member of the Bar who has not been faced at some time or other with the old and familiar question: 'How can you possibly defend a guilty man?' or some question of a similar kind. Such questions were asked at Athens in the days of Demosthenes and at Rome in the days of Cicero and they have been asked at every stage of our own legal history.

I quite realise how strange and indeed wrong it must seem to the ordinary citizen, that a man of honour and integrity and usually of great gifts should defend a man that he must know in his heart to be guilty of the crime with which he is charged and to be paid for doing so. 'How is it possible', men say, 'for an advocate to resist an argument that appears to be founded on truth and to seek to make the worse appear the better reason?' For, put quite starkly, the charge against the advocate is: that he cannot possibly be sincere or indeed honest in the conduct of his profession; for the ordinary citizen only espouses some particular cause because he believes in it, but the advocate espouses a cause because he is paid to do so, whether he believes in it or not. I do not think it is a sufficient answer to say that, theoretically at least, the advocate has no choice in the kind of case he will take up. In practice, if there are good reasons why an advocate should not undertake a certain case, he can quite easily decline it. But, as Erskine so eloquently said, 'If the advocate refuses to defend from what he may think of the charge or the defence, he assumes the character of the judge . . . and puts the heavy influence of perhaps a mistaken opinion into the scale against the accused, in whose favour the benevolent principles of English Law make all presumptions, and which command the very judge to be his counsel.'

Still, the charge against the advocate remains and was put into its most deadly form by that strange and erratic genius, Dean Swift, in *Gulliver's Travels*, when he said of the Bar that 'they were a society of men bred up from their youth in the art of proving by words multiplied for the purpose, that white is black and black is white according as they are paid'. Now the plain truth is that when the advocate is pleading in any case, *he is not stating his own view*, and indeed has no right whatever to do so. He is bound by very strict rules of conduct and an equally strict code of honour, expressly designed to allow him to discharge his duty in the administration of justice without being false to himself or to his conscience and without failing in his duty to the community in which he lives. The function of the advocate is to present one side of the case with all the skill he possesses, so that the judge, or the judge and jury, can compare *his* presentation with that of the counsel on the other side and then decide after full investigation, where the truth lies. In a criminal case many people suppose that an advocate who is prosecuting in a case of murder is trying to get the accused convicted at all costs. I speak with knowledge when I say that the duty of prosecuting counsel is to act as a minister of justice in the fullest sense. He must make sure that the evidence is relevant and admissible and is presented without bias. He must also make sure that the evidence in favour of the prisoner is before the court, and is given the same prominence and emphasis as the evidence tendered to show his guilt. And he will never omit to tell the jury that the duty of the prosecution is to prove the case against the accused beyond all reasonable doubt.

And what is the duty of the advocate who shoulders the heavy burden of *defending* the prisoner on this gravest of all charges? It is to devote himself completely to his task whatever he himself may think of the charges, and to lay aside every other duty, so that he may watch constantly in the interests of the accused, and say for him all that he would wish to say for himself, were he able to do so. The purpose of this procedure in English Law is not that a guilty person shall escape but to make certain, so far as human fallibility can do so, that no innocent person shall suffer. I sometimes hear it said that verdicts of not guilty are obtained from juries against the weight of the evidence by brilliant advocacy; and it may very well be so. But while human nature remains what it is, juries will *acquit* against the weight of the evidence, but they will not *convict* against the weight of the evidence, whatever the nature of the advocacy for the prosecution.

LORD BIRKETT: *Six Great Advocates*

Summarise this passage in 225 to 250 words, and provide a title.

Chapter 10

Summary III

In this chapter you will find eleven summary exercises, re-printed from the recent C.S.E. and G.C.E. O Level English Language papers of various Examinations Boards. Most of this work is easier than that towards the end of Chapter 9, and if you have worked through Chapters 8 and 9 you should find no difficulty in doing these exercises.

1   Read the following extract carefully and answer the question below.

'But the most exciting thing was when I flew my hawk free for the first time. I was frightened to death.'

'Do you want to hear about it?' said Mr. Farthing to the class. 'Yes, Sir,' came the chorus.

'Well, I'd been flying her on the line for about a week, and she was about ready to fly loose. So, on Saturday morning I thought right, if she flies off, she flies off, and it can't be helped. So I went down to the shed. She was dead keen, walking about on her shelf behind the bars, and screaming out when she saw me. So I took her out in the field and tried her on the line, and she came like a rocket. So I thought, right, this time, this time.

'I unclipped the line and let her hop onto the fence post. There was nothing stopping her now. I was terrified. I thought she's forced to go, she's forced to. But she didn't. She sat there looking while I backed off into the field. I went right to the middle, then held my glove up and shouted, "Come on, Kes!" Nothing happened at first, then, just as I was going to walk back to her, she came. You ought to have seen her. Straight as a die, about a yard off the floor. And what speed! She came twice as fast as when she had the line on, because it used to drag in the grass and slow her down. She came like lightning, head dead still, and her wings never made a sound, then wham! Straight up on to the glove, claws out grabbing for the meat.

'I was so pleased I didn't know what to do with myself, so I thought just to prove it, I'll try her again, and she came the second time just as good. Well, that was it. I'd done it. I'd trained her.'

Explain carefully how the boy in the extract managed to train the hawk and the sort of qualities he needed to do so.
Welsh Joint Education Committee C.S.E.

2   THE FILE ON JOHN WILKINSON

The two confidential reports were submitted in answer to a request for information about John Wilkinson who had applied for a position with a London firm.

Report A—from Mr. James Burr.

Mr. John Wilkinson

Mr. John Wilkinson was born in Bradford, Yorkshire, in April 1927. He was educated at Bexton Grammar School from September 1938 until July 1944 when he left having attained passes in five School Certificate subjects. During his time at the school he was the popular captain of the school football XI and, although he was involved in one or two typical schoolboyish pranks, his teachers found him to be a friendly boy with an acutely developed sense of humour. His work at this time was said to be satisfactory in all respects.

Outside school he showed keen interest in football and was an active member of two local youth clubs. Apart from a minor brush with the law over some 'scrumped' apples (for which no prosecution was brought), his character was above reproach.

Following temporary employment as a junior official in an insurance office, Mr. Wilkinson joined the Royal Air Force in November 1945. He returned to civilian life in January 1949 having attained the status of non-commissioned officer.

From 1949 until 1966 he was employed in the family firm of B. C. Wilkinson & Co., Wholesale Furnishers, of which his father was at that time Managing Director. He gained experience in all departments of the firm before earning control of the company when Mr. Wilkinson, senior, retired in 1964.

Adverse trading conditions in 1966 led to the bankruptcy of Wilkinson & Co., and for a time John Wilkinson was considering other offers of employment. Eventually he accepted a position as Export Manager with the Kenilworth Carpet Co. of Bexton where he has served efficiently until the present day.

Report B—from Mr. John Gale.

J. Wilkinson

Wilkinson, a native of Bradford, Yorkshire, is forty-six years of age. He attended Bexton Grammar School for six years where he had some success at football. He appears to have been a source of trouble at the school and was known for his facetious attitude to authority. His work generally was only 'satisfactory' as was borne out by his unremarkable attainment in the School Certificate Examination. Having failed the examination altogether in 1943, he re-sat a year later. Even then he acquired only the minimum five passes required for the award of a certificate.

In his leisure hours he seems to have had no enthusiasms beyond football and aimless fringe attachments to local clubs. At this time he became known to the police and, although he managed to avoid prosecution, was, at one time, suspected of theft.

After a period as an office clerk, Wilkinson was called-up for service in the Royal Air Force. In four years of service as an airman, he did not progress beyond the rank of corporal.

Following demobilisation, Wilkinson was fortunate enough to have guaranteed employment in a firm belonging to his family (Wilkinson & Co., Furnishers). Here, the influence of his father, who was Managing Director of the firm, was sufficient to give him advancement. Over the next fifteen years he was regularly moved from one department to another until, on his father's retirement, he was given the position of Managing Director.

By 1966 two years of mismanagement had plunged the company into liquidation. For many months thereafter Wilkinson was unemployed. At last, however, he managed to obtain work in a minor executive capacity with the Kenilworth Carpet Co., also of Bexton, where he has remained without distinction.

Imagine that you are an official of the firm to which John Wilkinson is now applying for employment. Make a list of the FACTS about him that you can gather from the two reports. Do not include any material which merely reflects the OPINIONS of the writers.
East Anglian Exams. Board C.S.E. Mode 1—North. English Paper 1 May, 1973

3   Here is the first chapter of a book on deep freezers – refrigerators which preserve food for long periods by keeping it at a temperature

below 0°F (-18°C). Read the chapter carefully and then follow the instructions beneath.

Advantages of Freezing

Many people who may be thinking of buying a freezer may wonder if they are going to get full value from their initial expenditure – relatively high compared with that on other pieces of kitchen and household equipment.

The initial outlay on freezing is admittedly greater than that on bottling or canning, but this can be offset by the efficiency of a freezer and the ease with which it may be used. Freezing methods are quick and simple and leave little to chance, while bottling and canning are subject to a variety of perfect conditions not always easily achieved in an ordinary kitchen. Many women, too, have little time for the sheer labour involved in more old-fashioned methods of food preservation, and have often been discouraged by poor results.

Of particular importance to the freezer owner is the fact that certain foods such as meat, fish, poultry and game are virtually impossible to preserve by any method other than freezing. Few vegetables preserve well, and most cakes and biscuits can only be kept for a few days. But now these foods can be perfectly preserved for use weeks and months ahead in a deep freezer.

In addition, there are the most positive advantages of saving time and money. The garden or farm can be planned to give the maximum amount of first-class produce for future use; even an unforeseen glut can be turned to advantage. But the freezer-owner of today is no longer only the farmer's wife; those in towns can take advantage of seasonal gluts at greengrocer, butcher or fishmonger to save money, yet give variety to meals months ahead.

Bulk buying gives another positive saving for the budget-conscious, not only in fresh produce but in commercially frozen food. Those with large families, or those who entertain a good deal, can use catering packs bought at budget prices, and can plan ahead for busy seasons when ready-cooked food will be a positive advantage.

For many people, the saving of time is more important than a tight budget, but as most of us know today of course time-saving can lead to money-saving. Shopping trips can waste petrol and can also be time-consuming to the housewife who may also be the family gardener or even a breadwinner too. Even the woman who has time to spare in her home will appreciate time saved for outside interests by being able to prepare a number of different meals each day by cooking in batches, making one day's cooking do the work of three or four future ones. Time taken to make an elaborate casserole for instance can be halved if a double quantity is prepared with a portion eaten on cooking day and the remainder frozen for use a week or month ahead.

Home baking in particular takes on a new aspect when three or four cakes can be prepared at a time, perhaps to be eaten months ahead, and this enables the cook to take full advantage of time-saving electric mixers and liquidisers.

Best of all, a freezer enables a family to be well fed on balanced meals, however busy the cook-shopper may be and whatever the weather or the price of fresh food.

MARY NORWAK: *Deep Freezing*

(*a*) First – List very briefly, *using not more than 5 words for each item*, the FIVE main advantages to the housewife claimed for a deep freezer.

(*b*) Then – Take each advantage in turn and summarize in your own words, *using not more than 30 words for each*, the arguments advanced in favour of the advantage claimed. You may write in note form using incomplete sentences, but they should be readily understandable.

West Midlands Examinations Board C.S.E.

4 Make a summary in your own words of the following passage. Do not use more than 100 words, and state the number of words you use.

The attitude of the traditional railwayman towards passenger traffic until about five years ago was that it was no more than the jam on the bread; the real lifeblood of the railways was freight. If passengers cared to travel on the morning milk train so much the better; but it was the milk that made the train run. Earlier statistics, such as less than 25 per cent of total revenue from passengers in the 1920s, supported this view.

In recent years it has been steadily eroded, however, by the increasing size and efficiency of the road transport industry, and by the increasing difficulty of providing competitive freight services in a large, rambling and inflexible rail system, with rapidly rising labour costs. For, however economical the trunk haul, freight still has to be handled on and off a train (unless in private sidings) and for distances of under about 200 miles the cost of handling, together with that of collection and delivery, can be great enough to lose the business.

The great merit of passengers in this respect is that they load and discharge themselves; there is no handling cost other than ticketing. And the second great advantage is that the typical inter-city distance in Britain, 200–300 miles, is ideal for rail as opposed to air on the one hand and car (for centre to centre travel) on the other.

Encouraged by such thoughts, and by the evident success of Midland services, British Rail threw themselves into developing the passenger business, with highly satisfactory results. While freight business barely held its own, passenger traffic grew by nearly 5 per cent a year during the late 1960s and revenue by over 10 per cent a year. In 1969 for the first time passenger traffic yielded more revenue than freight, a landmark in the history of the system.

The London to Southampton and Bournemouth route was electrified in 1967 – with a 15 per cent increase in traffic in the first year – and now two further electrification schemes are under way: Manchester to Glasgow, and the North London commuter services out of King's Cross to Hitchin and Royston. At the same time large quantities of new rolling stock, quieter, cleaner and more comfortable, are being built, and new signalling equipment installed to give greater safety and reliability.

From: *Going by Rail?* by MICHAEL BAILY
(Reproduced from *The Times* by permission.)
Southern Universities' Joint Board G.C.E.

5   Write a summary of the following passage in good continuous prose, using not more than 120 words. State at the end of the summary the number of words you have used. The passage contains 344 words.

For millions of years we have known a world whose resources seemed illimitable. However fast we cut down trees, nature unaided would replace them. However many fish we took from the sea, nature would restock it. However much sewage we dumped into the river, nature would purify it, just as she would purify the air, however much smoke and fumes we put into it. Today we have reached the stage of realising that rivers can be polluted past remedy, that seas can be overfished and that forests must be managed and fostered if they are not to vanish.

But we still retain our primitive optimism about air and water. There will always be enough rain falling from the skies to meet our needs. The air can absorb all the filth we care to put in it. Still less do we worry whether we could ever run short of oxygen. Surely there is air enough to breathe? However, we now consume about ten per cent of all the atmospheric oxygen every year, thanks to the many forms of combustion which destroy it: every car, aircraft and power station destroys oxygen in quantities far greater than men consume by breathing.

The fact is that we are just beginning to press up against the limits of the earth's capacity. We begin to have to watch what we are doing to things like water and oxygen, just as we have to watch whether we are over-fishing or over-felling. The realisation has dawned that earth is a space-ship with strictly limited resources. In the long run these resources must be re-created, either by nature or by man, and start their natural cycle afresh, just as the astronaut's expired air is regenerated to be breathed anew. Up to now, the slow pace of nature's own recycling has served, coupled with the fact that the 'working capital' of already recycled material was large. But the margins are getting smaller, and if men, in ever larger numbers, are going to require ever larger quantities, the pace of recycling will have to be artificially quickened.

G. R. TAYLOR

Associated Examining Board G.C.E.

6   The following passage is taken from a study of the effects of television on young children. *Using only the information in the passage,* write a summary consisting of *two* paragraphs:

(*a*) the varying reactions to Westerns of children of different ages and sex; and

(*b*) the reasons why violence in Westerns does not produce anxiety in most children.

Do not try to summarize everything in the passage, but select from it the material needed for your paragraphs. These should be written in clear, concise English, *and as far as possible in your own words*, although you may retain words and brief expressions which cannot be accurately or economically replaced.

Your whole summary should not exceed 140 words altogether, and at the end of it you must state the number of words used.

According to the mothers' reports, children under six were quite often frightened by the individual acts of violence and the noise of shooting in Westerns. They would hide behind chairs, rush out of the room, or, if the anxiety was not too great, climb on to their mothers' laps and from there continue to watch. Finding that the hero was still all right at the end, and that the others watching the programme had enjoyed it, the young child might look again on other occasions. Gradually the stereotyped pattern of the Westerns gets understood – not in detail, but in broad outline. At the same time, the children, boys in particular, rehearse the main elements of Westerns in play.

In general, it seems that the process of learning is related to the child's mental rather than to his chronological age, and that round about six or seven years the majority of children cease to be frightened by Westerns. Girls tend to be a little 'backward' here, not for want of intellectual understanding but because of different interests and different play-experiences. Girls play Westerns less often than boys, and, when they do, are rarely cast in the glorious and ultimately secure role of the cowboy hero. By about nine or ten, girls proved almost as interested in these programmes as boys. Anxiety about Westerns was rare well before the age of ten. In our survey, only seven children out of a thousand mentioned a Western when asked 'Have you ever been frightened by anything you have seen on television?'

Any remaining tension that younger children may experience, owing to the fact that they are more involved, tends to be worked off in play. These are not games of uncontrolled aggression, but are only versions of chasing and being chased – the oldest of childhood games, which were, of course, played long before television was thought of. They express the child's ingrained fondness for rules and for a clear differentiation between good and evil. The conventional cowboy films with their straightforward sides suit the play needs of children between six and ten, when they are testing out ideas about fair play and about friendship.

Enjoyment of Westerns is at its height where the format has been learnt sufficiently for tension not to mount too much, but where, at times during the showing, some element of doubt remains. Because children know that the ending will be happy, with no harm done to the hero, the violence does not matter. They gain security from the lack of variety in plot and solution, they enjoy being 'in the know'. When they stop playing at cowboys and similar games with clear-cut rules of good and evil, and even the momentary doubt during the showing has gone, they lose interest in Westerns, and criticise the stereotyped presentation which at first appealed to them so much. *University of London G.C.E.*

7   The passage below is from an article on girls' comics. Read it carefully and then answer the questions asked about it. Answer briefly and as far as you can in your own words. *Use only the information contained in the passage.*

Two million or so girls in Britain, mainly in the eight to thirteen age group, read comics regularly. For a title girls' comics usually rely on a Christian name only, such as *Bunty*, *Judy* or *Diana*, whereas boys' comics are called after virile qualities or associations – *Valiant*, *Smash*, *Lion*, *Victor* and so on. This may be partly because it is difficult to find adjectives expressing feminine qualities which do not have derogatory implications.

Girls enjoy stories which touch their feelings and are related to the life which they know. 'Sheer action' does not satisfy, as readers do not identify themselves with the characters unless there is a strong emotional appeal. The most popular stories are about nurses, orphans or animals, like 'Ross, Student Nurse' and 'Glen – a dog on a lonely quest'. A heroine who fights for personal justice, a relative's happiness, a friend or a pet, inspires instant sympathy.

Heroines (unlike heroes in boys' comics) always have their characters exposed in a very personal light. This seeming vulnerability always turns out to their advantage, however, as a favourite twist is to have a heroine with a defective character (she may be, for example, cowardly). She then gradually reveals the reasons for her dubious behaviour and proves herself a splendid type who has been misjudged. One editress stresses the realistic element in girls' comics – recent stories have included a comprehensive school going on strike, a coloured joint-heroine, and a hippie. She feels that this is to be applauded in contrast with the 'extreme fantasy' of boys' comics. Home and family are a constant background in girls' stories, and in a recent short-story competition for readers, 95 per cent of entries contained this element. Curiously, boys' comics appear to make every effort to banish the family and its related emotions altogether.

Women and girls almost never set foot in boys' comic stories. An editor's reason was, 'There's no bar, but from experience we have found the boys are not keen on heroines'. Girls' comics feature men

and boys quite prominently, and heroines are often given prominence through being associated with a more important male – thus,
'Lonely Sue Shields finds herself the centre of attraction when
her pop-singer brother signs an important recording contract'.
Although the leading characters, girls tend to be featured in suppor-
tive roles to the men.

Although girls' comics make much of girlhood, one cannot help
noticing the scarcity of adult women characters in them. In boys'
comics a very large percentage of heroes are adult males, already
invested with some kind of authority, like 'Zip Nolan – highway
patrolman'. In girls' stories, apart from the occasional sympathetic
teacher, there is little idealisation of the adult woman. In fact, there
is much 'putting down' of women because girls have a confirmed
preference for female villains.

'Interest features' in girls' comics tend to be miniature replicas of
what goes on in mother's magazines. Cookery and fashion articles
are particularly popular, and pictures of pop-stars are commonplace. Famous mothers are sometimes included, indicating that
motherhood is compatible with stardom. Several girls' comics run
problem pages because, as the editor of *June and School Friend* puts it,
'Girls do tend to agonise about themselves'.

It is just because girls' comic features are so similar to those in
women's magazines that the readership falls off rapidly after the age
of twelve. Girls progress to magazines such as *19* and *Petticoat*, or to
the romantic comics such as *Valentine* and *Romeo*. Boys' comics tend
to hold their readership longer, and there are more of them because
there is not the same progression for boys in terms of reading matter.

(*a*) What do you learn about the content of girls' comics? (Try to
answer in not more than 90 words.)

(*b*) In what ways do boys' comics differ from those of girls? (Use
about 80 words.)

(*c*) What, briefly, are you told by those who edit comics?
Welsh Joint Education Committee G.C.E.

8 Read the following passage carefully, and then answer the
questions on it in your own words.

There is a disarming, unprofessional charm about the Cawthorne Victoria Jubilee Museum. In what other museum would you
find the blasted boots of a village boy?

The pair which stands in a window-bottom of the village museum bears a card which explains: 'Boots worn by Tom Parkin when struck by lightning at Upper House Farm, Cawthorne, 1930'. Tom's nail-studded boots, ripped wide open from ankle to welt, have been gazed at by amazed visitors for nearly forty years. Most people, seeing them, assume that their owner perished, but he is alive and well and still living at Upper House Farm.

I found the indestructible Mr. Parkin hedge-cutting in one of his fields.

'I've come to see you about your boots,' I said. He looked puzzled. 'What boots?'

'Your boots in the museum.' He laughed.

'You're taking me back forty years. I was just twelve when the lightning struck. I was standing beside the old kitchen range and the lightning hit my legs. Fortunately, I was wearing thick, hand-knitted woollen socks to my knees. The doctor said the wool acted as a conductor. Otherwise my legs and feet would have been more severely burned.'

Mr. Parkin didn't know who presented his shattered boots to Cawthorne Museum. I left him chuckling over the idea of his boyhood boots bringing a complete stranger to visit him forty years later.

But Tom Parkin's boots aside, Cawthorne Museum is well worth careful scrutiny. It contains some surprising exhibits bequeathed not only by the gentry but by the villagers too. There is a community pride in this collection of bygones which you do not find elsewhere. The museum was founded by the village squirearchy, the Stanhopes of Cannon Hall. To commemorate Queen Victoria's jubilee, the cottage in which it was first housed was razed and the existing timbered building constructed by estate workmen.

The family originally used their museum to house hunting trophies which threatened to clutter up Cannon Hall. Friends were asked to bring back spoils of their big games hunts. So the one-room museum displays an odd juxtaposition of dead animals. The massive head of a Canadian moose stares curiously down at the perky head of a fox opposite. Maori spears, clubs and boomerangs share wall space with an assortment of Japanese swords.

When the last of the Stanhopes died in 1953, the villagers bought the museum and have run it ever since. There is evidence of the change of ownership in the exhibits which have since been introduced. For instance, a piece of the Emley Moor TV mast which collapsed in 1969 now lies in a display case alongside an Eskimo ice-chopping axe, an Indian idol carved in slate, and the beaks and webbed feet of two albatrosses killed off Cape Horn. As well as the perky fox, the Canadian moose now has another neighbour to wonder at – a two-headed calf born at a local farm. A villager has provided a hemlock stalk, ten feet tall and as thick as a man's forearm, dwarfing the foreign assegais and longbows presented by the gentry.

Because of lack of space, time and distance overlap in the Cawthorne Museum. A primitive Turkish toothbrush is close by a pair of wooden pattens 'worn in Cawthorne on washdays to keep the feet out of the water'. A glass-topped case contains grime-encrusted wine-bottles, put down in the cellars of Cannon Hall in 1659, and pop bottles of the 1920s with glass marbles in their necks. The same case also holds a piece of the first transatlantic telephone cable, and a lantern used by the village policeman. Near a horse's gall stone weighing 9 lb. 9 oz. is a delicate sailing ship in spun glass which bears the thought-provoking inscription: 'Made at Mexborough and commissioned by Alfred Hodgson for his bride, it was cared for by his second wife who bequeathed it to this museum'.

There is a small admission fee to the museum, but the sight of Tom Parkin's lightning-blasted boots is alone worth the few coppers that open up this homely treasure house.

(Note. In your answers to (a), (b) and (c) below you must not quote whole phrases from the passage. The length of answers suggested for (a), (b) and (c) is meant as a guide. There will be no penalty for not answering within the suggested limits.)

(a) The writer suggests that this museum is different from most. Using the evidence of the whole passage, show in what ways it differs. (Answer in about 100 of your own words.)

(b) Outline the early history of the museum and show how this accounts for the original exhibits. (Answer in about 70 of your own words.)

(c) Show how the change of ownership added a different type of exhibit. (Answer in about 50 of your own words.)
Joint Matriculation Board G.C.E.

9   Read carefully the following passage, and answer the questions set on it.

I remain perpetually divided in my mind on the question of the adaptation of classic novels for television. A short-sightedly literary education naturally prejudices me against the idea. A novel is written to be read; it cannot therefore be anything but diminished by being animated. I have previously convinced myself that as a general rule (of course there will be exceptions) the better the novel the less chance there is of its unique quality carrying over into television; for that quality will depend on its style, and a way has not yet been found for translating style into pictures.

But I admit that this is the view of a predominantly literary disposition. The majority of people have not been subjected to the same exclusive training in reading that I was forced to undergo as a student. And the evidence is there to show that one result of television adaptations is to increase enormously the number of new readers for the work adapted. So that is a clear gain, and one that we must not discount.

Then again, television has to fill out its immense stretches of time somehow or other, and the adaptation of good novels seems, on the face of it, a more profitable way of doing it than many one could list. So the question really seems to be, does the bad, or inferior, adaptation of a good novel do any actual harm? And there I find myself taking a puritan attitude and coming to the conclusion that it does. If it diminishes a work, the loss will hardly be offset by the number of new readers gained; they will be counted only in thousands, or more probably hundreds: the total viewers will be counted in millions. And one must consider, too, the effect the falsification of a bad adaptation has on the new reader when he comes to the novel in print.

What is the harm done, then? It is surely simply of selling the viewer short, of marking the package as containing a pound when the contents weigh only three-quarters, or less. A good novel, like any other work of good art, is a complete, unique and personal vision of the artist's, and so a complete, unique and personal experience for the recipient. If the adaptation fails to communicate just that – the completeness, the uniqueness, the personalness, difficult though that is – it is guilty of vandalism on the one hand, and of selling short on the other.

The failure may take one of several forms. Its effect may be to prettify, to vulgarise, to trivialise, to conventionalise, or to sentimentalise. It may reduce a novel celebrating a man's honour (as in Conrad) to the level of a mere adventure story. It may reduce the harshness and violence of Dickens to the conventionalities of a Christmas card view of him (as more than one BBC adaptation of him has seemed to me to do). It may reduce the stoic pessimism of

Hardy's view of nature to a holiday brochure picture of ye olde Englishe countryside. It may reduce the subtle moral elegance of a Henry James story (as did the authors of *The Heiress*) to a period melodrama.

The unwary and the untutored viewer imagines that he is being given the kernel of the book, when what perhaps he is being given is only a pre-digested product – an instant powder essence instead of the real thing. This is a form of devaluation, and the corruption may easily extend to those who are lured into reading the novel as well. For the animated images of the screen are a very powerful factor, and the new reader may easily be persuaded by them to bring to his reading of the novel just those falsifications which the adaptation has been guilty of. For it is no use pretending that the reading of the best novels is always an easy and comfortable distraction. It is often a strenuous and exhausting (though always a creative and rewarding) exercise.

T. C. WORSLEY: *Television: The Ephemeral Art*

(*a*) The writer allows that two things may be gained by adapting great novels for television presentation. Briefly, what are they?

(*b*) He then asks whether any harm may be done by a bad adaptation of a great novel, and decides that it may. In a passage of some 60–80 words, give his reasons for so deciding.
Oxford Local G.C.E.

10   Read the following passage carefully, and answer the questions that follow.

The house was strange – thus Edith pursued her thoughts – there was such a contrast between what went on inside and what went on outside. Outside it was all blare and glare and publicity, what with the posters, and the reporters still hanging about the area railings, and the talk of Westminster Abbey, and speeches in both Houses of Parliament. Inside it was all hushed and private, like a conspiracy; the servants whispered, people went soundlessly up and down stairs; and whenever Lady Slane came into the room everybody stopped talking, and stood up, and somebody was sure to go forward and lead her gently to a chair. They treated her rather as though she had had an accident, or had gone temporarily off her head. Yet Edith was sure her mother did not want to be led to chairs, or to be kissed so reverently and mutely, or to be asked if she was sure she wouldn't rather have dinner in her room. The only person to treat her in a normal way was Genoux, her old French maid, who was nearly as old as Lady Slane herself, and had been with her for the whole of her married life. Genoux moved about the house as noisily as ever, talking to herself as her custom was, muttering to herself about her next business in her extraordinary jumble of French and English; she still burst unceremoniously into the drawing-room in pursuit of her mistress, whoever might be there, and horrified the assembled family by asking, 'Pardon, miladi, est-ce que ça vaut la peine d' envoyer les shirts de milord à la wash?' They all looked at Lady Slane as though they expected her to fall instantly to pieces, like a vase after a blow, but she replied in her usual quiet voice that yes, his lordship's shirts must certainly be sent to the wash; and then, turning to Herbert, said, 'I don't know what you would like to do with your father's things, Herbert; it seems a pity to give them all to the butler, and anyway they wouldn't fit.'

Her mother and Genoux, Edith thought, alone refused to adapt themselves to the strangeness of the house. She could read disapproval in the eyes of Herbert, Carrie, Charles, and William; but naturally no disapproval could be openly expressed. They could only insist, implicitly, that their own convention must be adopted: Mother's life was shattered. Mother was bearing up wonderfully. Mother must be sheltered within the privacy of her disaster, while the necessary business was conducted, the necessary contact with the outside world maintained, by her capable sons and her capable daughter. Edith, poor thing, wasn't much use. Everybody knew that Edith always said the wrong thing at the wrong moment, and left undone everything that she was supposed to do, giving the excuse that she had been 'too busy'. Herbert, Carrie, William, and Charles stood between their mother and the outside world.

From time to time, indeed, some special rumour was allowed to creep past their barrier: the King and Queen had sent a most affectionate message – Herbert could scarcely be expected to keep that piece of news to himself. Huddersfield, Lord Slane's native town, desired the approval of the family for a memorial service. The King would be represented at the funeral by the Duke of Gloucester. The ladies of the Royal School of Embroidery had worked – in a great hurry – a pall. The Prime Minister would carry one corner of it; the Leader of the Opposition another. The French Government were sending a representative; and it was said that the Duke of Brabant might attend on behalf of the Belgian . . .

These bits of information were imparted to his mother by Herbert in driblets and with caution; he was feeling his way to see how she would receive them. She received them with complete indifference. 'Very nice of them, to be sure,' she said; and once she said, 'So glad, dear, if you're pleased.' Herbert both relished and resented this remark. Any tribute paid to his father was paid to himself, in a way, as head of the family; yet his mother's place, rightfully, was in the centre of the picture; those three or four days between death and burial were, rightfully, her own. Herbert prided himself on his sense of fitness. Plenty of time, afterwards, to assert himself as Lord Slane. Generation must tread upon the heels of generation – that was a law of nature; yet, so long as his father's physical presence remained in the house, his mother had the right to authority. By her indifference, she was abdicating her position unnecessarily, unbecomingly, soon. She ought, posthumously, for those three or four days, to rally supremely in honour of her husband's memory. So it ran in Herbert's code. But perhaps, chattered the imp in Edith, perhaps she was so thoroughly drained by Father in his lifetime that she can't now be bothered with his memory?

Adapted from *All Passion Spent* by V. SACKVILLE-WEST

(*a*) Edith clearly differs from her brothers and sister. From the evidence of this passage, describe, in about 100 words, the impression of Edith you have formed.

(*b*) Imagine that Herbert keeps a careful diary. In about 100 words write the entry in his diary for the day partly described in the passage. His selection of material and his comments on the day must reveal what seem to you his chief characteristics.

Oxford and Cambridge G.C.E. (adapted)

11 Read the following passage carefully and then answer **all** the questions which follow it.

'Pop' is the name given to a 'popular' cultural movement, at first concerned only with music but later covering a whole life-style and entertainment industry which, since its beginnings in the 1950s, has swept round the world. Surrounded by the increased prosperity of the post-war years, the newly affluent teenagers demanded new ways of amusing themselves, and rock'n'roll films starring singers like Bill Haley showed the pop generation 'raving' and 'having a ball' at the expense of their rather bumbling elders. Indeed, the old respect for one's 'elders and betters' was on the way out. With a contempt for adults which their Victorian great-grandfathers would have found incredible, the kids dismissed everyone over a certain age as 'square' (out of touch with their current ideas) and replaced, on their own terms, the 'square' opinions of the Establishment with their 'hip' ideas of increased freedom and mobility.

About the same time as pop appeared, it became commonplace in the press to talk of 'personalities' projecting their 'images' rather than themselves. This image was largely built up for them. The advertising profession, through photographs, film, music and carefully written copy, could create an image of comfort, masculinity or speed which people would identify with a particular product; it was inevitable that this technique would eventually be applied to people as well. Elvis Presley's career is a classic example. A spontaneous reaction from the young people who happened to hear his first recordings brought him his initial success; his style was what they wanted. As soon as it became obvious from the mood of the pop audience that Elvis Presley's potential could be practically unlimited if he was presented properly, his manager – Colonel Parker – took command of the singer's every move. Parker controlled Presley's movements and appearances better than those of any head of state. He appeared infrequently. He was heard and seen mainly on record and film (both media allowing for frequent rehearsals and re-takes to achieve the perfect performance or image) and made no public statements that were not carefully vetted. Colonel Parker knew that however great the current demand for his protégé, it would soon be exhausted by repeated public exposure. So Elvis, the personality, was carefully hoarded. The myth of the recluse was added to that of the pop star, and the image was kept untarnished. Elvis became 'king' not just because he was the best of his kind, but because he was unreachable.

According to the pop songs of the 50s human relationships went little deeper than a roving eye for a good-lookin' woman or for the wiggling movement of a girl's hips. The sorrows of this generation came to little more than the tell-tale traces of lipstick on a boyfriend's collar. Songs of powder puffs and candy kisses reflected the emphasis on superficial sex appeal and glamour which characterized early pop culture. But the juvenile sex symbols began to age, and the teenagers became slowly aware of what was happening to themselves. Bob Dylan became the mouthpiece of a disaffected generation. In a voice that could scarcely carry a tune Dylan wailed of social and sexual hypocrisy among the established generation. Through lyrics that were poetic and intricate, he drummed out the griefs and complexes of the lost generation – the young and dispossessed. Where previous pop songs represented a glamorized dream world in which the teenager was supposed to live, in the anguish and sarcasm of Bob Dylan's songs the 'hang-ups' – the awakening worries – of the pop generation began to show through. The teenagers were beginning to be concerned about what the manipulators were doing to them. A social change was taking place for the youth of the late 50s and early 60s.

Undirected energy of the first part of their rebellion found a direction, or rather many directions. In 1958 the first Aldermaston march was held in Britain to protest against nuclear arming by Britain and America. The movement which grew out of it, the Campaign for Nuclear Disarmament, merely foreshadowed the massive demonstrations against United States' involvement in Vietnam which developed in the latter part of the 60s. Youth became political, not – as had been customary before – as part of one of the existing parties, but more often as a kind of anarchistic splinter group. The majority of them held to no policy except a belief that peace was possible. Protest songs, which Bob Dylan had pioneered, became a genre of their own. The more conventional idealists in America and Britain joined the Peace Corps and the Voluntary Service Overseas organizations. These volunteers devoted themselves occasionally with great self-sacrifice, to the ideal of aid to underdeveloped countries. Others continued the fight for what they saw as right, often in the streets of their own cities. This fight became more bitter and violent as deeper grievances emerged and the passions of the young became more inflamed. Violence came into the struggle for the civil rights of the black minority in the States and for university reform in Paris. Western society was split more and more into two camps, the 'haves' and the 'have nots', the 'hawks' (for war) and the 'doves' (for peace), the young and the old. It was an updated, much less innocent version of the original 'hips' and 'squares' of the early pop days.

However, another youth movement arose in the latter part of the 60s which ran counter, if never violently so, to any previous ones – the 'hippy movement'. 'Hippy' is often used as an expression of contempt for people who are dirty, have long hair and are unemployed. However, their ideal is quite close to Christianity; hippies believe that, if life is to be lived fully, it must be lived simply. For them this means a turning away from selfishness, lavish comfort and business affairs: it is, in a sense, a deliberate return to the innocence of childhood. The fact that such attempts fail far more frequently than they succeed can be an indication of the materialistic and aggressive aspects of society as much as of the hippy's folly or lack of courage.

That pop culture would develop and diversify as it has done could not have been foreseen in its beginnings. But, as is often the case, it seems inevitable in retrospect.

(a) 'That pop culture would develop and diversify' was 'inevitable', says the author in his final paragraph. Summarise the course of this development and diversification which the author has described in paragraphs 3, 4, and 5.

Your summary must be in continuous prose and must not exceed 150 words. It must be in three paragraphs, corresponding to the three paragraphs in the passage.

You may use or adapt the language of the original where you think it advisable, but unintelligent copying of large extracts from the passage will be penalised.

Adapted from *University of Cambridge G.C.E.*

Acknowledgements

We are grateful to the following for permission to reproduce copyright material:
George Allen & Unwin Ltd for extracts from *The Book World Today* by Joseph
Trenaman, and *The Scientific Outlook* by Bertrand Russell; the author for an extract
from his article 'Soccer as it was writ' by John Arlott, published in *The Observer*;
Lady Isobel Barnett, Miss Marghanita Laski and Mr Frank Byers for extracts from
Any Questions published by Icon Books Ltd; B. T. Batsford Ltd for an extract from
Railways of Britain by O. S. Knock; A. & C. Black Ltd for an extract from *Approach
to Archaeology* by S. Piggott; The Bodley Head Ltd for extracts from *The Jenguin
Pennings* by Paul Jennings, and 'Down Pens' from *The Short Stories of Saki*; Borough
of Weston-super-Mare for an extract from *Weston Town Guide*; the author for an
extract from *Architecture* by Martin S. Briggs, published by Oxford University
Press; British Railways for an extract from their advertising copy; Jonathan Cape
Ltd for extracts from *The Reader Over Your Shoulder* by Robert Graves and Alan
Hodge and *Theory of Literature* by Rene Wellek and Austin Warren; Cassell & Co.
Ltd for extracts from *Style* by F. L. Lucas; Chatto & Windus Ltd for an extract
from *The Olive Tree* by Aldous Huxley; The Clarendon Press for an extract from
The Last Hundred Years by C. H. C. Blount; Miss D. E. Collins for an extract from
'The Tremendous Adventures of Major Brown' from *The Club of Queer Trades*
by G. K. Chesterton; Wm. Collins, Sons & Co. Ltd for an extract from *Cooking for
Pleasure* by Rupert Croft-Cooke; Conservative Political Centre for an extract from
'Science and Faith' by Norman St. John-Stevas, published in *Science and Society*;
Consumer's Association for an extract from *Which?*, August 1964; Council for the
Protection of Rural Wales for an extract from their 1963 report; The Daily Mirror
Newspapers Ltd for extracts from 'Daily English'; The Daily Telegraph and
Morning Post for an extract from *The Daily Telegraph*, 28 April 1964; Andre Deutsch
Ltd for an extract from *Tell Me, Josephine*, edited by Barbara Hall; E.M.I. Records
Ltd; Faber & Faber Ltd for extracts from *Coast to Coast* by James Morris; Samuel
French Ltd for extracts from *Dealing in Futures* and *Graft*, both by Harold Brighouse
and Granada Television for extracts from their television adaptations of these plays,
titled respectively *Vitriol* and *Fiddlers Four*; Geographical Publications Ltd for an
extract from *Applied Geography* by Sir Dudley Stamp; Granada Television for an extract from 'Newspapers' by Sir Leslie Plummer, M.P., from *Inquiry* published by
Manchester University Press and based upon a series of talks on Current Affairs originally transmitted by Granada; *The Guardian*; Hamish Hamilton Ltd for extracts from
Flowers and a Village by Wilfrid Blunt and *The Liberal Hour* by J. K. Galbraith; the
Controller of Her Majesty's Stationery Office for extracts from *Traffic in Towns*
and *15-18 Report of the Central Advisory Council for Education* (Crowther Report);
Hogarth Press Ltd for an extract from *This Island Now* by G. M. Carstairs; Hollis
& Carter Ltd for an extract from *Light on a Dark Horse* by Roy Campbell; Hoover
Ltd for an extract from their advertising copy; the author for extracts from 'Impei-
ious Caesar' by Michael Innes from *Appleby Talking*, published by Victor Gollancz
Ltd; Mr R. Johnson for his letter published in *The Guardian*, 11 August 1964;
London Transport for extracts from their advertising copy; the author for extracts
from *Juvenile Delinquency and the Law* by A. E. Jones; Longmans, Green & Co. Ltd
for extracts from *The Road to Tyburn* by Christopher Hibbert, *From Kitty Hawk to
Outer Space*, *From Steamcarts to Minicars*, *From Coracles to Cunarders* and *From Rocket
to Railway*, all by L. E. Snellgrove, and *English Social History* by G. M. Trevelyan;
Macmillan & Co. Ltd for extracts from *The Sources of Invention* by J. Jewkes, D.

Sawers and R. Stillerman; Mathematic Pie Ltd for extracts from *Topic*; the author for an extract from the Introduction to *The Complete Short Stories*, Vol. 3, by W. Somerset Maugham, published by William Heinemann Ltd; the author's agents for an extract from *Growing Up in New Guinea* by Margaret Mead; National Coal Board for their *N.C.B. Housewarming Plan* advertisement; The New English Library for extracts from *All You Need to Know About the Law* by Ewan Mitchell; Newman Neame Take Home Books Ltd for extracts from *Take Home Books*; Odhams Press Ltd for extracts from *Hitler, A Study in Tyranny* by Alan Bullock; Oxford University Press for an extract from *The Exploration of Outer Space* by Sir Bernard Lovell; Pan Books Ltd for extracts from *The Story of Language* by C. L. Barber, and *How to Study* by Henry Maddox; Penguin Books Ltd for extracts from *Six Great Advocates* by Lord Birkett, *At Your Service* by Elizabeth Gundrey, *Beyond the Microscope* by K. M. Smith, *Shakespeare: A Celebration* by John Russell Taylor and *Experimental Psychical Research* by R. H. Thouless, and for an extract from the blurb of the Penguin edition of *Animal Farm* by George Orwell; Pergamon Press Ltd for an extract from *The Journal of Education* edited by Boris Ford; the author's agents for an extract from *Journey Down a Rainbow* by J. B. Priestley and Jacquetta Hawkes, © J. B. Priestley and Jacquetta Hawkes 1955; the Editor of *The Review of English Literature* for an extract from Vol. 5, No. 1; Routledge & Kegan Paul Ltd for an extract from *Maxwell Knight Replies* by Maxwell Knight; Royal National Life-Boat Institution for extracts from *Life-Boat*; S.C.M. Press Ltd for extracts from *Teenage Religion* by Harry Loukes; Sidgwick & Jackson Ltd for an extract from 'Directive No. 16' of *Hitler's War Directives 1939–1945* and from *The Making of Prose* by R. Swann and F. Sidgwick; *The Sunday Telegraph* for an extract from an article entitled 'Experts Forecast 1984' by Nigel Calder, published in that paper 30 August 1964; The Times Publishing Co. Ltd for extracts from *The Times Educational Supplement*, 24 April 1964, and *The Times*, 14 February and 9 May 1964; The Twentieth Century for extracts from 'The Laughing Stock' by J. B. Morton and 'Writing for Hancock', published in *Comedy*, and an extract from 'What Christmas Means to Me' by C. S. Lewis, published in *Twentieth Century*; the author for an extract from 'The Hazards of Playgoing' from *Miscellany* by Kenneth Tynan; C. A. Watts & Co. Ltd for extracts from *Sport in Society* by P. C. McIntosh; George Weidenfeld & Nicolson Ltd for an extract from *The Image* by Daniel J. Boorstin, and the author for an extract from his article entitled 'Man in the Future' by W. T. Williams, published in *The Listener*, 14 May 1964.

We are grateful to the following Examining Boards for permission to reproduce questions from past Examination Papers:

The Associated Examining Board; East Anglian Examinations Board (Northern Sub Region); Joint Matriculation Board; Oxford and Cambridge Schools Examination Board; Oxford Delegacy of Local Examinations; Welsh Joint Education Committee; West Midlands Examinations Board; University of Cambridge Local Examinations Syndicate and University of London Entrance and School Examinations Council.

We are also grateful to the following for permission to reproduce copyright material:

Michael Joseph Ltd for an extract from *A Kestrel for a Knave* by Barry Hines; Thames and Hudson Ltd for an extract from *The Doomsday Book* by G. Rattray Taylor and Times Newspapers Ltd for an extract from an article 'Going by Rail' by Michael Baily from *The Times*. Reproduced from The Times by permission.